ぐんまの魅力を英語で伝えよう

おらが群馬のおもてなし英語

Hospitality English in Nostalgic Gunma

高崎商科大学 教授
渡邉 美代子

上毛新聞社

はじめに

　本書の目的は、観光県群馬の魅力を地域社会の人々に認識していただくとともに、世界に開かれた観光地を目指す地域社会の英語コミュニケーション力の向上に貢献することです。

　「温泉王国」「豊かな自然」「絹の里」で知られる群馬県は、都心から新幹線で1時間弱という便利な位置にあり、「すき焼き」の具材が全て県内産でそろうほど、農畜産物にも恵まれた観光県です。昨今、富岡製糸場と絹産業遺産群の世界遺産登録、北陸新幹線（高崎駅－金沢駅間）の開通、上野三碑のユネスコ世界の記憶への登録と拍車がかかり、「観光県群馬」としての堅固な礎が築かれつつあります。

　では、今、なぜ観光産業が脚光を浴びているのでしょうか。それは、観光が人の移動に伴い、地域の様々な産業と関わりを持つことにより、広範囲に経済の波及効果をもたらすためです。裾野の広い観光産業は、21世紀の成長産業の一つに位置付けられるとともに、経済活性化への有効な手段であると認められます。観光産業の興進によって、地域経済が活性化されれば、雇用機会の創出が図られると同時に、若者の県外流失を食い止めるという対策につながることが期待できるからです。

　筆者が教鞭をとる高崎商科大学では、群馬県出身学生が大部分を占め、学生たちには地元志向の強い傾向がうかがえます。つまり、卒業後は県内に就職し、家族のもとで地元の役に立ちながら生きていくことを理想とする地域密着型の若者たちという特徴です。このような若者たちが県内に就職口を見出せずに、不本意にも都心へ流失するという事態を回避するために、地域経済活性化と雇用創出は不可欠であるということができます。将来、地域を支える若者たちを地域につなぎ止めるために、裾野の広い観光産業の興進は必須であるわけです。

実際、本学卒業生の多くは観光・サービス業に従事することが本学統計から認められます。今後とも、この傾向は続くと予見されます。それは、群馬県におけるインバウンド政策が強化されつつあるとともに、外国人宿泊者数は年々増加していることが確認されるからです。

　インターネットを通して情報収集が容易な今日、人々は様々な関心・興味、あるいはこだわりを持って観光に出かけます。増え続ける訪日外国人旅行者は、東京、箱根、富士山、名古屋、京都、大阪などのゴールデンルートだけでなく、ディープジャパンを求めて地方へも足を運び始めています。例えば、地域の人々の暮らしぶり、継承されてきた食文化、地域の歴史や歴史秘話、伝承される祭りや慣習、地域産業や特産品など、地域の魅力や価値を体感するといった、これまでとは一味違う観光ルートが人気を呼んでいるようです。最近、高崎駅で観光客らしき外国人旅行者を頻繁に見かけるようになりました。今後とも、群馬県を訪れる外国人観光客数は増えていくことが予測されます。

　インバウンドの旅行者に対して、英語で接客・接遇できる人材が求められていることは、今日誰もが認めるところです。英語コミュニケーション力は仕事力の一環であり、不可欠な技能になりつつあるという認識に加え、海外からの訪問者/客を受け入れるおもてなしの精神として、地域全体の英語力の向上が求められる今日この頃です。

　本書は、なるべく文法用語を用いず、また文法的な説明を最小限にとどめるという方針のもと、日常的な表現や決まり文句を実際的な、自然な会話で紹介することを重視しました。文法の知識よりも、実際に英語コミュニケーションをとれることが肝要だからです。また、長い解説を避けるとともに、例文を紹介することで、使い方が一目でわかるようなアプローチをとりました。

　日常の英語会話においては、実際、中学校で学んだ基礎英語の知識で十分に間に合います。肝要なのは、話す内容を持っているというこ

とではないでしょうか。英語文法について熟知していても、話す中身を持っていなければ、英語コミュニケーションは成立しないといえます。つまり、英語コミュニケーション上達の秘訣は、伝えるべきこと、もしくは伝えたい内容を持つこと、というように思惟されるのです。「群馬よいとこ」「地域の魅力」について多くの知識や情報を有するとともに、それについて広く伝えたい、わかってもらいたいという願望を持つことが英語習得の動機であり、英語コミュニケーション上達の鍵ではないかというのが私見です。

　地域の魅力を再認識し、観光資源として積極的な活用を図るとともに、世界に開かれた観光地を目指すまちづくりにおいて、本書が何らかのかたちで貢献できることを願っています。

　本書の出版に際して、本学の各関係部署、殊に地域連携センターにおいては、前田拓生センター長をはじめスタッフの方々に多大なるご尽力をいただきました。地域連携センターは、本学の教育理念に基づき、地域社会の発展に貢献するという趣旨のもと、様々な取り組みを推進しています。本学における研究成果を地域社会へ還元することもその一環であり、この度、拙地域志向研究に対して出版企画が図られ、その実現に向けてお骨折りいただきました。編集では、上毛新聞社事業局出版部の富澤隆夫氏より、編集者として豊かな経験から、読者に届く誌面づくりにご助力をいただきました。また、本学地域連携センター所属、川又彩夏地域コーディネーターには、掲載写真に関する承諾の取得や校正作業の補佐など、いろいろと便宜を図っていただきました。加えて、各施設の関係者各位より掲載写真のご提供、並びに写真撮影と掲載においてご快諾をいただきました。

　ここに、ご協力をいただきました方々に心から感謝の意を表します。

平成31年2月

高崎商科大学教授　渡　邉　美代子

本書の使い方

　本書では、地域の魅力ある観光スポットを紹介するとともに、受付、案内、誘導、注文、金銭のやり取り、クレーム対応、体調不良者の対処など、観光・サービス業に携わる人々にとって必須な場面・状況が取り込まれています。

　本書は6章から構成されますが、一貫して同じ難易度ではありません。第1〜4章を初・準中級レベル、そして第5〜6章を中・準上級レベルと位置付けています。前者で要求されるのは、道案内、乗車券の買い方、店頭や飲食店および宿泊施設での接客に関する英語コミュニケーションですから、決まった表現で対応できる部分が多く含まれると見ることができます。それに対して、後者ではボランティア・ガイドとして案内を担当する設定ですから、地域に関する知識とそれを英語で説明するとともに、訪問者の質問にも対応できる英語コミュニケーション力を想定した内容になるため、中・準上級者向けということができます。

　それぞれの場面は、Conversation（会話）、Vocabulary（語彙）、English Points（英語のポイント）、Exercise（練習問題）、Tips（助言）から構成されています。まず、Vocabulary を確認した後、Conversation に挑戦してください。

　続く English Points では、会話における英語表現の要点および使い方について解説が加えられていますが、学生だけでなく一般の方々の使用も考慮し、難しい文法用語を極力使わないように解説を加えました。言葉の仕組みを理解することにおいて、どうしても文法用語が必要である場合を除き、平易な言葉での説明を心掛けました。

　Exercise は Conversation の一部を切り取った、あるいは関係した

内容で構成されていますので、学習を試みてください。繰り返すことで、自分のモノにすることが肝要です。

　地域について多くを知ることがまちづくりや地域創造の原点であるという見地から、**Tips** 欄には、さらなる英語の知識をはじめ、歴史・文化・社会的な観点から地域の特筆すべき情報やエピソードなどを紹介していますが、これらに関してもできる限り平易な語彙で表現するという斟酌を加えました。

　最後に、**付記**として、会話の日本語訳が掲載されていますので、日本語表現や会話の流れなどを確認する際に活用してください。

目　次

第 1 章　上信電鉄でお出かけ【交通編】
Transportation ……………………………………………… 1

1 - 1　高崎駅で──上信線乗り場への行き方 …………………… 2
At *Takasaki* Station: Directions to the *Joshin* line platform

1 - 2　上信線乗り場で──切符の買い方を説明する ……………… 5
At the *Joshin* line: Explaining how to buy a ticket

1 - 3　上州富岡駅で──乗客に対応する ………………………… 8
At *Joshu Tomioka* Station: Responding to a passenger

1 - 4　行き方を教える──〔1〕 ………………………………… 9
Giving directions：〔1〕

1 - 5　行き方を教える──〔2〕 ……………………………… 11
Giving directions：〔2〕

1 - 6　客を乗せる ……………………………………………… 14
Carrying a passenger

1 - 7　ぐるりんバスの乗り方を教える ………………………… 17
Explaining how to use the "*Gururin* Bus"

1 - 8　観光バスに関する情報を提供する ……………………… 20
Providing information on tour buses

第 2 章　物産店でお土産を買う【買い物編】
Shopping ……………………………………………………… 23

2 - 1　土産店で──〔1〕 ……………………………………… 24
At a souvenir shop：〔1〕

2 - 2　土産店で──〔2〕 ······················· 26
At a souvenir shop：〔2〕

2 - 3　土産店で──〔3〕 ······················· 28
At a souvenir shop：〔3〕

2 - 4　土産店で──〔4〕 ······················· 32
At a souvenir shop：〔4〕

2 - 5　土産店で──〔5〕 ······················· 36
At a souvenir shop：〔5〕

2 - 6　土産店で──〔6〕 ······················· 41
At a souvenir shop：〔6〕

2 - 7　土産店で──〔7〕 ······················· 44
At a souvenir shop：〔7〕

2 - 8　土産店で──〔8〕 ······················· 47
At a souvenir shop：〔8〕

2 - 9　薬局で ··· 51
At a pharmacy

第 3 章　おいしい郷土料理【飲食編】
Food and Drink ·································· 55

3 - 1　ファーストフード店で ····················· 56
At a fast food restaurant

3 - 2　群馬の郷土食 ································· 59
Comfort food for *Gunma* people

3 - 3　食事処で ····································· 63
At a restaurant

3 - 4　すき焼きの具材は全部メイド・イン・グンマ ·············· 68
All the ingredients for *sukiyaki* are made in *Gunma*

第4章　温泉旅館に泊まる【温泉・宿泊編】
Onsen and Accommodations ································· 73

4-1　チェックイン ·· 74
Check-in

4-2　予約なしのチェックイン ······························· 78
Check-in without a reservation

4-3　客を部屋へ案内する ····································· 83
Showing a guest to their room

4-4　貴重品は金庫に保管する ······························ 86
Putting valuables in the safe

4-5　地図で場所を説明する ·································· 88
Explaining a place on a map

4-6　泉質と効能について説明する ·························· 92
Explaining the *onsen* quality and its effects

4-7　問題を処理する——部屋が寒すぎる ················ 96
Handling a problem: The room is too cold

4-8　給仕をする——〔1〕 ································· 100
Waiting on tables：〔1〕

4-9　給仕をする——〔2〕 ································· 101
Waiting on tables：〔2〕

4-10　朝食の時間を確認する ································ 102
Confirming breakfast time

4-11　朝食バイキング ··· 103
Breakfast buffet

4-12　フロントで部屋の鍵を預かる ······················· 105
Keeping the room key at the front desk

4-13　宿泊客に情報を提供する ···························· 107
Providing a hotel guest with information

4 -14　チェックアウト ························· 111
Check-out

第5章　世界遺産の見学【富岡製糸場編】
Tomioka Silk Mill ······························· 117

5 - 1　窓口で来場者に対応する ················· 118
Responding to a visitor at the counter

5 - 2　初対面で自己紹介する ···················· 122
Introducing yourself in the first meeting

5 - 3　瓦職人、煉瓦を焼く ······················· 128
Roof tile craftsmen made bricks

5 - 4　東置繭所で ································· 131
At the East cocoon warehouse

5 - 5　繰糸所で ·································· 133
At the Silk-reeling plant

5 - 6　繰糸所内で──〔1〕 ···················· 136
In the Silk-reeling plant：〔1〕

5 - 7　繰糸所内で──〔2〕 ···················· 139
In the Silk-reeling plant：〔2〕

5 - 8　ブリュナ館で──〔1〕 ···················· 141
At the Brunat House：〔1〕

5 - 9　ブリュナ館で──〔2〕 ···················· 145
At the Brunat House：〔2〕

5 -10　寄宿舎で ································· 148
At the Dormitories for female workers

5 -11　工女たちの作業着 ························· 151
Work clothes of female workers

5 -12　見解を示す ································ 152
Expressing one's opinion

5 -13 養蚕と群馬の女性 ··· 154
Sericulture and women in *Gunma*

5 -14 お手洗いの場所を説明する ··· 156
Explaining a restroom's location

第6章　おすすめパワースポット【周辺観光編】
Sightseeing Spots ·· 157

6 - 1 貫前神社はユニーク！ ·· 158
The *Nukisaki* Shrine is unique!

6 - 2 城下町小幡はカッコイイ！ ··· 162
Castle town *Obata* is cool!

6 - 3 群馬県立自然史博物館 ··· 167
The *Gunma* Museum of Natural History

6 - 4 アドバイスをする──〔1〕 ··· 170
Giving advice：〔1〕

6 - 5 アドバイスをする──〔2〕 ··· 174
Giving advice：〔2〕

6 - 6 高崎のバス観光をすすめる──〔1〕 ··························· 177
Recommending a bus tour in *Takasaki*：〔1〕

6 - 7 高崎のバス観光をすすめる──〔2〕 ··························· 181
Recommending a bus tour in *Takasaki*：〔2〕

6 - 8 高崎のバス観光をすすめる──〔3〕 ··························· 186
Recommending a bus tour in *Takasaki*：〔3〕

6 - 9 吹割の滝で ··· 189
At *Fukiware* Falls

付記 ··· 195

会話（日本語訳）··· 196

解答 ··· 223

第1章　上信電鉄でお出かけ
【交通編】

Transportation

1-1 高崎駅で——上信線乗り場への行き方
At *Takasaki* Station: Directions to the *Joshin* line platform

Takasaki Station（高崎駅）

Visitor: Excuse me. I would like to go to the *Tomioka* Silk Mill, a World Heritage Site. Can [Could] you tell me which line to take?

Passer-by: You should take the *Joshin* line. You can take the train from track No. 0 [Zero]. You'll find the entrance to the *Joshin* line when you go down the stairs. Go straight for approximately 100 [a hundred] meters and then you'll see the ticket gate.

Visitor: I see. Thank you.

Passer-by: You're welcome. You can ask one of the station staff about how to use the ticket (vending) machines because they are different from those of JR.

Visitor: OK, I will. Thanks for your advice.

Passer-by: Sure. Have a nice trip!

Visitor: Goodbye.

Vocabulary

line　　　　　（鉄道・バスなどの）線　　　silk mill　　　（絹）製糸工場
World Heritage Site　　世界遺産　　※site は敷地、用地の意味
passer-by　　通行人
track　　　　車両が走行する線　　※日本ではプラットフォームという呼び方が一般的
approximately　　約、ほぼ（about のかしこまった言い方）
ticket gate　　改札口　　　　　　　　　　station staff　駅員
ticket (vending) machine　　切符販売機

English Points

- visitor は、「訪問者／客」の意です。日本語の「客」は、あらゆる客を言い表すことのできる便利な言葉ですが、英語の場合、客の種類によって使い分けなければなりません。

    customer ……… デパートや商店、レストランなど、商品やサービスの提供を受ける客。
    guest ………… 招待客。ホテル・旅館の宿泊客。レストランの客（丁寧な呼び方）。
    passenger ……… 飛行機、電車、タクシーなどの乗客。
    client ………… 医師、弁護士、会計士などの依頼客。カウンセリングを受ける来談者。
    visitor………… 動物園、博物館、教育機関、公共施設、会社などの訪問客。
    tourist / traveler 観光客。旅行客。
    audience ……… 映画、演劇などの観客。音楽会、講演会などの聴衆。
    spectator ……… スポーツや催し物などの観客。祭りや行事の見物客。

- would like to～（～したい）は want to～と同じように使うことができますが、やや控えめなニュアンスのため、後者の直接的な、強い願望表現よりも、丁寧な印象を与えます。相手に「～したいですか」と尋ねる場合も、Do you want to～？よりも Would you like to～? を用いる方が、相手を成人として見ているニュアンスや丁寧さを表現することができます。

    ・I want to have a glass of water.（水を一杯、もらいたい。）
    ・I would like to have a glass of water.（水を一杯、いただきたい。）
    ・Do you want to go to the park?（公園へ行きたい？）
    ・Would you like to go to the park?（公園へ行きたいですか。）

- Can you～？と Could you～？ のニュアンスも、同様に丁寧さの違いです。カジュアルに表現しても問題ない場合は、見知らぬ相手に対してでも Can you～？を使えます。丁寧に依頼したい場合は、Could you～？の言い回しが好まれます。

    ・Can you tell me the way to the station?（駅に行く道を教えてもらえますか。）
    ・Could you tell me the way to the station?（駅に行く道を教えていただけますか。）

Exercise

目的地を示して、最寄り駅と使用する線の情報を入手しましょう。

```
A: I would like to go to_____. Can [Could] you tell me which line to take?
B: Take the_____line. The nearest railway station is_____.
```

Provide information

	1	2	3	4
目的地	*Shikishima* Park	*Rakusan-en*	*Fukiware* Falls	*Mizusawa Kannon*
最寄り駅	*Maebashi* Station	*Joshu Fukushima* Station	*Numata* Station	*Shibukawa* Station
路線	the *Ryomo* Line	the *Joshin* Line	the *Joetsu* Line	the *Joetsu* Line

	5	6	7	8
目的地	*Nukisaki* Shrine	*Isobe Onsen*	Japan Snake Center	*Takaragawa Onsen*
最寄り駅	*Joshu Ichinomiya* Station	*Isobe* Station	*Iwajuku* Station	*Minakami* Station
路線	the *Joshin* Line	the *Shin-etsu* Line	the *Ryomo* Line	the *Joetsu* Line

Practical application：次の路線図を用いて、さらなる練習をしよう。

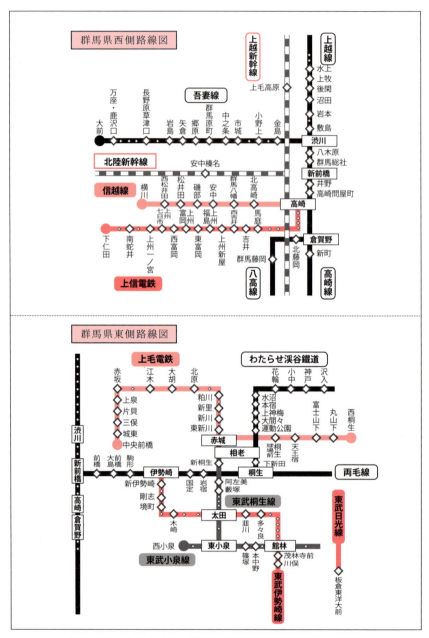

「駅からのりかえガイド」（群馬県庁交通政策課提供画像を修正）

1-2 上信線乗り場で──切符の買い方を説明する

At the *Joshin* line: Explaining how to buy a ticket

The *Joshin* line（上信線）

Ticket (vending) machine（切符販売機）

Visitor: Excuse me. Could you help me with this ticket (vending) machine? I have no idea how to use it.

Station staff: Sure, I'll be with you in a minute... First, confirm the destination and the charge on the screen. What is your destination?

Visitor: The *Tomioka* Silk Mill, a World Heritage Site. Which is the closest station?

Station staff: Buy a ticket for *Joshu Tomioka*. 〈On the screen〉 All station names on the *Joshin* line are also displayed in roman letters, as you see. The fare is under each station name. Here's the *Joshu Tomioka* Station.

Visitor: I see, it says 790 [seven hundred (and) ninety] yen.

Station staff: Then insert the fare into the slot, and select the number of people and the arrival station. That's it!

Visitor: This is a little different from the JR ticket (vending) machine.

Station staff: Yes, it is. But as the operation is easy, anyone can use it.

Visitor: I see. By the way, how long does it take to get to *Joshu Tomioka?*

Station staff: It takes about 40 minutes. Get off at the thirteenth station, *Joshu Tomioka*.

Visitor: Got it. Thank you so much for your help.

Station staff: You're welcome. Enjoy the scenery on the local line.

Vocabulary

explain	〜を説明する	confirm	〜を確かめる
destination	目的地	charge	（課される）料金、手数料
display	〜を表示する	fare	料金
insert A into B	A を B に入れ込む	operation	操作
get off	下車する		

English Points

■ 料金の呼び方は、その内容によって異なります。

(1) 交通機関を利用する場合の乗車料金、運賃：
- train fare ……………………… 電車賃
- bus fare …………………………… バスの運賃
- taxi fare ………………………… タクシー料金
- one-way fare ………………… 片道料金

(2) 博物館や美術館などの入場料や入園料、施設を利用する際の使用料：
- admission fee ………………… 入場料　　※ admission のみでも使用
- entrance fee ………………… 入場料、入学金
- tuition fee …………………… 授業料
- parking fee ………………… 駐車場代

(3) 一定の基準を有する料金：
- hotel rate …………………… ホテル宿泊料金
- postal rate…………………… 郵便料金　　※ postage, postal charge も使用
- parking rate ………………… 駐車料金
- ※ rate は基本的に discount rate（割引率）や exchange rate（為替相場［レート］）のように「率」「割合」「歩合」といった意味で、一定の基準に基づいた料金を表す。

(4) サービス対する料金は、charge が広く用いられます。
- service charge ………………… サービス料
- free of charge ………………… 無料
- no extra charge ……………… 追加料金なし
- cover charge…………………… 飲食店などの席料、テーブルチャージ
- telephone charge……………… 通話料金
- delivery charge ……………… 配送料

(5) 道路や橋の通行料は、toll が用いられます。
- highway / expressway toll…… 幹線道路／高速道路料金
- bridge toll …………………… 橋銭
- canal toll …………………… 運河通航料

6

■ Can [Could] you help me with〜?（〜を助けていただけますか）は、依頼の表現です。また、Can[Could] you help me（to）V〜? でも使えます。

・Can [Could] you help me with | this?（これを助けていただけますか。）
　　　　　　　　　　　　　　　　 | my homework?
　　　　　　　　　　　　　　　　 |（宿題を手伝っていただけますか。）

・Can [Could] you help me | clean the living room?
　　　　　　　　　　　　　 |（居間を掃除するのを手伝っていただけますか。）
　　　　　　　　　　　　　 | carry the bags?
　　　　　　　　　　　　　 |（かばんを運ぶのを手伝っていただけますか。）

※ help は使役動詞ではありませんが、米英語においては「help ＋目的語＋（to）do」の用法が一般的であるようです。因みに、原形不定詞（to なし不定詞）は、使役動詞（make, have, let）あるいは知覚動詞（see, hear, feel, watch, smell）の構文に表れます。

■ 「わかりません」を伝えたいとき、I don't know. ではぶっきら棒な印象を与えてしまいます。I'm not sure.（よくわからないなぁ）や I have no idea.（見当がつかない）の表現が丁寧です。

■ How long does it take to get to 〜?（〜へはどれくらい時間がかかりますか）の質問に対して、It takes about 〜（〜くらいです）と返答します。どちらも、決まりきった表現です。

 Exercise　Prepare を答えた後、枠内のパターンを用いて質問と応答の練習をしましょう。

A: How long does it take to get to＿＿＿＿＿ from your house?
B: It takes about＿＿＿＿＿ | by train / bus / car.
　　　　　　　　　　　　　　 | on foot.

※ by train / bus / car は、交通手段を表します。ただし、「徒歩で」は on foot を用います。

Prepare
(1) from your house to the nearest station:　　　　＿＿＿minutes [hours] by/on＿＿＿
(2) from your house to the high school you went to:＿＿＿minutes [hours] by/on＿＿＿
(3) from your house to the university you go to:　 ＿＿＿minutes [hours] by/on＿＿＿
(4) from your house to the post office:　　　　　　＿＿＿minutes [hours] by/on＿＿＿
(5) from your house to the city [town] hall:　　　 ＿＿＿minutes [hours] by/on＿＿＿
(6) from your house to the nearest supermarket:　　＿＿＿minutes [hours] by/on＿＿＿
(7) from your house to the convenience store:　　　＿＿＿minutes [hours] by/on＿＿＿
(8) from your house to your favorite *ramen* shop: ＿＿＿minutes [hours] by/on＿＿＿

1-3 上州富岡駅で──乗客に対応する
At *Joshu Tomioka* Station: Responding to a passenger

Joshu Tomioka Station（上州富岡駅）

Visitor: Excuse me, where is the information center?

Station staff: It's on your right after you pass through the ticket gate. You can see it over there.

Visitor: Are there any guides?

Station staff: No, not on weekdays. The volunteer guide is present on Saturdays and Sundays. You'll find some free town maps and pamphlets over there.

Visitor: Okay, I'll stop by and see. Thanks a lot.

Station staff: Don't mention it.

Vocabulary

respond to	〜に対応する	pass through	〜を通り抜ける
over there	あそこに、すぐそこに	free	無料の
stop by	〜に立ち寄る	mention	〜をちょっと言う、言及する

English Points

■ お礼の言い方とその返し方には、カジュアルから丁寧な表現までいろいろあります。表現が長くなるほど丁寧さが増すとみることができます。

Thanks. …………………ありがとう。		That's OK.………… 大丈夫。	
Thanks a lot.……………どうもありがとう。		No problem.……… 問題ないよ。	
Thank you. ……………ありがとうございます。		Sure, any time.……… いつでも、どうぞ。	
Thank you so much. … どうもありがとうございます。		Don't mention it.……お礼はいりません。	
Thanks a million. ………どうもありがとうございます。		You're welcome. ……どういたしまして。	
I really appreciate it. ……本当に感謝しています。		(It was) My pleasure. …どういたしまして。	

1-4 行き方を教える──〔1〕

Giving directions：〔1〕

《At *Joshu Tomioka* Station》

Station staff: Hello. <u>Here's</u> a rough map of how to get to the *Tomioka* Silk Mill.

Visitor: Thanks. Oh, <u>this is</u> great. The route is easy to understand and it's only about "15 minutes on foot."

Station staff: It's quicker to take a taxi, but it's within walking distance.

Visitor: <u>I'd rather walk</u> because I want to look around the town.

Station staff: Sounds great. Have a nice day!

Visitor: Thanks. You too.

Vocabulary

rough map	略図	understand	理解する
distance	距離	look around	見て回る、見て歩く

👉 English Points

■ Here's 〜／Here're 〜（〜をどうぞ、ここに〜があります）は、何かを渡したり、すすめたりする表現です。
- ・Here's my card. ………… 名刺をどうぞ。
- ・Here's the menu. ……… メニューをどうぞ。
- ・Here're some cookies. …クッキーをどうぞ。

■ This is〜は、便利な表現です。This is <u>a pen</u>. のように名詞が続けば、「これは○○です」という説明の表現になります。また、形容詞が続く場合、this が指し示すものを評価する言い回しになります。

　This is ＋名詞
- ・This is a *sensu*, a Japanese hand fan.
（これは扇子、日本の携帯用送風器です。）
- ・This is a *bonsai*, a minature potted tree.
（これは盆栽、小型の鉢植えの木です。）

　This is ＋形容詞
- ・This is good [delicious, tasty].（これはおいしい。）

- This is great [wonderful, terrific].（これはすごい［素晴らしい、素敵だ］。）

■ I'd rather～（～する方が良い、むしろ～したい）は、選択の判断や志向を言い表します。
- I'd rather have tea than coffee.（私はコーヒーよりもむしろお茶を飲みたい。）
- I'd rather stay home and watch TV this evening.
  （今晩は家にいてテレビを見る方がいい。）
- I'd rather not talk about it.（私は、それについて話したくありません。）

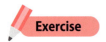 **Exercise** Prepare を答えた後、枠内のパターンを用いて質問と応答の練習をしましょう。

```
A: Would you like to_____?
B: I'd rather_____than_____.
```

Prepare

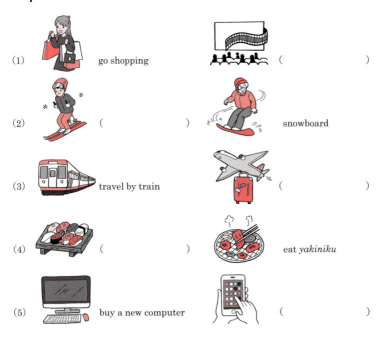

(1) go shopping ( )

(2) ( ) snowboard

(3) travel by train ( )

(4) ( ) eat *yakiniku*

(5) buy a new computer ( )

ski / buy a new smartphone / eat *sushi* / go to a movie / travel by plane [air]

1-5 行き方を教える──〔2〕

Giving directions：〔2〕

Transportation

1

交通編

《After leaving *Joshu Tomioka* Station》

Visitor: 〈Talking to oneself〉 I think I lost the way. I'd better ask someone.

《Looking around》

Visitor: Excuse me. <u>Could you tell me the way to the *Tomioka* Silk Mill?</u>

Passer-by: Sure. <u>Go straight for one block.</u> <u>Then turn [to the] right and go one more block.</u>

Visitor: Got it. How much longer does it take? Looking at some of the shops on the map, I have no idea how far I've walked from the station.

Passer-by: You're almost there. When you turn right at that corner, you'll see a brick building in front of you. <u>You can't miss it.</u>

Visitor: Good! I'm almost there. Thank you.

Passer-by: Don't mention it.

Vocabulary

lose the way	道に迷う
go straight	まっすぐに進む
block	街区
turn to the right / turn right	右へ曲がる
brick	煉瓦
miss	～を逃す

📢 English Points

■ 「○○を教えてください」の表現は、「何をどのように教える」のかによって用いる動詞が異なります。次の例文の下線部を参照してください。

- Could you <u>tell</u> me where the restaurant is?（言葉で教える）
- Could you <u>show</u> me where the restaurant is on this map?
  （地図などを用いて視覚的に教える）
- Please <u>teach</u> me how to write a report.（知識や技術を教える）
- Please <u>explain</u> why you want to become a nurse.（理由等を教える＝説明する）

■ 道を教える基本的な言い回しです。

- Go straight | for one block.（まっすぐ1ブロック進んでください。）
  about 100 meters.
  （まっすぐ100mほど進んでください。）
  until you get to the first set of traffic lights.
  （一つ目の信号までまっすぐ行ってください。）
- Go down this street and then take the third left.
  （この通りをまっすぐ行って、三つ目の角を左に曲がってください。）
- Go past the Washington hotel and then turn right at the Gusto Family Restaurant.
  （ワシントンホテルを通り過ぎて、ガスト・ファミリーレストランを右に曲がってください。）
- Turn right [left] at the second corner.
  （二つ目の角を右［左］に曲がってください。）
- Cross the intersection and go two more blocks.
  （あの交差点を渡って、もう2ブロック行ってください。）

■ 位置関係を表す場合、下線部の決まり文句を用います。

- The building is <u>in front of</u> the station.（そのビルは駅<u>の前</u>にあります。）
- The parking lot is <u>next to</u> the department store.
  （駐車場はデパート<u>の隣</u>にあります。）
- The convenience store is <u>just around that corner</u>.
  （コンビニは<u>その角を曲がった</u>ところです。）
- The post office is <u>across from</u> the park.
  （郵便局は公園<u>の向かい側</u>にあります。）
- Bus stop number 10 is <u>on the other side of</u> the station.
  （10番バス停は駅<u>の向こう側</u>です。）
- The hospital is <u>opposite</u> the bank.（その病院は銀行<u>の反対側</u>にあります。）

■ You can't miss it. は、〈あなたはそれを見逃すことはできない〉という直訳になりますが、「見逃すことはありませんよ」や「（すぐに）わかりますよ」といった意味合いで用います。

Exercise Prepareを答えた後、枠内のパターンを用いて質問と応答の練習をしましょう。

⟨At the west exit of *Takasaki* Station⟩
A: Could you tell me the way to＿＿＿＿＿＿＿＿＿?
B: Sure. *Go straight for＿＿＿＿block(s). Then turn right/left and go＿＿＿＿more block(s).
　*目的地によっては、別の表現も必要。English Points（前頁）を参照。

Prepare

　JR高崎駅周辺地図を参考に、次の目的地への行き方を確認してください。

(1) the town hall ＿＿＿＿＿＿＿＿＿＿＿＿＿＿＿＿＿＿＿＿＿＿＿＿＿＿＿＿＿＿
(2) a restaurant ＿＿＿＿＿＿＿＿＿＿＿＿＿＿＿＿＿＿＿＿＿＿＿＿＿＿＿＿＿＿＿
(3) the Music Center ＿＿＿＿＿＿＿＿＿＿＿＿＿＿＿＿＿＿＿＿＿＿＿＿＿＿＿
(4) ○○ bank ＿＿＿＿＿＿＿＿＿＿＿＿＿＿＿＿＿＿＿＿＿＿＿＿＿＿＿＿＿＿＿＿
(5) a convenience store ＿＿＿＿＿＿＿＿＿＿＿＿＿＿＿＿＿＿＿＿＿＿＿＿＿＿
(6) ○○ hospital ＿＿＿＿＿＿＿＿＿＿＿＿＿＿＿＿＿＿＿＿＿＿＿＿＿＿＿＿＿
(7) ○○ clinic ＿＿＿＿＿＿＿＿＿＿＿＿＿＿＿＿＿＿＿＿＿＿＿＿＿＿＿＿＿＿
(8) ○○ hotel ＿＿＿＿＿＿＿＿＿＿＿＿＿＿＿＿＿＿＿＿＿＿＿＿＿＿＿＿＿＿
(9) ○○ square ＿＿＿＿＿＿＿＿＿＿＿＿＿＿＿＿＿＿＿＿＿＿＿＿＿＿＿＿＿
(10) ○○ department store ＿＿＿＿＿＿＿＿＿＿＿＿＿＿＿＿＿＿＿＿＿＿＿＿

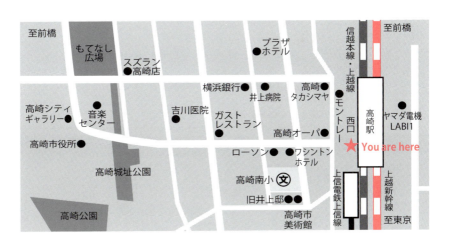

1-6 客を乗せる
Carrying a passenger

Taxi driver: Hello. <u>Where to</u>?

Passenger: <u>Can you take me to</u> the *Umenoi Ryokan* on *Yukimi* Street, please?

Taxi driver: Sure. Do you have any baggage?

Passenger: Yes. One suitcase.

Taxi driver: Please <u>get in (the car)</u> and fasten your seat belt. I'll put your suitcase in the trunk.

Passenger: How long does it take to get to the *ryokan*?

Taxi driver: It's about twelve minutes without traffic.

《After a while》

Taxi driver: <u>Here we are</u>.

Passenger: How much is it?

Taxi driver: (It's) 1,810 [one thousand eight hundred and ten] yen.

Passenger: <u>Here's 2,000 [two thousand] yen. Keep the change.</u>

Taxi driver: Thank you. Have a good day!

Passenger: Thanks. You too.

Vocabulary

baggage　　荷物
fasten　　　～を締める
traffic = traffic jam [congestion]　交通渋滞
keep the change　　お釣りを取っておく

English Points

- タクシー乗車の際に耳にする Where to? の表現は、Where are you going?／Where would you like to go?（どちらまで行かれますか）の省略形です。

- Can you take me to〜, please? は、依頼の表現ですが、目的地のみを告げる To the *Umenoi Ryokan* on *Yukimi* Street.（雪見通りの梅乃井旅館まで）の簡単な表現も頻用されます。

- suitcase または bag は可算名詞ですから、2つ以上は -s をつけて用います。これに対して、baggage もしくは luggage は「（まとまった）荷物」の意味で用いられ、不可算名詞の扱いになります。数える場合は two pieces of baggage [luggage] になります。因みに、luggage はイギリス、baggage はアメリカで使われる傾向にありますが、どちらの語を用いても通じます。

《At the airport check-in counter》
（空港のチェックインカウンターで）

Ground staff

Do you have any baggage [luggage] to check in?
（預けるお荷物はありますか。）

Passenger

I have two suitcases [bags].
（スーツケース［鞄］2つです。）
three pieces of baggage [luggage].
（3つの荷物があります。）

- 「〜に乗る」「〜から降りる」は、get on〜 get off〜とは限りません。移動の方向によって、言い回しが異なります。

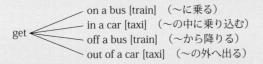

get ─┬─ on a bus [train] （〜に乗る）
　　　├─ in a car [taxi] （〜の中に乗り込む）
　　　├─ off a bus [train] （〜から降りる）
　　　└─ out of a car [taxi] （〜の外へ出る）

- Here we are. は、「さぁ、着きましたよ」を意味する決まり文句です。モノを渡す際の Here you are.（はい、どうぞ）と似ていますが、これらはそれぞれ用途が異なる表現です。

- チップを渡す感覚で、Keep the change.（お釣りは取っといて）という表現があります。1万円札で支払う場合、Here's 10,000 [ten thousand] yen. Can I have 8,000 [eight thousand] yen back? And you can keep the change.（1万円で。8千円を戻して、あとの釣りは取っといて）という表現は便利です。

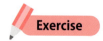

Exercise p.13の地図を見て、枠内のパターンを用いて接客の会話を練習をしましょう。

Taxi driver: Hello. Where to?

Passenger: Can you take me to_____, please?

Taxi driver: Sure. Do you have any baggage?

Passenger: Yes._____.

Taxi driver: Please get in (the car) and fasten your seat belt. I'll put your_____ in the trunk.

1-7 ぐるりんバスの乗り方を教える
Explaining how to use the "*Gururin* Bus"

Gururin Bus（ぐるりんバス）

Passenger: Excuse me. I'd like to go to *Kannon-yama*. Which [Which number] *Gururin* bus should I take?

Passer-by: Take the number 13 or 14 bus. You can catch the bus at bus stop 8 over there.

Passenger: Thanks a lot.

Passer-by: Don't mention it.

《Confirming the route with the bus driver》

Passenger: Hi. Does this bus go to *Kannon-yama*?

Bus driver: Yes, it does. What's your destination?

Passenger: Let me see... the bus stop near the statue of *Takasaki Byakue Dai-kannon*. How long does it take to get there?

Bus driver: The nearest bus stop is "*Byakue Kannon-mae*," which means "in front of *Byakue Kannon*." It takes about 25 minutes to get there. Please push the button when you hear your stop being announced.

Passenger: All right. Uh, one more question... Where do I buy a ticket?

Bus driver: No ticket is needed. <u>All you have to do is</u> drop 200 [two hundred] yen into the machine when you get off. It's a flat rate.

Passenger: I pay 200 [two hundred] yen <u>no matter where</u> I go. That's great!

Bus driver: By the way, it's almost time to leave. You'd better get on the bus.

Passenger: Oh, okay. Thanks for the information.

Bus driver: No problem.

Vocabulary

bus stop　　バス停留所
near　　　　〜の近くに
drop A into B　　A を B に落とす
flat rate　　一律料金

English Points

■ All you have to do is 〜は、〈しなくてはならないことのすべては、〜である〉という直訳ですが、「〜しさえすればいい」の表現として用います。

- All you have to do is (to) push this button.
  （あなたはこのボタンを押しさえすればいい。）
- All you need to do is (to) sign this contract.
  （あなたはこの契約に署名しさえすればいい。）
- All I want to do is (to) see my family.（家族に会えさえすればいい。）

be 動詞の後に名詞がくる場合もあります。

- All we need is love.（愛さえあればいい。）
- All they want is freedom.（彼らが望むのは自由だけです。）

■ no matter の後には、疑問詞（where / what / who / when / which / how）が続きます。

- No matter where you go, I'll find you.
  （あなたがどこへ行こうと、私はあなたを見つけ出します。）
- No matter what I do, it's none of your business.
  （私が何をしようと、あなたには関係がない。）
- No matter who does this, the result will be the same.
  （誰がこれをやっても、結果は同じでしょう。）
- No matter how busy he is, he keeps his promises.
  （どんなに忙しくても、彼は約束を守ります。）

Exercise　枠内のパターンを用いて会話の練習をしましょう。

> *Passenger:* Excuse me. I'd like to go to_____.
> Which [Which number] Gururin bus should I take?
>
> *Passer-by:* Take the number_____ bus. You can catch the bus
> at bus stop_____ over there.
>
> *Passenger:* Thanks a lot.
>
> *Passer-by:* Don't mention it.

Provide information

Place of destination	Bus number / name	Bus stop number / place
Takasaki Arena	Shuttle bus	6
Gunma-no-mori	9 or 10	in front of the police station at the east exit
Takasaki University of Commerce	11 or 12	8
Shorinzan Daruma-ji Temple	1 or 2	4
Takasaki City University of Economics	3 or 4	4
Saint Pierre Hospital	11 or 12	8

Tips:

■ "*Gururin*" is the name of the circle buses in *Takasaki* City. A flat-fare system is used on the city buses, with adults costing 200 yen and children below elementary school age costing 100 yen. In certain sections (Downtown Circulation Line, *Takasaki Arena* Shuttle Bus, etc.) the fare is only 100 yen for adults and 50 yen for children.
　「ぐるりん」は高崎市内を循環するバスの名称です。ぐるりんバスは一律料金で200円ですが、小学生以下の子どもは100円です。一部の運行区間（都心循環線および高崎アリーナシャトルなど）に限って、大人100円、子ども（小学生以下）50円になります。

■ Only coins are accepted on buses. It is possible to exchange 500-yen coins and 1,000-yen notes at the money changer near the driver's seat. Please use the money changer when the bus has stopped because it is dangerous to use it on a moving bus.
　料金はお釣りのないように用意してください。運転席近くの両替機で500円硬貨と1,000円札を両替することができます。走行中の両替機の使用は危険ですので、停止しているときに利用してください。

■ One-day passes (unlimited rides available on all *Gururin* routes) are available for 510 yen. They can be purchased from the bus driver when you board or at a *Basu sougou annai-jo* (Bus information office) at the west exit of *Takasaki* Station.
　ぐるりんバス専用の1日フリー乗車券が510円で利用できます。その乗車券は、乗車の折にバスドライバーから、または高崎駅西口のバス総合案内所で購入することができます。

■ The date is stamped on the one-day pass when you make the purchase. Every time you get off a *Gururin* bus, please show the pass to the driver.
　購入の際に、1日フリー乗車券に利用日がスタンプされます。ぐるりんバスを降車するたび、ドライバーに提示してください。

1-8 観光バスに関する情報を提供する
Providing information on tour buses

Takasaki Station west exit
(高崎駅西口)

Bus information office
(バス総合案内所)

Guide: You know what... As route buses cover a large area of *Takasaki* City, people can go to their destinations by bus, but the service frequency is not so good.

Visitor: Local people <u>seem to</u> go by car. Tourists need to depend on public transport [transportation] though.

Guide: That's true. Now I'd like to give you some useful information. Regular tour bus services run on weekends. For example, the tour bus that departs from *Takasaki* Station and stops at the main tourist spots such as Lake *Haruna*, the *Haruna* Shrine, the *Daruma* Temple, and the *Takasaki Kannon* is very convenient as you can visit them all in one day.

Visitor: That's great! How much is it [the fare]?

Guide: I remember that it's pretty reasonable.

Visitor: I'll just have to schedule my tour then.

Guide: I hope you enjoy it.

Vocabulary

cover	（範囲が）〜に及ぶ
frequency	頻度、回数
depend on	〜に頼る
public transport [transportation]	公共交通機関
useful	役立つ、有用な
regular service	（バス・列車などの）定期運行
convenient	便利な、都合のよい

English Points

■ seem と look は、どちらも「〜に見える、〜らしい」の意で用いられますが、これらの使い方には違いがあります。look が様子や状況から客観的な判断を示すのに対して、seem は話し手の主観に基づいた判断を述べる場合に用いられます。seem の使い方は、次の通り。

(1) seem (to be) ＋形容詞　　※このパターンでは to be の省略が可能

・She seems (to be) nice [kind, difficult, smart].
（彼女はいい［親切な、難しい、賢い］人らしい。）
・The man seems (to be) sick.（あの男の人は病気のようです。）

(2) seem to be ＋名詞　　※このパターンでは to be の省略は不可

・That woman seems to be a lawyer.（あの女性は弁護士だと思われます。）
・He seems to be a serious student.（彼はまじめな学生らしい。）
・It seems to be an international problem.（それは国際的な問題に見えます。）

(3) seem to ＋動詞（原型）

・The audience seemed to enjoy the game.（観客は試合を楽しんだようだ。）
・The students seem to have gone home.（学生たちは帰宅したようです。）

Tip:

■ As some of the regular tour bus services are not offered over the winter season, please confirm with the bus companies.
定期観光バスは、冬季に運行しないルートもありますので、バス会社に確認してください。

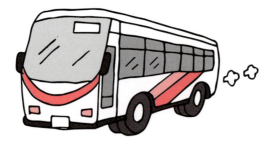

第2章　物産店でお土産を買う
【買い物編】

2-1 土産店で——〔1〕
At a souvenir shop：〔1〕

E'site *Takasaki* souvenir shops in *Takasaki* Station
（高崎駅　E'site 高崎土産店）

Salesclerk: Hello. <u>How may I help you</u>?

Customer: Just looking, thanks.

Salesclerk: Please take your time. <u>Let me know if</u> you need any help.

Customer: I will, thank you.

Vocabulary

souvenir	土産、記念品
salesclerk	店員
take one's time	（急がずに）ゆっくりやる

English Points

■ 日本語の「いらっしゃいませ」の場合、お客は応えることを期待されていませんので、黙って店の中に入り、店内を見歩くといった光景は珍しくありません。英語の May I help you? は「お手伝いしましょうか」という意味ですから、Yes, I'm looking for 〜. / No, I'm just looking. のように応えることが期待されています。簡単に、Yes./No. だけの応答も行われます。How may I help you? は、「どのようにお手伝いしましょうか」の意味合いですから、お客の求めているものを聞きたいという気持ちが表れた、丁寧な表現になります。Yes./No. ではなく、具体的な内容を引き出す表現として用いられます。

■ Let me know if 〜（もし〜なら、お知らせください）は、相手に対して強制力を伴わない婉曲的な表現です。これに対して、Tell me 〜（［必要な情報を］教えてください）というのは、相手に情報を切望するニュアンスが含まれるため、行き方を尋ねたり、話をせがんだりする際の表現です。

- Please let me [us] know | if you have any questions.
  （質問があれば、お知らせください。）
  when is convenient for you?
  （ご都合のよい日時をお知らせください。）

- Could you tell me how to get to the *Gunma* Music Center?
  （群馬音楽センターへの行き方を教えていただけますか。）
- Please tell me [us] about your trip to *Nikko*.
  （あなたの日光への旅行について話してください。）

2-2 土産店で──〔2〕
At a souvenir shop：〔2〕

Customer: Excuse me, could you help me?

Salesclerk: Sure. How may I help you?

Customer: <u>I'd like to see the one on the shelf over there.</u>

Salesclerk: Okay, I'll get it for you. <u>Which one?</u>

Customer: <u>The second one from the left in front</u>.

Salesclerk: This one?

Customer: Yes, that's it.

Salesclerk: Here it is. Would you like to buy this?

Customer: I think I like it. Sure, I'll take it.

Vocabulary

shelf	棚

👉 English Points

■ 手の届かないところにある商品を手にとって見たいときの表現です。

- I'd like to see the one | on the shelf over there.
（そこの棚の上にある商品を見たいのですが。）
in the window.
（ウインドーに飾ってある商品を見たいのですが。）
in the showcase [display case].
（陳列ケースにある商品を見たいのですが。）

■ Which one?（どれですか）は、Which one would you like to see? の省略形です。使われる状況によってニュアンスの違いは生じますが、次の表現のどれも Which one? の省略形で間に合います。

- Which one (do you want)?（どれが欲しいですか。）
- Which one (will you take)?（どちらを取りますか。）
- Which one (is better for you)?（あなたにとってどちらがいいですか。）

■ 具体的な場所を言い表す。

- It's over there. (そこにあります。)
- It's on the far right [left] of the display case.
  (陳列ケースの右［左］端にあります。)
- It's the one on the right [left]. (右［左］側のものです。)
- It's the second [third, fouth...] one from the right [left].
  (右［左］から2番目［3番目、4番目...］のものです。)
- It's the second one from the right [left] in front.
  (前の列の右［左］から2番目のものです。)
  ＝ It's the second one in front from the right [left].
- It's the third one from the right [left] in back.
  (奥の列の右［左］から3番目のものです。)
  ＝ It's the third one in back from the right [left].

 Exercise Prepare を答えた後、枠内のパターンを用いて質問と応答の練習をしましょう。

Customer: I'd like to see the _____ in the showcase.
Salesclerk: Okay, I'll get it for you. Which one?
Customer: The _____.

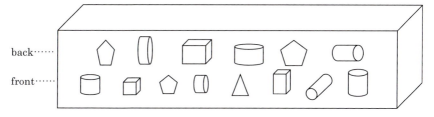

back……
front……

Prepare
続く商品に下の枠から英語名を選び、記入しなさい。

(1) (　　　) (2) (　　　) (3) (　　　) (4) (　　　)

(5) (　　　) (6) (　　　) (7) (　　　) (8) (　　　)

| wooden chopsticks | *kokeshi* doll | silk ties | glassware |
| *Daruma* doll | silk scarf | wooden cup | *Gunma-chan* good |

2-3 土産店で——〔3〕

At a souvenir shop：〔3〕

Customer: Excuse me. <u>How much is this?</u>

Salesclerk: <u>It's 2,980 [two thousand nine hundred (and) eighty]
yen with tax.</u>

Customer: Can you give me a <u>discount</u>?

Salesclerk: These are already at discounted prices.

Customer: The same item was <u>on sale</u> at the other store. But I
prefer this color compared to the other one. It's
classy, too.

Salesclerk: It's quite a <u>bargain</u>.

Customer: I'll <u>stop by again</u> on my way back. I'll probably
purchase it if I don't change my mind.

Salesclerk: I'll see you again then.

Vocabulary

discount	割引、安くすること	on sale	特売で
compared to	〜と比べ、比較すると	classy	粋な、シックな
bargain	安い買い物	stop by	立ち寄る
purchase	〜を購入する　[＝ buy]	change one's mind	心変わりする

English Points

■ 「いくらですか」の決まり文句に関しては、次の表現が一般的です。

- How much? (いくら。)
- How much is this [that]? (これ［あれ］はいくらですか。)
- How much would it be? (それはおいくらですか。)
- What's the price of this? (これの値段はいくらですか。)

　※ price が「(商品の) 価格」であるのに対して、cost は「(〜かかる) 費用」の
　　意ですから、使い方が異なります。

- How much does this *cost? (この費用はいくらですか。)　　　*cost (動詞)
- How much does the trip *cost? (旅行費用はいくらですか。)　　　〃

28

■ 「税込み［抜き］で、○○円です」という説明は、次のようになります（単位を表す thousand, hundred は複数形にならないことに注意を要します）。

- It's 2,980 [two thousand nine hundred (and) eighty] yen with [without] tax.
（税込み［抜き］で、2,980円です。）
- It's 1,450 [one thousand four hundred (and) fifty] yen plus tax.
（1,450円に税金がプラスされます。）
- That's the price after [before] tax.（それは課税後［前］の金額です。）
- Prices are displayed on the items and all prices include [exclude] tax.
（価格は商品に表示され、すべての表示価格は税込み［抜き］です。）

■ 上記の会話では、discount（値引き、割引）は名詞として使われていますが、この語は形容詞や動詞としても用いられます。

- This is an outlet shop. You can buy goods at a discount.
（ここはアウトレット店です。ディスカウントで商品を買うことができますよ。）
- Discount prices are available for group travel.
（グループ旅行に割引価格が利用可能です。）
- The price of this item is discounted by ten percent.
（この商品の値段は10％の値引きになっています。）

■ on sale には、「販売中」と「安売り、特売中」の両方の意味が含まれます。これに対して、bargain は「お買い得品」の意で、商品そのものを指し示します。

- The new model goes on sale next month.
（その新しい機種が来月販売になります。）
- Canned foods were on sale at the supermarket, so I stocked up (on them).
（スーパーで缶詰類が特売だったので、それらをまとめ買いしました。）
- This brandname bag was a bargain. I couldn't resist buying it.
（このブランド・バッグはお買い得品でした。買わずにはいられませんでした。）

■ I'll stop by again on my way back.（また寄ります）と同様の意味で、I'll come back later on my way back.（後ほど戻ります）の表現も使用できます。

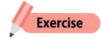 **Exercise** Prepare を答えた後、枠内のパターンを用いて質問と応答の練習をしましょう。

Customer: Excuse me. How much is this?
Salesclerk: It's _____ with [without] tax.

Provide information

- ￥680−（税込み）
- ￥2,980−（税抜き）
- ￥12,530−（税抜き）
- ￥3,790−（税抜き）
- ￥24,800−（税抜き）
- ￥67,320−（税込み）
- ￥116,741−（税込み）
- ￥98,300−（税抜き）

Prepare

数字に直しなさい。
(1) two hundred (and) fifty-seven ……………………………………………… (   )
(2) four thousand six hundred (and) twelve [=forty-six hundred (and) twelve] …… (   )
(3) sixty-eight thousand nine hundred (and) seventeen ……………………… (   )
(4) three thousand five hundred (and) seventy-eight [=thirty-five hundred (and) seventy-eight] … (   )
(5) twenty-five thousand seven hundred (and) forty ……………………… (   )
(6) thirteen thousand six hundred (and) forty-one ……………………… (   )

Tips:

■ thirteen と thirty、fourteen と forty といった似通った読み方の数字が紛らわしく、注意を要します。それぞれ13と30、14と40という異なる数字を指しますから、-teen と -ty の規則性を次の表から把握してください。

Number	English	Number	English	Number	English
1	one	11	eleven	21	twenty-one
2	two	12	twelve	22	twenty-two
3	three	13	thirteen	23	twenty-three
4	four	14	fourteen	24	twenty-four
5	five	15	fifteen	25	twenty-five
6	six	16	sixteen	26	twenty-six
7	seven	17	seventeen	27	twenty-seven
8	eight	18	eighteen	28	twenty-eight
9	nine	19	nineteen	29	twenty-nine
10	ten	20	twenty	30	thirty

```
        30  …… thirty
        40 …… forty
        50 …… fifty
        60 …… sixty
        70 …… seventy
        80 …… eighty
        99 …… ninety-nine
       100 …… a [one] hundred
       101 …… a [one] hundred (and) one
       200 …… two hundred
       900 …… nine hundred
     1,000 …… a [one] thousand ───────────── 1千
    10,000 …… ten thousand ─────────────── 1万
   100,000 …… a [one] hundred thousand ──── 10万
 1,000,000 …… a [one] million ───────────── 100万
10,000,000 …… ten million ───────────────── 1千万
100,000,000 …… a [one] hundred million ──── 1億
```

■ 今や、値引き交渉は当たり前のように行われているようです。「もう少し〜」と迫るお客の要求表現と、その対応表現は次の通りです。

customer

Could you give me[us] an additional 10% [ten percent] discount?
（もう10％値引きしていただけますか。）
　= Could you take an additional 10% [ten percent] off?
Could you give me[us] a bigger discount?（もっと値引きしていただけますか。）
Could you discount it a little more?（もう少し値引きしていただけますか。）
Could you make it ¥8,000 [eight thousand yen]？（それ、8,000円になりませんか。）

clerk

We cannot discount it any more.（これ以上の値引きはできません。）
　= We cannot make it any lower.
We cannot offer a lower price.（これ以上の低価格では提供できません。）
This is our best price.（これが提供できる最高の価格です。）
¥8,500 [eighty-five hundred yen] is our final offer.（8,500円が最終提案です。）

2-4 土産店で――〔4〕
At a souvenir shop：〔4〕

Various *konnyaku* products
（コンニャク製品各種）

Customer: Excuse me, what is this dark jelly-like lump? <u>A kind of</u> *tofu*?

Salesclerk: No, it isn't. It's a yam cake. We call it *konnyaku* in Japanese. It has a jelly-like texture. The texture does not change even if it's boiled or baked.

Customer: How does it <u>taste</u>?

Salesclerk: As *konnyaku* doesn't have a <u>flavor</u>, the flavor depends upon the seasoning used.

Customer: Tasteless food is not interesting to me.

Salesclerk: But it's very popular as a diet food because *konnyaku* has few calories and a lot of dietary fiber. It's a well-known product in *Gunma*.

Customer: Oh, is that so?

Salesclerk: *Gunma* Prefecture is famous for *konnyaku-imo* as it produces 90% [percent] of the total Japanese production. Yam noodles, *shirataki* in Japanese, which is used for *sukiyaki*, is also *konnyaku*.

Customer: Well, that means I have eaten *konnyaku* before. I like *sukiyaki* very much. If we use a lot of yam noodles in it, *sukiyaki* would be a diet dish, right?

Salesclerk: Good idea!

Vocabulary

lump	塊り
a kind of	一種の、〜のような
yam	芋
texture	食感
taste	味がする
flavor	味、風味
depend upon	〜次第である
seasoning	調味料
tasteless	味のない
popular	人気のある
dietary fiber	食物繊維
prefecture	県
produce	〜を生産する

※ product　　生産物
※ production　　生産

English Points

■ What is this?（これは何ですか）と聞かれて、It is a kind of ○○．（それは一種の ○○です）と説明する表現ですが、ここでは「○○の一種ですか」と質問する表現として使われれいます。同カテゴリーに属していると判断される場合に a kind of 〜が用いられるのに対して、視覚的・感触的に似ている場合は like〜 が用いられます。

　・A *Shamisen* is a kind of musical instrument.（三味線は楽器の一種です。）
　・*Hiyamugi* are a kind of noodles.（ひやむぎは麺の一種です。）
　・*Takuwan* is a kind of pickled food.（たくわんは漬物の一種です。）

　・*Okonomiyaki* is like pizza.（お好み焼きはピザのようなものです。）
　・*Takoyaki* are like dumplings with octopus pieces.
　　（たこ焼きはタコ入りの団子のようなものです。）

■ 味覚表現は多様です。まず、「おいしい」それとも「まずい」の二項選択で表現するのが、端的で明解です。その後に、「甘い、酸っぱい、塩辛い／しょっぱい、苦い、辛い」という味覚の表現、もしくは風味（flavor）や食感（texture）で具体性が伝わります。

　・How does it taste? = How is the taste?（味はどうですか。）
　　——It tastes good [terrible]. = It's great [awful].（おいしい［まずい］。）

←——————————————→

excellent（とてもおいしい）　　　　　terrible（散々な）
delicious（とてもおいしい）　　　　　awful（ひどい）
great（おいしい）　　　　　　　　　　disappointing（がっかりさせる）
(so) good（おいしい）　　　　　　　　bad（まずい）
tasty（味のある）　　　　　　　　　　tasteless（味のない）
savory（味のよい、風味のある）　　　bland（味気ない）
flavorful（風味豊かな）　　　　　　　plain（あっさりした、味気ない）
yummy（おいしい）　※俗語、幼児語　yuck（気持ち悪い、見たくない）※俗語

- -

It tastes　｜ sweet（甘い）
It's　　　　｜ sour（酸っぱい）
　　　　　　｜ salty（塩味の、しょっぱい）
　　　　　　｜ hot（辛い）
　　　　　　｜ bitter（苦い）
　　　　　　｜ rich（濃厚な）

- -

・Flavor（風味）　　　　　　　　　　　・Texture（食感）

It tastes　｜ sugary（砂糖味の甘い）　　　It's　｜ soft（柔らかい）
It's　　　　｜ juicy（ジューシーな）　　　　　　 ｜ tender（柔らかい）
　　　　　　｜ fruity（フルーツ味の）　　　　　　｜ moist（しっとりした）
　　　　　　｜ nutty（ナッツ風味の）　　　　　　 ｜ mushy（柔らかい、ドロドロした）
　　　　　　｜ cheesy（チーズ味の）　　　　　　　｜ creamy（滑らかな、クリーム状の）
　　　　　　｜ buttery（バター風味の）　　　　　 ｜ gooey（ベタベタの、ねばねばした）
　　　　　　｜ spicy（スパイスの利いた）　　　　 ｜ crunchy（ポリポリした、カリカリした）
　　　　　　｜ fishy（魚の匂いの、生臭い）　　　 ｜ crispy（サクサクした）
　　　　　　｜ greasy（脂っこい）　　　　　　　　｜ chewy（噛み応えがある）
　　　　　　｜ oily（脂っこい）　　　　　　　　　｜ dry（パサパサした、辛口の（酒））
　　　　　　　　　　　　　　　　　　　　　　　　　｜ hard（硬い）

Exercise 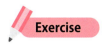 Prepare を答えた後、枠内のパターンを用いて会話の練習をしましょう。

Example: *C:* Excuse me, what is this, saying *sansyo* here?
         S: Sansho is a kind of Japanese pepper.
         C: I see. Thanks.

Customer: Excuse me, what is this, saying _____ here?

Salesclerk: _____ is a kind of _____ .

Customer: I see. Thanks.

Prepare

続く説明に合致するものを下の枠内から選びなさい。

(1) (　　　　　　) is a kind of Japanese pepper.
(2) (　　　　　　) is a kind of dumpling made of vegetables.
(3) (　　　　　　) is a kind of *sashimi*, seared bonito in English.
(4) (　　　　　　) is a kind of pickle, pickled plums in English.
(5) (　　　　　　) is a kind of flute made of a bamboo stem.
(6) (　　　　　　) is a kind of fire festival burning New Year's decorations.

umeboshi	*dondoyaki*	*sansho*	*oyaki*
shakuhachi	*katsuo-no-tataki*		

Tips:

■ コンニャクは、英語では devil's tongue あるいは Japanese yam cake と呼ばれ、馴染みの薄い食品でした。最近、日本食の浸透により、*konnyaku, konjac, konjak* というように日本語の発音に基づいて表記されています。

■ コンニャクは群馬県の特産品の一つで、原料となるコンニャク芋は下仁田町とその周辺地域、利根郡、北群馬郡、吾妻郡で栽培されています。近年、豊富な食物繊維、低カロリーという特徴を生かして様々に加工されていますが、中でもコンニャクゼリーはダイエット菓子として好評を博し、ヒット商品の座にあります。コンニャクゼリーは、*konnyaku* jelly や jelly made from a devil's tongue と説明することができます。

2-5 土産店で——〔5〕
At a souvenir shop：〔5〕

Konnyaku jelly
（コンニャクゼリー）

Customer: Excuse me, I'm looking for <u>*konnyaku* jelly in bite-size plastic cups</u>. Do you have them here?

Salesclerk: Yes, we do. They're on the rack over there. There are several kinds, so you can choose the flavor you like.

Customer: Okay. Do you have any lemon flavored (*konnyaku* jelly)?

Salesclerk: I'm sorry, we're out of stock. It'll take a few days before the next shipment arrives. <u>How about</u> the grapefruit flavored ones?

Customer: They must be popular items.

Salesclerk: The pineapple flavored ones are very popular, too. Peach, apple, and Muscat grape flavors are also popular. I recommend them all.

Customer: Okay then, I will take one bag of each flavor.

Salesclerk: Is it for yourself, or a gift? We can wrap them as a gift if you want.

Customer: I'<u>m gonna</u> use them at a party at home, so no special wrapping is necessary. I'm serving my friends *konnyaku* jelly as dessert so that they'll praise my low-calorie dessert. Most of my friends are obsessed with dieting.

Salesclerk: *Konnyaku* jelly is made from yams, so it's <u>healthier than</u> animal gelatin jelly.

Customer: After all, I buy them because they taste good.

Salesclerk: I'm sure all of your friends will like the low-calorie sweets.

Customer: I hope so.

Vocabulary

bite-size	一口サイズの
rack	置き棚、網棚
choose	～を選択する
out of stock	在庫切れ
shipment	出荷
recommend	～をすすめる
wrap	～を包む
praise	～を称賛する
be obsessed with	～に取りつかれている、思い込む
healthy	健康的な

English Points

■ *konnyaku* jelly in bite-size plastic cups は、スナック用に開発された「プラスチックカップに入った一口サイズのコンニャクゼリー」を言い表します。

■ ○○味のコンニャクゼリーという表現は、○○ flavored *konnyaku* jelly、あるいは *konnyaku* jelly with ○○ flavor になります。

　・lemon [peach, apple, grape, pineapple, mango......] flavored *konnyaku* jelly
　・*konnyaku* jelly with lemon [peach, apple, grape, pineapple, mango......] flavor
　（レモン［桃、リンゴ、ブドウ、パイナップル、マンゴー……］味のコンニャクゼリー）

■ How about～?（～はいかがですか）の表現は、相手に何かを勧めたり、提案したりするときに用います。

　How about ＋ 名詞 ?
　・How about this tapestry?（このタペストリーはいかがですか。）
　・How about lunch tomorrow?（明日、ランチはいかがですか。）

　How about ＋ V-ing ?
　・How about going on a hike next Saturday?
　　（今度の土曜日にハイキングへ行くのはいかがですか。）
　・How about buying some eggs for breakfast?
　　（朝食用に卵を買うのはいかがですか。）

■ 会話では (be) gonna, wanna, gotta のように省略した言い回しが頻繁に使われます。

(be) going to　→　(be) gonna
・I'm gonna buy this key holder for my nephew.
（甥にこのキーホルダーを買うつもりです。）
・He's not gonna take on the job. （彼はその仕事を引き受けるつもりはないです。）

want to　→　wanna　　　※　wants to の省略形ではないことに注意。
・I wanna go home and watch a soccer game on TV.
（家に帰ってテレビでサッカーの試合を見たいです。）
・Do you wanna go to the party? （そのパーティーに行きたいですか。）
・She's studying English because she wants to become a tour guide.
（彼女は観光ガイドになりたくて、英語を勉強しています。）

have to, (have) got to　→　gotta
・I gotta go now. The meeting starts from 1 o'clock.
（さて、行かなくちゃ。会議が 1 時から始まるので。）
・It was a wonderful experience staying in the Japanese-style inn. You gotta try it.
（その旅館に滞在したことはすばらしい経験でした。あなたも試してみて。）
・She's gotta(=has to) finish her report by next Wednesday.
（彼女は来週水曜日までに報告書を仕上げなければならないので。）

■ A is healthier than B. は比較級表現です。2 つのものの性質や状態などの程度の違いを述べる際に用いますが、形容詞（もしくは副詞）の長さによって -er または more の使用が決まります。2 音節以上の語は、原則として長い単語とみなされますが、多少の例外が含まれます（詳しくは、p.40の Prepare を参照）。

短い形容詞──A is ○○ -er than B.
・Winter in *Kyoto* is colder than in *Tokyo*. （京都の冬は東京より寒いです。）
・The population in *Takasaki* City is larger than in *Tomioka* City.
（高崎市の人口は富岡市よりも多いです。）

長い形容詞──A is more ○○ than B.
・This chair is more comfortable than that one.
（この椅子はあの椅子よりも座り心地がいい。）
・Silk soap is far more expensive than ordinary soap, but it moisturizes the skin.
（シルク石鹸は普通の石鹸よりもはるかに高価ですが、肌を保湿する効果があります。）

 **Exercise** Prepare を答えた後、枠内のパターンを用いて質問と応答の練習をしましょう。

Example: *A:* Which is stronger, a lion or a tiger?
B: I think a lion is stronger than a tiger.

A: Which is _____ , _____ or _____ ?
B: I think _____ is _____ than _____ .

Provide information
(1) friendly ············ a cat or a dog
(2) tall ············ the Eiffel Tower or Tokyo Tower
(3) popular ············ baseball or football
(4) fast ············ a cheetah or a jaguar
(5) dangerous ············ sky diving or hang glider
(6) fascinating ············ Tokyo Disneyland or Universal Studios Japan

Prepare

次の説明を読み、続く形容詞を比較級に変化させなさい。

(1) 規則的に変化する形容詞

比較級のつくり方において、「短い・長い」語と判断するのは、音節数によってです。音節というのは専門的な響きがありますが、一つのまとまった音として意識される音の単位です。例えば、tall は 1 音節、beau-ti-ful は 3 音節という具合です。

- ・ 1 音節の語の場合、語尾に -er を付ける。

- ・ 2 音節の語の大部分は、more を前置するが、次の例外がある。
  ※ 2 音節の語でも、-y, -er, -le, -ow などで終わる語には -er を付ける。
    (eas-y, clev-er, sim-ple, nar-row → easier, cleverer, simpler, narrower)

  ※ -er と more のどちらへも変化する語も一部に認められる。
    (pret-ty → prettier / more pretty, hand-some → handsomer / more handsome)

- ・ 3 音節以上の語は、more を前置する。

原級の和訳	原　　級	比　較　級
	high	
	short	
	old	
	small	
	exciting	
	heavy	
	interesting	
	fast	
	young	
	important	
	early	
	difficult	

(2) 不規則に変化する形容詞

原級の和訳	原　　級	比　較　級
	many	
	much	
	little	
	good	
	well	
	bad	

2-6 土産店で——〔6〕

At a souvenir shop：〔6〕

Customer: Excuse me. I want to purchase this <u>*happi* coat</u>, but I can't find the size.

Salesclerk: It's <u>one-size-fits-all</u>. Why don't you try it on?

Customer: This size fits me. But <u>this is a little flashy</u>. I want one that's <u>not as bright as</u> this.

Salesclerk: People wear these *happi* coats at events to make them feel cheerful and merry, so an outstanding pattern is preferable.

Customer: I see. Then I'll take this one.

Salesclerk: <u>How would you like to pay for it?</u>

Customer: <u>Can I pay by credit card?</u>

Salesclerk: What credit card do you have?

Customer: Visa.

Salesclerk: Sure, we accept Visa.

Vocabulary

one-size-fits-all	フリーサイズ
flashy	派手な
bright	明るい
cheerful and merry	元気に楽しく
outstanding pattern	目立つ柄
preferable	好ましい
accept	～を受け入れる

English Points

■ free size（フリーサイズ）は和製英語です。正しくは、one-size-fits-all または one size fits all と言い表します。

■ 衣類に関する表現は多種多様です。次の使用頻度の高い、基本的な表現が使われています。

Shopping

2

買い物編

・This is a little | flashy | for me.（これは私には、少し派手です
This is too | bright | ／派手すぎます。）
| loud |
| gaudy |
| showy |

　　※「派手な」と言っても、flashy（パッとした）　bright（明るい）　loud（目
　　にうるさい）　gaudy（俗っぽい）　showy（人目を引く）のニュアンスの違
　　いがあります。

・That is a little | plain | for you.（それはあなたには、少し地味です
That is too | subdued | ／地味すぎます。）
| quiet |
| conservative |

　　※「地味な」も同様に、plain（飾り気のない）　subdued（抑えられた）
　　quiet（落ち着いた）　conservative（保守的な）のニュアンスの違いがあり
　　ます。

・You look | good | in the dress.（その服はあなたに似合います。）
| modest | 〃 （〃はあなたを控えめに見せます。）
| sophisticated | 〃 （〃であなたは洗練された人に見えます。）

■ as 〜 as（〜と同じ程度に）に対して、否定の場合は not as 〜 as（〜ほど〜では
ない）の意になることに注意を要します。

・This tomato is <u>as</u> sweet <u>as</u> fruit.（このトマトは果物と同じくらい甘いです。）
・I'm <u>not as</u> skillful <u>as</u> you in cooking.
（料理において私はあなたほど器用ではありません。）

■ 商品購入の支払いに際して使われる主な表現は次の通り。

clerk

How would you like to pay for it?（お支払いはどうされますか。）
How will you be paying for this?（　　〃　　）
Would you like to pay by cash or by credit card?
　（お支払いは現金それともクレジットカードになさいますか。）
Will that be cash or charge?
　（お支払いは現金それともクレジットカードでしょうか。）
Cash or charge [credit]?（現金、それともクレジットカードですか。）

customer

I'll pay | cash.（現金を支払います。）
　　　　| in cash.（現金で支払います。）
　　　　| by credit card.（クレジットカードで支払います。）

・クレジットカードが使えるかどうかを確認したいときは…

Can I pay by credit card?（クレジットカードで支払えますか。）
Do you accept [take] credit cards?（クレジットカードを受け入れますか。）
Can I use VISA?（VISAは使えますか。）

Tip:

■「法被（はっぴ）」を英語で言い表すと *happi* coat ですが、もう少し詳しい説明を求められることも少なくありません。

A "*Happi* coat" is a Japanese traditional costume worn by craftsmen. Usually, the employer's name or crest is printed on it. Also, at festival time people in the town wear the same patterned *happi* coat to show solidarity.
　「法被」は職人たちが着る日本の伝統的な衣装です。たいてい雇い主の名前または家紋がプリントされています。また、祭りの時に町内の人々は連帯を示すために同じ柄の法被を着用します。

2-7 土産店で——〔7〕
At a souvenir shop: 〔7〕

Daruma dolls
（達磨人形）

Customer: What's this? Can I touch it?

Salesclerk: Sure, go ahead.

Customer: How do I use this?

Salesclerk: A *Daruma* doll is a kind of lucky charm. It's believed that this figurine brings good luck. People purchase a *Daruma* doll at the beginning of the New Year and pray for peace, health, success, and so on.

Customer: Good manners and customs, but why are the eyes blank?

Salesclerk: You paint the left eye black and pray. When your wish comes true, you paint the right eye. It's a mascot that wins by all means because it rights itself (to the upright position) when knocked over.

Customer: How come the *Daruma* doll doesn't have any hands or feet?

Salesclerk: *Daruma* was a great Buddhist priest. He was known to be a person who meditated for many years. However, because his arms and legs were hidden under his clothes, he looked like a round shape when he meditated.

Customer: I see. This doll teaches us that we should never give up.

Salesclerk: That's right.

Customer: I think it is a good souvenir. I'll take one.

Salesclerk: Thank you.

Vocabulary

touch	～に触れる
go ahead	（ためらわずに）どうぞ
lucky charm	幸運のお守り
figurine	小立像、人形
pray for	～のために祈る
custom	慣習
blank	空白の
wish	願い、願望
come true	実現する
by all means	何としてでも
right oneself	起き上がる、元の姿勢に戻る
Buddhist priest	仏教の僧、仏僧
meditate	瞑想する　　※ meditation　　瞑想
arms and legs	腕と脚、四肢
hide under	～の下に隠す
round shape	丸い形

Shopping

2

買い物編

English Points

■ How do I [you] ～?（～はどうやるのですか）は、やり方を尋ねる表現です。相手もしくは自分の視点に立つかの違いが、you または I の選択に表れますが、どちらを用いても同じ内容の質問になります。

・How do I [you]
　play this game?（このゲームはどうやって遊ぶの。）
　open this?（これをどうやって開けるの。）
　pronounce this word?（この単語、どのように発音しますか。）
　operate this washing machine?
　（この洗濯機、どうやって操作するの。）
　use this Japanese high-tech toilet?
　（この日本のハイテクトイレ、どうやって使うのですか。）

次の表現もよく使われます。

・How does this work?（これはどのように作動しますか。）
・What's it used for?（それは何に使われますか。）

■ 慣習・慣行や伝話・伝承などには、説明不可能な部分も少なくありません。その場合、It's believed that～（～と信じられています）、または It's said that～（～と言われています）の言い回しは有用です。同時に、これらは○○ is believed to～／○○ is said to～の表現に置き換えることができます。

・It's believed that this herb is effective for skin burns.
　= This herb is believed to be effective for skin burns.
　（この薬草は火傷に効くと信じられています。）

45

- It's believed that this stone has spiritual power.
  = This stone is believed to have spiritual power.
  （この石には霊力があると信じられています。）

- It's said that the composer was a genius.
  = The composer is said to have been a genius.
  （あの作曲家は天才だったと言われています。）

■ How come? は、Why? と同じように「どうして」「なぜ」と理由を尋ねる場合の口語体表現です。How did that come about～?（どのようにして～が起こったのか）という文が省略された表現です。How come に続く文章は疑問文にならないことがポイントです。

- How come she's angry? = Why is she angry?
  （どうして彼女は怒っているの。）
- How come the accident occurred? = Why did the accident occur?
  （どうしてその事故は起こったの。）

Tip:

■ ダルマはそもそも達磨大師（だるまだいし）のことですから、英語で Dharma と記されます。よって、達磨人形は Dharma doll ですが、最近は *Daruma* doll と表記される傾向にあり、発音も日本語の〈ダルマ〉で通じます。

2-8 土産店で──〔8〕
At a souvenir shop:〔8〕

Souvenirs and confectionery in *Gunma*
(群馬のお土産・お菓子)

Customer: Can I see the Godzilla T-shirt over there?

Salesclerk: Sure. What's your size?

Customer: I usually wear a medium, but I don't know my size in this country. I'm a tourist as you can see.

Salesclerk: I think that a medium will do. Why don't you try it on?

Customer: Yeah, I think I should. Where is the fitting room?

Salesclerk: This way.

Customer: This is a little small for me. Is there a bigger size?

Salesclerk: Then the large size will probably fit you.

Customer: And one more thing, this is not my color. Does this come in any other colors?

Salesclerk: Yes, they come in red and blue. Please try these on, too.

Customer: This size is just right, and I think I look good in blue. Okay, I'll take this blue one.

Salesclerk: Thank you. I'll ring it up. That'll be 4,800 [four thousand (and) eight hundred] yen with tax.

Customer: I'm going to see a Godzilla movie in this T-shirt.

Salesclerk: Good! We all need to enjoy our lives.

Vocabulary

medium size	Mサイズ
will do	間に合う
fitting room	試着室
probably	多分、おそらく
fit	～にぴったり合う
ring it up	（売り上げを）レジに記録する

English Points

■ 衣服のサイズに関するやり取り表現は、次の通りです。

clerk

What's your size?（サイズはいくつですか。）
What size are you?（　　〃　　）
What size do you take [wear]?（どのサイズを着用しますか。）

customer

I'm a size 9.（9号です。）
I take [wear] a size 9.（9号を着用してます。）
I wear a small [medium, large].（S［M、L］サイズを着ます。）

※ XS（Extra Small） S（Small） M（Medium） L（Large） XL（Extra Large）の サイズ表記については、国際的に使用されています。もう一方で、洋服のサイズ 表記に関しては、国によって異なるという認識が必要です。例えば、日本では女 性服のサイズは7、9、11、13、15号というように奇数で表記されますが、米 国においては4、6、8、10、12というように偶数が用いられています。

・In my country I'm a size ○○. What size is that here in Japan?
（自国では私のサイズは○○号です。ここ日本ではどのサイズになりますか。）
・I'm not sure of my size. What size do you think I am?
（自分のサイズがわからない。どのサイズだと思いますか。）
・Can I try this on?（これを試着できますか。）

■ This way. の表現は、The fitting room is this way, please.（試着室はこちらです） の省略形です。また実際に案内する場合、Please follow me.（ついて来てくださ い）の表現が使われます。

■ 欲しいサイズを求めるときは…

・Do you have a smaller [bigger] one?（もっと小さい［大きい］ものはありますか。）
・Do you have this in | a smaller [bigger] size?
（もっと小さい［大きい］サイズはありますか。）
Small [Medium, Large]?
（これでS［M、L］はありますか。）
the next size up [down]?
（ひとサイズ大きい［小さい］ものはありますか。）

Exercise 枠内のパターンを用いて、各自の情報に基づいて会話を練習をしましょう。

Salesclerk: What's your size?

Customer: I usually wear a _____ , but I don't know my size in this country.

Salesclerk: I think that a _____ will do. Why don't you try it on?

Customer: Yeah, I think I should. Where is the fitting room?

Salesclerk: This way.

Tips:

- *Onsen manju* is a Japanese sweet (a steamed bun stuffed with *azuki*-bean paste) sold in hot-spring resorts. It is also called *yunohana manju*. It's one of the most popular souvenirs for an *onsen* visitor.
  温泉まんじゅうは、温泉地で売られている和菓子（小豆餡が詰まった蒸しパン）です。湯の花まんじゅうとも呼ばれます。温泉を訪れる客に人気のお土産品の一つです。

- *Karinto manju* is fried *manju,* which tastes like a fried dough cake, called *karinto* in Japanese. *Karinto* is often described as being similar to the taste of a donut. Although it's a recent product, *karinto manju* has become popular because of its good taste.
  かりん糖まんじゅうは、かりん糖のような味がする、油で揚げたまんじゅうです。かりん糖はしばしばドーナツの味に似ていると言い表されます。かりん糖まんじゅうは最近の商品ですが、そのおいしさから人気を得ました。

- "*Gunma-chan*" is a costume character from *Gunma* Prefecture. Though he was produced in 1994, he's a 7-year-old pony forever. He has been working hard to improve the image of *Gunma* Prefecture and became the manager of *Gunma* Prefecture Advertising Dept. on December 21, 2012. At souvenir shops, various *Gunma-chan* goods are sold such as *Gunma-chan* stuffed toys, T-shirts, aprons, clear files, tote bags, key holders, stationery, cookies, and so on.
  「ぐんまちゃん」は群馬県の着ぐるみマスコットです。1994年に生み出されましたが、永遠に7歳のポニーです。群馬県のイメージアップに尽力し、2012年12月21日に 群馬県宣伝部長に就任しました。土産店では、ぐんまちゃん縫いぐるみ、Tシャツ、エプロン、クリアファイル、トートバッグ、キーホルダー、文房具、クッキーなど、様々なぐんまちゃんグッズが売られています。

- Known for the *Tomioka* Silk Mill, *Gunma* Prefecture has been producing raw silk since ancient times, and it is still the best in Japan. "*Gunma* Silk" is recognized as an original brand of high quality. Various daily goods, including clothing, are produced from this high-quality raw silk such as silk scarves and stoles, neckties and socks, pajamas and underwear, wallets and hats, etc. In addition, daily necessities such as silk soap and cosmetics are also being developed.
  富岡製糸場の存在からもわかるように、群馬県は昔から生糸の生産が盛んで、現在も日本一です。「ぐんまシルク」はオリジナル・ブランドとして、その質の高さが認められています。

その良質な生糸から、衣類をはじめ様々な日用品がつくり出されています。シルク・スカーフやストール、ネクタイや靴下、パジャマや下着、財布や帽子など。また、シルク石鹸や化粧品といった日用品も開発されています。

■ *Kokeshi* is a traditional craft from *Gunma* Prefecture. Creative *kokeshi* is made from logs such as Dogwood, Cherry, Zelkova, and Chestnut, and its production volume is the highest in Japan. *Kokeshi* is a traditional doll, but *Gunma's kokeshi* has a free shape and design with new features being constantly created.

こけしは群馬県の伝統工芸品の一つです。ミズキ、サクラ、ケヤキ、クリといった原木から創作こけしがつくられ、その生産量は日本一を誇ります。こけしは伝統的な人形ですが、群馬のこけしは形状や図柄が自由で、常に新しいものが生み出されているのが特徴です。

■ *"Takasaki Daruma"* is produced in *Takasaki* City as its name suggests. It is also called *"fuku Daruma"* or *"engi Daruma,"* which means *"lucky Daruma,"* because there are two auspicious animals on the face. Its eyebrows are cranes, and the nose to the mouth and beard are turtles. It accounts for most of the nation's production. *Gunma's* dry wind is good for *Daruma* doll making, which it has been manufacturing for 200 years. Today, a wide variety of *Daruma* dolls are made, including those that pray for a prosperous business, family safety, passing an exam, and so on.

「高崎だるま」は、その名前の通り高崎市で生産されています。眉毛は鶴、鼻から口ヒゲは亀というように、縁起の良い動物が顔に描かれた「高崎だるま」は、「福だるま」あるいは「縁起だるま」とも呼ばれ、全国生産シェアの大半を占めています。群馬の空っ風がだるま人形づくりに適しているといわれ、200年間続いてきたものづくりです。現在では、商売繁盛、家内安全、試験合格を祈願するだるまをはじめ、多種多様なだるま人形が作られています。

■ *Konnyaku* is a low-calorie food. A variety of *konnyaku* diet products have been developed because of these characteristics. For example, *konnyaku sashimi, konnyaku* noodles, *konnyaku* rice, *konnyaku* dessert, etc.

コンニャクは低カロリー食品です。その特徴を生かして、様々なコンニャクダイエット製品が開発されています。例えば、コンニャク刺身、コンニャク麺、コンニャク米、コンニャクデザートなど。

2-9 薬局で
At a pharmacy

Pharmacist: Hi. May I help you?

Customer: Yes. I seem to <u>have caught a cold</u>. Could you recommend a good cold medicine?

Pharmacist: Do you have a prescription?

Customer: No, I don't.

Pharmacist: Then I can recommend you an <u>over-the-counter medicine</u>. Could you tell me a bit more about your symptoms?

Customer: <u>I have a sore throat and runny nose</u>.

Pharmacist: Okay. Do you have a fever?

Customer: Yes. <u>I have a slight fever.</u>

Pharmacist: Do you take any other medication?

Customer: No.

Pharmacist: Okay. Do you have any drug allergies?

Customer: Not that I know of.

Pharmacist: Okay, then any over-the-counter cold medicine will do.

Customer: Where are they?

Pharmacist: They're all along this aisle, on the right shelf. I'll show you.

Customer: Thanks.

《In front of the shelf》

Pharmacist: These are all cold medicines.

Customer: It's all Greek to me. Which one would you

recommend?

Pharmacist: Well, these are tablets. Take two tablets, three times a day after a meal. And this one is a powder. Take one sachet, twice a day before meals.

Customer: Do they have any side effects?

Pharmacist: There are no serious side effects, but they can make you sleepy, so please don't drive after taking them.

Customer: I won't drive while I'm staying in Japan anyway. Then, I'll take the tablets please.

《Receiving the item after paying at the cash register》

Customer: Okay, thanks.

Pharmacist: I hope you feel better soon.

Vocabulary

pharmacy	調剤薬局	※ pharmacist	薬剤師
catch a cold	風邪をひく		
cold medicine	風邪薬		
prescription	処方せん	※ prescribed medicine [drug]	処方薬
over-the-counter medicine [drug]	〔医師の処方せんなしで買える〕市販薬		
symptom	症状		
sore throat	痛い喉、ヒリヒリする喉		
runny nose	鼻水		
fever	熱	※ slight fever	微熱、少しの熱
take medication	薬剤投与を受ける、薬を服用する		
allergy	アレルギー		
aisle	(旅客機や劇場などの座席間の)通路		
It's all Greek to me.	〔私にはすべてギリシャ語です⇒〕さっぱりわからない		
tablet	錠剤		
sachet	小袋		
side effect	副作用		

👉 English Points

■ drugstore も pharmacy と同じく「薬局」の意ですが、薬以外に化粧品や雑貨なども扱う薬局を指します。

■ I caught a cold. (風邪をひきました) に対して、I have a cold. (風邪をひいている) は病状を言い表します。

have 動詞で様々な病状を言い表すことができます。

- I have | a fever [temperature]. … 熱があります。
  | a cough. ……………… 咳が出ます。
  | a headache. ………… 頭が痛いです。
  | a stuffy [blocked] nose. … 鼻がつまっています。＝ My nose is stuffy [blocked].
  | a stomachache. ……… お腹が痛いです。
  | a toothache. ………… 歯が痛いです。
  | sore muscles. ………… 筋肉痛です。
  | diarrhea. ……………… 下痢をしてます。

- I don't feel very well. …………… あまり調子が良くないです。
- I'm not feeling well. ………… 具合が悪いです。
- I'm constipated. ………………… 便秘です。

- I feel | very chilly. …………… 寒気がします。
  | tired. ………………… 疲労感があります。
  | exhausted. …………… だるいです。
  | nauseous. …………… 吐き気がします。
  | like vomiting [throwing up]. … 吐き気がします。

- My eye hurts. ………………… 目が痛い。
- My leg hurts. ………………… 足が痛い。
- My body hurts [aches]. ………… 身体が痛い。

■ over-the-counter medicine は、〈カウンター越しの薬〉という直訳ですが、つまり医師の処方せんなしで買える市販薬を指します（短縮して OTC medicine と呼ばれることもあります）。それぞれ国の薬事法が違うことから、薬の摂取量に関しては必ずしも同じではありませんし、また海外では薬局で簡単に手に入る薬が、日本では市販薬になっていない場合もあります。さらに、座薬に嫌悪を示す外国人もいますので、薬に関しては、対応が難しいと言わざるを得ません。

Tips:

Shapes and types of medicine
（薬の形状と種類）

- tablet（錠剤）
- capsule（カプセル）
- pill（丸薬）
- granule（顆粒剤）
- powdered medicine / powder（粉剤）
- liquid medicine（液剤）

internal medicine（内服薬）

- medicine for stomachache（腹痛の薬）
- medicine for diarrhea（下痢止め）
- medicine for fever（熱さまし）
- medicine for cough（咳止め）
- painkiller（痛み止め）
- aspirin（鎮痛剤）
- lozenge（薬用ドロップ）

application（外用薬）

- ointment（軟膏）
- ointment for itching（かゆみ止め）
- eye drops（目薬）
- compress（湿布）
- plaster（絆創膏）/ Band-Aid（バンドエイド）
- gauze bandage（ガーゼ包帯）
- cotton swab（綿棒）
- bug (protect) spray / insect repellent（虫よけスプレー）
- sunscreen [sun protection] lotion（日焼け止めローション）

第3章　おいしい郷土料理

【飲食編】

Food and Drink

3-1 ファーストフード店で

At a fast food restaurant

Restaurant staff: Next, please.

Customer: Hi.

Restaurant staff: Hi. <u>What would you like (to have)?</u>

Customer: 〈Looking at the menu〉 <u>I'll have</u> one cheeseburger, a small French fries, and a medium coffee, please.

Restaurant staff: We have hot and iced coffee. <u>Which do you prefer?</u>

Customer: Hot coffee.

Restaurant staff: <u>For here or to go?</u>

Customer: For here, please.

Restaurant staff: <u>Anything else?</u>

Customer: No, that's all.

Restaurant staff: Okay. That'll be 768 [seven hundred (and) sixty-eight] yen.

Customer: Here is 1,000 [a thousand] yen.

Restaurant staff: Your change is 232 [two hundred (and) thirty-two] yen. Please take this number and wait at your table. We'll call your number when your order is ready.

Customer: All right.

《In a couple of minutes》

Restaurant staff: Forty-five! One cheeseburger, a small French fries, and a medium hot coffee. Have a nice day!

Customer: Thank you. You too.

Vocabulary

For here or to go?	こちらで召し上がりますか、それともお持ち帰りですか。
iced coffee	アイスコーヒー　　　※ ice coffee ではないことに注意
prefer A to B	B より A を好む
wait	待つ
ready	用意ができた

English Points

■ 注文をとる際、May I～? の丁寧な言い方に対して、What would you～? はカジュアルな言い回しになりますが、どちらも多用される表現です。

Formal
- ・May I take your order, please? (注文をおとりしてもよろしいですか。)
- ・Are you ready to order now? (ご注文はお決まりですか。)

Causal
- ・What would you like (to have)? (何を召し上がりますか。)
- ・Ready to order? (注文は決まりましたか。)

■ 次のいずれもの表現も「○○と○○をいただきます」の意味合いになります。

- ・I'll have ○○, and ○○ , please.
- ・I think I'll have ○○, and ○○.
- ・I'd like ○○, and ○○.

■ 飲み物の注文には、アイスまたはホット、どのサイズといったやり取りが伴います。

- ・What would you like to drink? (お飲み物は何になさいますか。)
- ・We have hot and iced tea with lemon. Which do you prefer?
  (レモンティーはホットとアイスがございますが、どちらになさいますか。)
- ・We have three sizes of Coke, Small, Medium and Large. Which size would you like?
  (コーラには、S、M、L の 3 サイズございますが、どのサイズになさいますか。)

■ ファーストフード店では、持ち帰りか否かを確認することが求められます。

- ・For here or to go?
  (こちら [＝店内] でお召し上がりですか、それともお持ち帰りですか。)
- ・Eat here or take away? (　　　　　　　　　　　〃　　　　　　　　　　　)
- ・Eat in or take away? (　　　　　　　　　　　　〃　　　　　　　　　　　)
- ・Will that be for here or to go? (　　　　　　　　　〃　　　　　　　　　　)
- ※ イギリス英語では、to go の代わりに take away が一般的

Food and Drink

3

飲食編

57

■ 客の注文を確認する表現です。

・Anything else?（他にご注文は。）
・Will that be all?（それで全部ですか。）

・I'll confirm your order.（ご注文を確認させていただきます。）
・Let me check your order.（ご注文をチェックさせてください。）

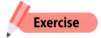 **Exercise** メニューを見ながら、枠内のパターンを用いて注文をとる練習をしましょう。

Restaurant staff: Hi.《ご注文は何にいたしましょうか。》
  Customer: I'll have _____ , _____ and _____ , please.
Restaurant staff:《こちらで召し上がりますか、それともお持ち帰りですか。》
  Customer:《選択して答える。》

Provide information

Genki Burger Shop					
Burger				Side	
Regular beef burger	¥320	Cheeseburger	¥250	French fries S size	¥150
Double beef burger	¥490	Fish burger	¥340	M size	¥200
Bacon & lettuce burger	¥320	Shrimp burger	¥450	L size	¥250
Teriyaki chicken burger	¥360	Avocado burger	¥430	Onion rings	¥180
				Chicken nugget (5 pcs)	¥270
Beverage					
Coca-Cola S size	¥150	Orange juice S size	¥150	Coffee	¥150
M size	¥200	M size	¥200	Iced coffee	¥150
L size	¥230	L size	¥230	Cafe au lait	¥200
				Tea	¥150

Tip:

■ ハンバーガーやピザなどのファーストフードは世界中どこにでもあるという理由で敬遠されることはなく、むしろ日本食に飽きてしまった場合や、移動中の手軽な食事として重宝されている観があります。

3-2 群馬の郷土食
Comfort food for *Gunma* people

Yakimanju & related item
(焼きまんじゅうと関連商品)

Customer: Smells good. What are they?

Salesclerk: These are *yakimanju*, a regional food *Gunma* people love. Would you like to try one?

Customer: They look like a dumpling, but is there anything inside?

Salesclerk: These dumplings are basically made from wheat flour and yeast. They are steamed first. Then they are stuck on bamboo skewers and baked while being coated with sweet soybean paste.

Customer: The smell makes me hungry. It's irresistible. How much is it?

Salesclerk: One skewer is 300 [three hundred] yen.

Customer: Well, I'll try one. Can I pay by credit card?

Salesclerk: I'm sorry, but we don't accept credit cards.

Customer: Okay, I'll pay by cash then.

Salesclerk: For here or to go?

Customer: For here. And can I have a cup of green tea?

Salesclerk: Sure. Green tea is free.

Salesclerk: Here you are. Enjoy the *Gunma* food.

Customer: Thanks.

Vocabulary

smell	匂う
regional food	郷土の食べ物
dumpling	団子
wheat flour	小麦粉
yeast	イースト菌
steam	蒸す
stick	〜を突き刺す　　※ stick-stuck-stuck
bamboo skewer	竹串
bake	〜を焼く
coat with	〜で覆う、〜を塗る
soybean paste	味噌（みそ）
irresistible	抵抗できない、抑えられない

English Points

■　It smells good. この it は、何か（something）を指し示し、Something smells good.（何かがいい匂いですね）の解釈になります。It tastes good.（いい味ですね）と同種の文型です。

・It smells

delicious.	（おいしそうな匂いがする。）
sweet.	（甘い匂いがする。）
exotic.	（エキゾチックな匂いがする。）
fresh.	（爽やかな匂いがする。）
bad.	（嫌な匂いがする。）
terrible [awful].	（すごく嫌な匂いがする。）
foul.	（悪臭がする。）　　※ foul は「汚い」「不潔な」の意
fishy.	（生臭い。）　　※比喩表現で「うさん臭い」の意

・My hands	smell of	soap.（私の手は石鹸の匂いがする。）
・This soup	smells of	garlic.（このスープはニンニクの匂いがする。）
		herbs.（このスープは薬草の匂いがする。）

・The perfume	smells like	the sea air.（その香水は海のような匂いがする。）
・Durian		rotten onions. （ドリアンは腐ったタマネギのような匂いがする。）
・This leaf		sesame.（この葉っぱはゴマのような匂いがする。）
・It		something's burning. （何かが焦げている匂いがする。） ＝ I smell something burning.

・I smelled curry in the school cafeteria.（学食ではカレーの匂いがしました。）
・I can smell an apple pie baking.（アップルパイを焼く匂いがする。）

■　焼きまんじゅうは群馬県人のソウルフードと言われますが、英語で soul food は「アフリカ系米国人の伝統料理」を指すため、意味が伝わりません。要するに、ソ

ウルフードは和製英語であるわけです。その地域に特有の食べ物、またその地域で親しまれてきた食べ物という意味合いでは、regional food（郷土の食べ物）もしくは comfort food（懐かしい食べ物）と言い表します。続く表現も同様の意味で使えます。

- *Yakimanju* is an iconic food from *Gunma*.
  （焼きまんじゅうは群馬の象徴的な食べ物です。）
- *Udon* is a signature food from *Gunma*.（うどんは群馬の代表的な食べ物です。）

■ 「～される」という受身（= 受動態）をつくる場合、「be 動詞 + 動詞の過去分詞」の形をとります。なお、規則動詞の過去分詞は、動詞に –ed を付けてつくりますが、不規則動詞の場合は様々に変化しますので、動詞ごとに原型・過去形・過去分詞の変化を把握する必要があります。

Snow covers Mt. *Asama*.（雪が浅間山を覆う。）

Mt. *Asama* <u>is covered</u> with snow.（浅間山は雪に覆われる。）
※ be 動詞は主語と時制によって決まる

- Snow covered Mt. *Asama*.（雪が浅間山を覆いました。）
- Mt. *Asama* <u>was covered</u> with snow.（浅間山は雪に覆われました。）

- Snow will cover Mt. *Asama*.（雪が浅間山を覆うだろう。）
- Mt. *Asama* <u>will be covered</u> with snow.（浅間山は雪に覆われるだろう。）

Exercise　Prepare を答えた後、受動態のパターン練習をしましょう。

(1) Our next door neighbor keeps that big dog.
That big dog _____ _____ by our next door neighbor.

(2) The children ate one hundred hamburgers.
One hundred hamburgers _____ _____ _____ the children.

(3) *Yasunari Kawabata* wrote "*The Izu Dancer*."
"*The Izu Dancer*" _____ _____ _____ *Yasunari Kawabata*.

(4) Pablo Picasso painted "*Guernica*" in 1937.
"*Guernica*" _____ _____ _____ Pablo Picasso in 1937.

(5) The *Meiji* government hired many foreign advisors from the West.
Many foreign advisors from the West _____ _____ by the *Meiji* Government.

Prepare

続く規則動詞と不規則動詞の活用について答えなさい。

規則動詞の活用

	意　味	原　形	過　去　形	過去分詞
1		clean		
2		close		
3		hire		
4		paint		
5		stop		
6		study		

不規則動詞の活用

	意　味	原　形	過　去　形	過去分詞
1		catch		
2		cut		
3		drink		
4		eat		
5		find		
6		give		
7		keep		
8		know		
9		read		
10		see		
11		take		
12		write		

Tip:

■ *Gunma* Prefecture produces two crops a year. As wheat is grown in winter, a flour-based food culture with items such as *udon* noodles, *okkirikomi* dumplings, and buns has developed. One of *Gunma's* local foods [delicacies] is *yakimanju*, which is baked while sweet *miso* sauce is applied to the dough, which is made from wheat flour mixed with rice malt. Even when called *manju*, buns usually don't have bean paste. It should be explained that steamed bread is baked with *miso* sauce. *Yakimanju* stalls, which have a great aroma, are always present at festivals.

群馬県は二毛作地帯です。冬季に小麦が栽培されることから、うどんやおっ切り込みなどの麺類やまんじゅう類など小麦粉を用いた食文化が発達しています。焼きまんじゅうは小麦粉を麹で発酵させた生地に甘辛い味噌だれを塗りながら焼いたもので、群馬の郷土料理の一つです。まんじゅうといっても、餡の入ってないものが一般的で、蒸しパンを味噌だれで焼いたものという説明ができます。お祭りには必ず焼きまんじゅうの屋台が出て、香ばしい匂いを漂わせています。

3-3 食事処で
At a restaurant

Waitperson: <u>Hello</u>. Please take any table you like.

Customer: Okay.

Waitperson: <u>Here's the menu</u>. I'll be back in a few minutes to take your order.

《In a few minutes》

Waitperson: Are you ready to order now?

Customer: <u>Do you have any recommendations?</u>

Waitperson: All dishes are good, but *tonkatsu-teishoku*, the pork cutlet set meal, is quite popular. A pork cutlet, rice, *miso* soup, and pickles are served together as a set.

Customer: Does that <u>come with</u> salad?

Waitperson: There is no salad, but the pork cutlets <u>are served with</u> shredded cabbage.

Customer: All right. I'll take that.

Waitperson: One *tonkatsu-teishoku*. Anything else?

Customer: Can I have a glass of water?

Waitperson: Sure, right away.

Food and Drink

3

飲食編

Vocabulary

waitperson / wait staff	給仕人、接客係	
take a table	テーブルに座る	
recommendation	おすすめ、推薦	
pickle	漬物	
be served	（料理が）出される	※ serve（食事）を提供する
come with	〜が付いている	
shredded cabbage	千切りキャベツ	

👉 English Points

■ ホテル等で宿泊客を迎える際、Welcome to ～. の表現をしばしば耳にしますが、飲食店では Hello. や Good morning [afternoon, evening]. が一般的です。このことから、Welcome to ～. の言い回しは、丁寧でフォーマルであることがうかがえます。どこで接客するのかを見据えて、相応しい言い方を選ぶことがポイントです。

■ メニューを渡す際の表現は…

・Here is the [our, your] menu.（こちらがメニューでございます。）
・Here are the [our, your] menus.（　　〃　　）

・I'll be back in a minute to take your order.（後ほどご注文を取りに伺います。）
・I'll be back to take your order in a moment.（　　〃　　）
・Please let me know when you've decided.
（お決まりになりましたらお知らせください。）

■ メニューに目を通しながらも、「おすすめは何ですか」と尋ねてくるお客は少なくありません。

customer

What do you recommend?（何がおすすめですか。）
What dish do you recommend?（どの料理がおすすめですか。）
What's today's special?（今日のおすすめは何でしょうか。）
Do you have any recommendations?（おすすめ料理はありますか。）
Do you have any regional dishes?（地元の料理はありますか。）

waitperson

I highly [strongly] recommend the chow mein.
（焼きそばを強くおすすめします。）
I think curry and rice is the best.（カレーライスは最高だと思います。）
Our specialty is fried prawn.（特別おすすめは海老フライです。）

■ ライフスタイルや宗教の違いから、口にすることのできない食材があるということを認識しておく必要があります。

customer

Can you recommend any vegetarian dishes?
（ベジタリアン料理のおすすめはありますか。）
Do you have a special menu for vegetarians?
（ベジタリアン向けの特別メニューはありますか。）

※ vegetarian（菜食主義者）は一括りできない状況にあります。肉類だけでなく、卵や乳製品など、一切の動物性食品を避ける完全菜食主義者は vegan（ヴィーガン）と呼ばれ、その呼び方は veg(etari)an から生じています。さらに、肉は口にしないが魚介類は食す、あるいは卵や乳製品は摂取するというように、いくつかのタイプに分類されます（詳しくは、第 4 章、4-2. : Tips 欄を参照）。

customer: Does this restaurant have Halal certification？
（このレストランはハラル認証を受けていますか。）

waitperson: We're currently applying for that. I hear that Muslims don't eat pork, so I recommend a chicken and egg rice bowl.
（現在、申請中です。イスラム教徒は豚肉を食べないと聞いていますので、親子丼をおすすめします。）

※イスラム教は戒律が厳しいことで知られています。食に関しても食べてはいけないものが聖典に記されています（詳しくは、第4章、4-2.：Tips欄を参照）。また、ハラル認証とは、イスラム法に則り処理された食品であることを認定するシステムを指します。

■ come with～（～と一緒に来る）は、ここでは「AにBが付いてくる」という意味合いで用いられています。また、be served with～もほぼ同じ意味で使われます。

- At lunch time, all meals come with soup, salad and rice.
（ランチの時間帯は、すべての食事にスープ、サラダ、ライスが付いてきます。）
- *Tempura* is served with dipping sauce.
（天ぷらにはつけ汁が添えられています。）
- Cakes are served with tea or coffee.
（ケーキには紅茶やコーヒーが添えられます。）

Exercise メニューを見ながら、枠内のパターンを用いて注文をとる練習をしましょう。

Waitperson: Are you ready to order now?

　Customer: Sure. I'll take ＿＿＿＿＿＿＿＿＿＿＿＿＿＿＿＿＿＿＿＿＿＿＿.

Waitperson: One＿＿＿＿＿＿＿＿＿《Repeat》＿＿＿＿＿＿＿＿ . Anything else?

　Customer: Can I have ＿＿＿＿＿＿＿＿＿＿＿＿＿＿＿＿＿ ?

Waitperson: Sure, right away.

Provide information

「料理メニュー（**Menu**）」各種

Curry and Rice　カレーライス
Potato Croquette　ポテトコロッケ
Fried Chicken　鶏唐揚げ
Fried Prawn [Shrimp]　海老フライ
Fried Oyster　牡蠣フライ

Grilled Dumplings　焼き餃子
Soy Sauce [Salt, *Miso*, Pork Bone Broth]
　Ramen　醤油［塩、味噌、豚骨］ラーメン
Dipping Noodles　つけ麺
Chow Mein　焼きそば
Cold Noodle Salad　冷やし中華

Chicken and Egg Rice Bowl　親子丼
Beef Rice Bowl　牛丼
Salt-grilled Salmon　鮭の塩焼き
Tuna *Sashimi*　マグロの刺身
　※Sliced Raw Fish　刺身
Squid *Sashimi*　イカの刺身
Mixed *Sashimi* Platter　刺身盛り合わせ
Seared Bonito　カツオのたたき
Chilled *Tofu*　冷やっこ
Meat and Potato Stew　肉じゃが

Chilled *Udon* Noodles　ざるうどん
Udon Noodle Soup with fried *Tofu*　キツネうどん
Chilled *Soba* (Buckwheat) Noodles　ざるそば
Tempura Soba Noodle Soup　天ぷらそば
Soba (Buckwheat) Noodle Soup with bits
　of deep-fried *Tempura* Batter　たぬきそば

Tips:

■ 「B 級グルメ（B-grade gourmet）」は和製英語ですから、用いる際に a cheap, delicious regional dish（安くておいしいローカル料理）や a dish loved by people in the region（地域の人々に愛される料理）の説明を要します。A、B、C の成績をつけるやり方で料理を評価しているといった説明を加えると、さらにわかりやすい説明になります。

"B-grade gourmet" means "a cheap, delicious regional dish" or "a dish loved by people in the region." In an educational institution, the B-grade is pretty good, if not as good as A. People evaluate dishes in the same way. Though it is not high quality, the dish is cheap, delicious, and one of the locals' favorites because of the local ingredients.
　「B 級グルメ」というのは、「安くておいしいローカル料理」あるいは「地域の人々に愛される料理」を意味します。教育機関では、B の成績は A の優秀とまでいかなくとも、それなりによい成績を表します。そのやり方で料理を評価しているわけです。決して高級ではないけれど、地元の食材が用いられた、安くておいしい地域の人々のお気に入り料理のことです。

B-grade gourmet in *Gunma*
（群馬の B 級グルメ）

■ *Mizusawa udon*……One of the pleasures of visiting *Ikaho Onsen* is eating *udon* in the *Mizusawa Kannon* nearby. *Mizusawa udon*, which has been offered to temple visitors for 400 years, is an additive-free natural food made only with wheat flour from *Gunma*, salt, and the water of *Mizusawa*. The dish has been ranked as one of the three major *udon* in Japan along with *Inaniwa udon* of *Akita* and *Sanuki udon* of *Kagawa*. *Mizusawa udon* is served as *zaru-udon* (chilled *udon* noodles) and is eaten after being dipped in a sesame-flavored sauce or a soy-flavored sauce.

> 水沢うどん……伊香保温泉を訪れる楽しみの一つは、近くの水澤観音でうどんを食すること でしょう。400年にわたり参拝客に提供されてきた水沢うどんは、地元産の小麦粉、塩、水沢 の水だけでつくられる無添加の自然食です。そのおいしさは、秋田の稲庭うどん、香川の讃 岐うどんと並び、日本三大うどんの一つとして称賛されるほどです。水沢うどんはざるうど んで出され、ごまだれや醤油味の漬け汁につけて食べます。

■ *Takasaki* pasta……There are many Italian restaurants in *Takasaki* because of the large amount of wheat production in the region; therefore, because noodles such as *udon* or *okkirikomi* have been eaten for many centuries, Italian pasta culture was easily adopted in this region. Now *Takasaki* is a hotspot for pasta, and a King of Pasta event is held every year. It naturally follows that the quality of *Takasaki* pasta is pretty high.

> 高崎パスタ……高崎にはイタリアンレストランが多いです。その理由は、地域の小麦生産量 が多いことと関係しています。つまり、この地域では昔からうどんやおっ切り込みなどの麺 が食されてきたために、イタリアの食文化、パスタが容易に受け入れられたのです。現在、 高崎はパスタ激戦区で、キング・オブ・パスタを決定するイベントが毎年行われています。 高崎パスタはレベルが高いわけです。

■ *Ota Yakisoba* is stir-fried soba noodles and is similar to chow mein. There are various types of local *yakisoba* throughout Japan. *Ota yakisoba* features thick noodles with a dark-colored sauce. The taste is lighter than it looks.

> 太田焼きそばは炒めた麺で、チャーメン（五目中華焼きそば）に似ています。様々な焼きそ ばが日本各地にあります。太田焼きそばは、太麺でソースの色が濃いことが特徴です。味は 見た目ほど濃くなく、あっさりしています。

■ Sauce *Katsudon* is a dish common in *Gunma*. It features a deep-fried pork cutlet (*tonkatsu*) seasoned with a Worcester-like sauce, therefore the name "sauce *katsudon*" on a bowl of rice. Depending on the area, shredded cabbage is laid between rice and pork cutlets. For comparison, ordinary *Katsudon* is a bowl of rice topped with *tonkatsu*, which is cooked lightly with some vegetables and an egg. It is seasoned with soy sauce, sugar, sweet *sake* (*mirin*), and *sake*.

> ソースカツ丼は、群馬では一般的な料理です。ウスターソース系のソースで味付けしたトン カツが特徴で、それがソースカツ丼と呼ばれる理由です。地域によってはご飯とトンカツの 間に千切りキャベツが敷かれています。ちなみに、普通のカツ丼はご飯の上に、野菜と卵と 一緒に軽く煮たトンカツが乗っています。カツ丼は醤油、砂糖、みりん、酒で味付けされま す。

3-4 すき焼きの具材は全部メイド・イン・グンマ

All the ingredients for *sukiyaki* are made in *Gunma*

Staff: The iron pan on the table-top stove is for *sukiyaki*. Have you had *sukiyaki* before?

Guest: Yes, I have. I couldn't believe it when I saw raw eggs on the table for the first time. It's not common to eat raw eggs in my country.

Staff: It's safe to eat raw eggs in Japan.

Guest: And I also found that hot meat and vegetables taste so good when they are dipped in a raw, beaten egg right before being eaten.

Staff: May I make the *sukiyaki* now?

Guest: Sure.

Staff: This marbled meat is *Joshu Wagyu*. *Joshu* is another name for *Gunma*, so *Joshu Wagyu* is the branded beef from Japanese cattle raised in *Gunma* Prefecture.

Guest: I have never seen such beautiful marbled beef.

Staff: How would you like your beef?

Guest: Medium-rare, please.

《Cooking the *sukiyaki* in front of the guest》

Staff: Here you are. Please be careful because it's hot.

Guest: So good! The *Wagyu* melts in my mouth. Good flavor, too.

Staff: Another key to delicious *sukiyaki* is the seasoning. Soy sauce, sugar, *sake*, and *mirin*, which is sweet *sake*, are mixed into this stock.

Guest: Yummy.

Staff: These are *Shimonita* green onions, edible chrysanthemum, *shiitake* mushrooms, *konnyaku* noodles, and grilled *tofu*. All these ingredients for the *sukiyaki* are also from *Gunma*.

Guest: So *sukiyaki* is the dish recommended to visitors in *Gunma*.

Vocabulary

ingredient	具材	iron pan	鉄鍋
table-top stove	卓上コンロ	dip in	〜に浸す
raw, beaten egg	溶いた生卵	marbled meat	霜降り肉
cattle	〔集合名詞〕畜牛	(be) raised	育てられた
melt	溶ける	seasoning	調味料
green onion	長ネギ	edible chrysanthemum	食用の菊
grilled *tofu*	焼き豆腐		

English Points

■ Have you + 動詞の過去分詞 + before?（以前に〜したことはありますか）は、経験を尋ねる表現です。これに対する基本回答は、Yes, I have. / No, I haven't.（はい、あります／いいえ、ありません）ですが、会話においては具体的な展開が期待されます。

・Have you been to *Kamakura*?（鎌倉へ行ったことはありますか。）
——Yes, I saw the Great Buddha and also visited *Enoshima* Island.
（ええ、大仏を見物して、江の島へも行きました。）

・Have you ever eaten glaze-grilled eel?
（照り焼きにしたウナギを食べたことはありますか。）
——You mean *kabayaki*. At first I was reluctant to eat it, but actually it was so good.（蒲焼のことね。最初は戸惑ったけれど、実際に食べてみたら、すごくおいしかったです。）

・Have you ever seen *Kabuki*?（歌舞伎を見たことはありますか。）
——No, I've never seen it. Where can I buy that ticket?
（一度もないですね。チケットはどこで買うの。）

■ How would you like〜?（〜はいかがいたしますか）は、相手の好みを尋ねる丁寧な表現です。

staff member

How would you like your steak?（ステーキはいかがいたしますか。）
= How would you like your steak done [cooked, prepared]?
（ステーキをどのように調理してもらいたいですか。）

guest

I'd like it | rare, | please.（レアでお願いします。）　※表面だけを焼く
         | medium-rare, | （ミディアム・レアでお願いします。）
         | medium, | （ミディアムでお願いします。）※中位に焼く
         | well-done, | （ウェルダンでお願いします。）※十分に焼く

staff member

How would you like your eggs?（卵はいかがいたしますか。）

guest

Sunny-side up, please.（片面焼きの目玉焼きで。）
Over easy, please.　（両面焼きの目玉焼きで。）※ひっくり返して軽く焼く
Omelet, please.　　（オムレツで。）
Scrambled, please.　（スクランブル［= かき卵］で。）
Soft boiled, please.　（半熟ゆで卵で。）
Hard boiled, please.　（固ゆで卵で。）
Poached, please.　　（ポーチドエッグで。）
　※殻を割った卵を酢を入れた湯に落とし、半生状態で取り出したもの

Prepare を答えた後、枠内のパターンを用いて質問と応答の練習をしましょう。

```
A: What kind of ingredients do we need to cook _____ ?
B: I think we need _____ , _____ , and _____ .
```

Prepare

Ingredients for a dish

(1) *Okkirikomi*: _____ _____ _____ _____ _____

(2) Chicken Curry: _____ _____ _____ _____ _____

(3) Chow Mein: _____ _____ _____ _____ _____

(4) *Temaki-zushi*: _____ _____ _____ _____ _____

(5) Spaghetti with meat sauce: _____ _____ _____ _____ _____

(6) *Shabu-shabu*: _____ _____ _____ _____ _____

Ingredients:

beef　　ground beef　　pork　　chicken　　cabbage　　bean sprouts　　cucumber
taro　　sheet of dried seaweed　　egg　　tomato　　sesame paste　　vinegared rice
Japanese radish　　wide udon noodles　　green onion　　*shiitake* mushroom
carrot　　onion　　spaghetti noodles　　avocado　　tuna　　salmon　　shrimp
garlic　　curry powder　　chow mein noodles　　Worcester-like sauce……

Tips:

■　In Japan, eggs are produced under strict management standards, so raw eggs are safe to eat.
　　日本では厳しい管理基準のもとに卵が生産されていますから、卵を生で食べても安全です。

　　※日本養鶏協会によると、日本における卵の賞味期限は生食できる期限を示すものです。賞味期限を過ぎた卵は加熱して食することができます。生卵を食する習慣があるため、徹底した安全管理が行われていることがうかがえます。生卵を食する国は、日本の他にもありますが、多くはありません。諸外国では、食中毒を懸念して生卵を避けるのが普通です。すき焼きを機に生卵を食するようになる外国人は少なくありませんが、こと食に関しては強要しないことを心得なくてはなりません。（参考資料：日本養鶏協会「たまごの知識」）

■　*Gunma* Prefecture has abundant water resources and long sunshine hours, which helps farm produce grow well.
　　群馬県は水資源と日照時間に恵まれ、農作物がよく育ちます。

■　*Gunma* is well-known as a vegetable production center. Of the many vegetables produced here, *Shimonita* green onion, *Tsumagoi* cabbage, and *Kokufu* Chinese cabbage are branded vegetables.
　　群馬は野菜の産地としてよく知られています。いろいろな野菜がつくられていますが、中でも、下仁田ネギ、嬬恋キャベツ、国府白菜はブランド野菜です。

■　*Gunma* has two cropping cycles in a year. During summer rice is grown, and in the same field in winter wheat is grown. A number of the food products that use rice and wheat flour are local specialties such as *sake* (rice wine), *udon* noodles, and pasta.
　　群馬は二毛作地帯です。夏に稲作する土地で、冬の間は小麦が栽培されます。米や小麦粉を使った様々な食品、たとえば酒、うどん、パスタなどが地元の特産品です。

■　Raising stock is also a prosperous industry in *Gunma* and includes *Joshu* beef, *Joshu mugi* pork (the pigs are mainly fed on barley, *mugi* in Japanese), meat products such as ham or sausage, and dairy products such as cheese and ice cream, all of which are recommended.
　　群馬は畜産業も盛んです。上州牛や上州麦豚（麦類を中心にした飼料で育てられた豚）をはじめ、ハムやソーセージなどの肉製品、チーズやアイスクリームなどの乳製品もおすすめです。

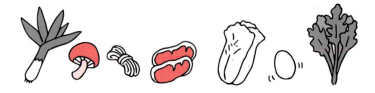

第4章　温泉旅館に泊まる
【温泉・宿泊編】

4-1 チェックイン
Check-in

「温泉」はそのまま *onsen* で通じる！

「温泉」に対して、hot spring と spa の二つが用いられ、ガイドブックやホームページにおいても温泉を意味する英語表記は統一されていない現状にあります。hot spring は「熱水線、源泉」の意で、spa というと、「温泉療養、療養施設」を指しますが、どちらの意味も含めて「温泉」という語が使われている訳ですから、温泉を英語に置き換えることに無理があることがうかがえます。

最近は日本文化の世界的な浸透により *onsen* で通じるため、英訳せずに、そのまま *onsen* が使用される傾向にあり、観光庁のウェブページでも *onsen* と表記されています。よって、このテキストにおいても *onsen* の呼び方で統一しています。

(参考資料：国土交通省観光庁「観光立国実現に向けた多言語対応の改善・強化のためのガイドライン」)

Guest: Hi. I'd like to check in, please.

Front clerk: Sure, <u>do you have a reservation, sir?</u>

Guest: <u>Yes, I do.</u> <u>My name is</u> Andrew Jones.

Front clerk: One moment, please.

《Checks a list of reservations》

Front clerk: Yes, Mr. Jones. We do have your reservation. One person for two nights, starting today.

Guest: That's right.

Front clerk: Please fill out this form.

Guest: Sure... Here you are.

Front clerk: Your room is called *Hagi-no-ma* on the second floor. Here's the room key. We'll take you to the room now.

Guest: Is the view from the room good?

Front clerk: It sure is. <u>The room faces</u> the Japanese garden.

Guest: Great!

Front clerk: We hope you enjoy the view.

Vocabulary

front clerk	フロント係
reservation	予約
fill out	～に記入する
face	～に面する

English Points

■ Do you have a reservation, sir / ma'am?（お客様、予約はございますか）のように、最後に敬称をつけることで丁寧な表現になります。英語の敬称は、男性に対しては sir、女性には ma'am が用いられます。

これに対して、予約してある場合は…

・Yes, I do. My name is Andrew Jones.
（はい。名前はアンドリュー・ジョーンズです。）
・Yes. I have a room booked under Jones.
（はい。ジョーンズで部屋を予約してあります。）

■ I [We] would like a quiet room with a nice view.（眺めがよく、静かな部屋がいいです）と要望する宿泊客は、少なくないようです。眺めは部屋の良し悪しを決める一つの要素であるということができます。部屋からの景色について説明を加えることがポイントです。

・The room faces	Lake *Haruna*.	（部屋は榛名湖に面しています。）
	Mt. *Myogi*.	（ 〃 　妙義山　　 〃 　　 ）
	the *Kannon-yama* Family Park.	
		（ 〃 　観音山ファミリーパーク 〃 ）
	the courtyard.	（ 〃 　中庭　　　 〃 　　 ）
	the golf course.	（ 〃 　ゴルフ場　 〃 　　 ）

・The room has | a fine view of Mt. *Akagi*.
（その部屋からは赤城山の見事な景色が見えます。）
a nice view of the valley.
（その部屋からは渓谷の美しい景色を眺められます。）
a wonderful view overlooking the whole city.
（その部屋から街全体を見下ろす素晴らしい景色が一望できます。）

Exercise Prepare を答えた後、枠内のパターンを用いて質問と応答の練習をしましょう。

A: Do you know what _____《日本語での呼び方》_____ is called in English?

B: I think it's _____ (in English).

A: What do they do?

B: _____.

Prepare

ホテル・旅館スタッフの英語名を下の枠内から選び記入し、仕事内容とマッチングさせなさい。

(1) (   ) receptionist　　　(A) They are owers of the inn. They greet guests and make sure the guests feel welcome.

(2) (   ) general manager　　(B) They take drink orders, and mix and serve drinks for guests.

(3) (   ) porter　　　　　　(C) They answer telephones and give information to guests.

(4) (   ) wait staff　　　　(D) They assist guests with everything they need, such as providing information and making tour reservations.

(5) (   ) housekeeping staff　(E) They take guests and their baggage to their room.

(6) (   ) proprietress　　　(F) They are responsible for every aspect of the hotel, including the staff and the guests.

(7) (   ) bartender　　　　(G) They prepare and cook food in a restaurant or a hotel.

(8) (   ) concierge　　　　(H) They tidy the rooms, and clean and polish the toilets, bathtubs and mirrors.

(9) (   ) cook　　　　　　(I) They take customer orders and deliver food and beverages.

給仕人　　総支配人　　コンシェルジェ　　荷物を運ぶ係　　受付
バーテンダー　　女将　　料理人　　客室係

Tips:

Ryokan, traditional Japanese-style inns, are very different from Western-style hotels.
（旅館は伝統的な和式の宿で、西洋式のホテルと違う）

■ _Ryokan_ have Japanese-style guest rooms, and hotels have Western-style rooms; therefore, _ryokan_ guests sleep on a futon, a Japanese-style mattress, which is usually rolled out in a _tatami_ room.

　　ホテルの客室は洋式であるのに対して、旅館では和式です。つまり、旅館客は畳の部屋に敷かれた布団で眠るということです。

■ Each hotel guest room has a Western-style bathroom or a shower room. However, in most _ryokans_, as there are many bathing facilities such as _onsens_ and outdoor baths, there are often no private bathing facilities in the guest rooms.

　　ホテルの各客室には、洋式浴室またはシャワー室がついています。しかし旅館では、温泉や露天風呂の施設が充実しているので、各客室に入浴設備のないケースもあります。

■ Hotel rates are usually only the room charge. While there are many hotels that have breakfast, hotel guests need to make their own dinner arrangements. At _ryokans_, the accommodation rate usually includes two meals for each overnight stay (dinner and breakfast).

　　ホテル料金は基本的に部屋代です。朝食付のホテルも少なくないですが、夕食は宿泊客が自分で手配するのが通例です。旅館の場合、宿泊料金に2食（夕食と朝食）が含まれているのが普通です。

■ Hotel guests can eat meals at any time they like; however, mealtimes are fixed at a _ryokan_. As mealtimes vary depending on a _ryokan_, guests are advised to confirm the timings in advance. However, a _ryokan_ staff member usually asks guests about their preferred dinner time during check-in.

　　客の好きな時間に食事のとれるホテルに対して、旅館では食事の時間帯が決められています。時間帯はそれぞれの宿ごとに同じではないので、あらかじめ確認することをすすめます。とはいえ、旅館ではチェックインの際、担当者が客に夕食時間の希望を尋ねるのが普通です。

■ A guest is treated in the spirit of _"omotenashi,"_ Japanese-style hospitality, in a _ryokan_. During their stay, guests are taken good care of by a _nakai-san_, a personal room attendant who is in charge of general services for guests such as serving meals and preparing the futon. Guests can expect higher-quality hospitality in a traditional _ryokan_.

　　旅館では、客におもてなしの心で接します。滞在中、仲居さん（部屋付きの接客係）が細かい気配りをしてくれます。仲居さんは、食事の配膳や布団の用意など、お客様へのサービス全般を担当しています。伝統的な旅館では、宿泊客はより質の高いおもてなしを期待できます。

4-2 予約なしのチェックイン

Check-in without a reservation

Guest: Hi. I don't have a reservation. Do you have a room available for tonight?

Front clerk: Just one person for tonight?

Guest: Uh-huh.

Front clerk: One moment, please.

《Checks on room availability》

Front clerk: <u>We can provide a room for you</u>. The room rate is 14,000 [fourteen thousand] yen, including dinner and breakfast.

Guest: That'll be fine. Do I pay it in advance or when I check out?

Front clerk: Either way is fine. Please fill out this form.

Guest: All right... Here you are.

Front clerk: Mr. Jones, could you <u>let us know if there are</u> any foods you can't eat for medical or religious reasons?

Guest: No, there aren't.

Front clerk: <u>Are there any Japanese foods you don't like?</u> Do you like *sashimi* and *natto*? In other words, raw fish and fermented soybeans.

Guest: I love *sushi*, so I think I can eat raw fish, too. But I don't think I would like fermented soybeans.

Front clerk: Okay, we'll give you another side dish instead of *natto* for breakfast.

Guest: Thanks.

Vocabulary

available	利用可能な	※ availability	利用できること
provide	〜を提供する		
include	〜を含む		
in advance	前もって		
either way	(二通りの) どちらでも		
medical	医学的な		
religious	宗教的な		
reason	理由		
fermented soybeans	納豆	※ fermented	発酵した
side dish	副菜		
instead of	〜の代わりに		

English Points

■ 空室がある場合は、上述の We can provide a room for you. (お部屋をご用意できます) の対応になりますが、空室がない場合の断りの表現は…

・Unfortunately, we have no rooms available tonight. Please look for another inn.
(あいにく今晩は空いている部屋はございません。他の旅館を当たってください。)

■ Let us know if there is[are] 〜 (もし〜があるなら、教えてください) という婉曲的な表現に対して、Is[Are] there any〜? (〜はありますか) は直接的な表現になります。

・Let us know if there are any clues.
(何か手がかりがある場合はお知らせください。)
・Let us know if there is anything we can do for you.
(私たちに何かできることがあれば教えてください。)

・Are there any places you really want to visit?
(あなたが心底訪れたい場所はありますか。)
・Is there any chance he can pass the Tourism English Proficiency Test?
(彼が観光英語検定に合格する可能性はありますか。)

個人的な嗜好やアレルギーのために避けたい、もしくは避けなくてはならない食品を確認する際、上述の言い回しを含めて、次のようなやり取りが行われます。

staff member

Are there any foods you can't eat? (食べられないものはありますか。)
Are there any foods you're allergic to?
(アレルギーのある食べ物はありますか。)
Are you allergic to any food? (何らかの食品にアレルギーがありますか。)
Do you have any allergies? (何かアレルギーはありますか。)

guest

There is no particular food I can't eat.
(食べられない食品は特にないです。)
I'm allergic to eggs [milk, wheat...].
(卵［牛乳、小麦…］にアレルギーです。)
I have an allergy to peanuts. (落花生にアレルギーです。)
I have an allergic reaction to shellfish such as crab, lobster, and shrimp.
(カニ、ロブスター、エビなどの甲殻類にアレルギー反応を起こします。)
I have severe allergies to soy and sesame.
(大豆とゴマに重度のアレルギーを持っています。)
I have a life-threatening food allergy to buckwheat.
(蕎麦に対して生命を脅かす食物アレルギーを持っています。)

※ al-ler-gy（名詞）と al-ler-gic（形容詞）のアクセントの違いに注意。太字の部分を強く発音。

 Prepare を答えた後、枠内のパターンを用いて質問と応答の練習をしましょう。

A: Are you allergic to any food?

B: Yes. / No. _____.

A: Are there any Japanese foods you don't like?

B: Yes. / No. _____.

Prepare

各自の情報に基づいて、次の質問に答えなさい。

・I'm allergic to _____.

・Japanese foods I don't like include _____.

Tips:

Vegetarian（菜食主義者）のタイプ

➢ Vegan（ヴィーガン）
肉類だけでなく、卵や乳製品など一切の動物性食品を避ける完全菜食主義者で、Pure-vegetarian（ピュア・ベジタリアン）とも呼ばれる。Vegan の呼び名は、veg(etari)an から生じている。食用・衣料用などの目的のために動物を苦しめたり、命を奪ったりすることを嫌い、獣肉・魚介類・卵・乳製品を口にしない。また、動物製品（皮製品・シルク・ウールなど）を身に付けることもしない。

➤ Lacto-vegetarian（ラクト・ベジタリアン）
植物性食品に加え、乳汁・乳製品などを食べる。肉類・魚介類・卵は食べない。

➤ Ovo-vegetarian（オボ・ベジタリアン）
植物性食品に加え、卵を食べる。肉類・魚介類・乳製品は食べない。

➤ Lacto-ovo-vegetarian（ラクト・オボ・ベジタリアン）
植物性食品に加え、牛乳やチーズなどの乳製品と卵を食べる。肉類・魚介類は食べない。
　※国際ベジタリアン連合（The International Vegetarian Union）は、このタイプを基本的なベジタリアンとして認めている。

➤ Pesco-vegetarian（ペスコ・ベジタリアン）
植物性食品に加え、魚を食べる。獣肉は食べない。

➤ Pollo-vegetarian（ポーヨー・ベジタリアン）
植物性食品に加え、鶏肉を食べる。赤身の肉は食べない。

➤ Fruitarian（フルータリアン）
果食主義者。穀物や根菜は刈り取って収穫し、植物の生命を絶つことから食べない。果実はもぎ取っても植物の生命を奪うことにはならないことから、食べてもよいという考え方に基づいた菜食主義者である。

（出典：国土交通省　総合政策局　観光事業課「多様な食文化・食習慣を有する外国人客への対応マニュアル」(pp.67-71)）

イスラム教における食に対する禁止事項と嫌悪感

豚、アルコール、血液、宗教上の適切な処理が施されていない肉、うなぎ、イカ、タコ、貝類、漬け物などの発酵食品

➤ 特に注意が必要な食材は「豚」「アルコール」「血液」「宗教上の適切な処理が施されていない肉」である。

➤ 豚は食べることだけでなく、見ることも嫌悪する人が多い。

➤ 「ブイヨン」「ゼラチン」「肉エキス」には豚の肉や骨が使われており、調理時に注意する必要がある。ソースやスープには「豚エキス」が使われることが多い。

➤ 「ラード」（豚の脂肪）は、調理時に注意する必要がある。「植物性油」を代用するとよい。

➤ 厳格なイスラム教徒には、豚肉を料理した調理器具が使われることを忌避する人もいる。

➤ 水餃子などの「豚を想起させる名称の料理」は、たとえ食材に豚が使用されていない場合も感覚的に拒絶されるため、注意が必要である。

➤ アルコールは「料理酒」「調味料」（みりんなど）「香り付け」「デザート」など様々な料理に使われることがあり、特に注意が必要である。

➤ 「アルコールの使用を想起させるもの」も感覚的に拒絶されるため、注意が必要である。例えば、コース料理では、ワイングラスがテーブル上に置かれていることにさえ嫌悪感を表す人もいるため、アルコールを飲まないお客様のワイングラスはあらかじめ下げておく必要がある。…〈中略〉…

➤ 血液は不浄なものとして忌避される。肉類や魚の焼き具合と調理方法には気をつける方がよい。

- 厳密には「宗教上の適切な処理が施されていない肉」（自然死、病死、事故死した肉を含む）も食べることができないため、厳格なイスラム教徒は食べることを忌避する場合もある。しかし実際は、豚肉以外の肉類ということで、牛肉、鶏肉、羊肉を食べるイスラム教徒も多い。また、魚料理は食べられる（ただし生魚を食べる習慣がない人が多い）。
- イスラム教で適切な処理を施した食材は「ハラルミール」と呼ばれ、購入することが可能な食材である。
- 「うなぎ」「イカ」「タコ」「貝類」「漬け物などの発酵食品」については宗教上の教義で禁じられているわけではないが、嫌悪感を示されるので、料理の食材として扱うことは避ける方がよい。「ウロコのある魚」と「エビ」は食べられる。イカ、タコ、貝類は酢の物などに使われることがあるため、注意が必要である。
- 日本の料理で扱う食材としては一般的ではないが、「爬虫類」「昆虫類」「肉食動物」も嫌悪感を示されるので、料理の食材として扱うことは避ける方がよい（宗教上の教義で禁じられているわけではない）。
- なおコーランの中では、「死獣の肉」「血液」「豚肉」「異神に捧げられたもの」を食べることが禁じられている。

　　※イスラム暦9月に1カ月にわたる断食期間（ラマダンと呼ばれる）がある。断食期間中は、夜明けから夜になるまで、一切の飲食が禁じられる（水も飲んではいけない）。…〈中略〉…この期間の食事は、通常、夜明け前と夜の2回である。

（出典：国土交通省　総合政策局　観光事業課「多様な食文化・食習慣を有する外国人客への対応マニュアル」(pp.72-77)）

4-3 客を部屋へ案内する
Showing a guest to their room

Staff: Please take off your shoes at the entrance. You can wear these slippers anywhere, but please don't wear them on the tatami, which are the straw mats.

Guest: Okay.

Staff: I'll take you to the room. This way, please.

Guest: Sure.

Staff: This is your room. Because it has a *tatami* floor, please take off your slippers here.

Guest: No slippers on the *tatami* mats. Got it.

Staff: I'll put your baggage here. The bathroom and toilet are over there. Please make yourself at home. I'll make tea for you now.

Guest: Thanks. 〈Looking out the window〉 What a beautiful garden that is!

Staff: Just by watching the Japanese garden you feel relief from stress.

Guest: The peaceful space relaxes my mind.

Staff: That's good. Now here's some tea.

Guest: Thank you.

Onsen and Accommodations

4

温泉・宿泊編

Vocabulary

take off	～を脱ぐ	at the entrance	入り口で
wear	～をはく、～を着用する		
straw mat / *tatami* mat	畳	make oneself at home	くつろぐ
feel relief	ホッとする、安心する		
relax one's mind	心をリラックスさせる、気が緩む		

☞ English Points

■ make oneself at home は、そもそも〈○○自身を家にいるように気楽にする〉の意ですが、客や友人などに対して Please make yourself at home.（ぞうど、くつろいでください）の表現として用いられます。同じ意味合いの表現として…

・Make yourself comfortable.（楽にしてください。）
・Please have a seat and relax.（座って、リラックスしてください。）
　——I felt at ease, thank you.（緊張がほぐれました。ありがとうございます。）

■ I'll make tea for you. または I'll make you some tea. で「お茶を入れます」を表します。make は名詞を伴い、多様に使用される動詞です。

・I make
coffee	every morning.（私は毎朝コーヒーを入れます。）
my breakfast	（ 〃 　自分の朝食をつくります。）
my bed	（ 〃 　自分のベットを整えます。）
sandwiches	for lunch.　（昼食にサンドイッチをつくります。）

・I'll make
money	as a babysitter.（ベビーシッターとしてお金を稼ぎます。）
room	for you on the couch.
	（ソファにあなたが座れるよう席を詰めます。）

・make a(n) ＋名詞 で行動・動作を表現することができます。

make an appointment	（人と会う約束をする）
make a reservation	（予約する）
make a phone call	（電話する）
make an excuse	（言い訳する）
make a mistake	（間違える）
make a decision	（決定する）
make a promise	（約束する）
make a change	（変更を加える、修正する）
make a choice	（選ぶ）
make a deal	（取引をする）
make an attempt	（試みる）
make an agreement	（合意する）
make a suggestion	（提案する）
make a calculation	（計算する）
make an investment	（投資する）

■ 「なんと〜でしょう！」の感嘆文は、how あるいは what で始まります。疑問文と区別するポイントは、語順の違いと文末の「！」（感嘆符：exclamation mark）です。

疑問文
- How old is this shrine?（この神社はどれくらい古いですか。）
- What do you do for a living?（何の仕事をしていらっしゃいますか。）

感嘆文
- How old the shrine is! = What an old shrine it is!
  （その神社はなんと古いのでしょう！）
- How kind you are! = What a kind person you are!
  （あなたはなんと親切なのでしょう！）

 Exercise 次の how または what で始まる文が疑問文なら「？」、感嘆文なら「！」を記入しなさい。

(1) What a big room this is (　　　)
(2) How old is the turtle (　　　)
(3) What are you looking for (　　　)
(4) How tall your brother is (　　　)
(5) What a delicious apple this is (　　　)
(6) How much is this chocolate (　　　)
(7) How hard she works (　　　)

4-4 貴重品は金庫に保管する
Putting valuables in the safe

Staff: There is an attached safe in the TV stand. Please put your valuables in the safe. <u>Even if you are not in the room,</u> we come in and out of this room for cleaning or bed making. It's good to use the safe.

Guest: How do I use it?

Staff: You open the safe door, put your valuables in here, and lock it. That's it.

Guest: It's easy. But what should I do with this key when I get into the *onsen*?

Staff: Like this, you can wear it as a bracelet. And you won't lose the key.

Guest: That's a good idea!

Staff: Thank you. Or you can leave your valuables at the front desk.

Guest: Japan is such a safe country, and people are honest. The other day, <u>I left my camera behind in the restroom</u> of a restaurant, and I was surprised I got it back. It's almost impossible in other countries.

Staff: Of course, our inn is safe, but just in case, we warn our guests not to leave their valuables unattended.

Guest: You're absolutely right.

Vocabulary

valuables	［複数形］貴重品		
attached safe	備え付けの金庫	※ safe（形容詞）	安全な
even if	たとえ〜でも	bracelet	ブレスレット
lose	〜を紛失する	honest	正直な
leave behind	〜を置き忘れる	restroom	トイレ
be surprised	驚く	impossible	不可能な
warn	警告する	just in case	念のために
leave 〜 unattended	〜を置いたままにする		
absolutely	絶対に		

👉 English Points

■ even if（たとえ〜でも）は、逆説的な仮定を表す表現です。

- ・Even if we don't like someone, we should be polite to them.
  （たとえ相手のことが好きでなくとも、丁寧に対応するべきです。）
- ・They have to follow the company policy, even if they disagree with it.
  （たとえ彼らが反対であっても、会社の方針に従うべきです。）

■ 「○○を置き忘れる」は、leave behind または leave が用いられます。「地図を忘れた」という場合は、I forgot the map. と言い表すことができます。しかし、「部屋に地図を忘れた」という場合は、I left the map in my room. の表現になります。場所との関係性で leave が用いられるためです。

- ・I left my umbrella on the train.（電車に傘を置き忘れました。）
- ・I accidentally left my bag in the taxi.
  （うっかりタクシーにカバンを置き忘れました。）

  ※ I cannot find my glasses.　I must have misplaced them.
  （眼鏡が見つからない。どこか（いつもと違う場所に）に置き忘れたに違いない。）

Tip:

■ There is a locker with a key for valuables in the changing room, so you can put the safe key or your glasses in there when you take a bath.
　脱衣場には鍵付きの貴重品用ロッカーがありますので、そこに金庫の鍵や眼鏡などを保管して入浴できます。

4-5　地図で場所を説明する

Explaining a place on a map

Staff: Dinner will be ready after 5:30p.m. <u>What time would you like to have dinner?</u> We'll bring the dinner to your room.

Guest: Then at 6:30. Now, I want to take a dip in the *onsen* before dinner.

Staff: You can use the private bath in this room, but there's a large communal bath, too.

Guest: Since it's such a rare chance, <u>I might as well try the large bath.</u> Where is it?

Staff: Here is a map of the building. 〈Pointing to the large bath room on the map〉 The large bath room is right here on the first floor.

Guest: I see. Thank you.

Staff: There are *yukata* on the shelf over there. For first time use, a guide to bathing etiquette for the large communal bath is attached to it. Please read it.

Guest: Okay. I'll do that.

Staff: Please ask me any questions anytime. I'll be happy to answer you.

Vocabulary

bring	～を持ってくる
take a dip	ひと浴びする
private bath	（各部屋に付いている）専用浴室
communal	共用の
rare chance	めったにない機会
might as well	～した方がよい、～しても悪くない
bathing etiquette	入浴エチケット　　※ etiquette　礼儀作法
attach	添付する

English Points

■　夕食の提供の仕方は宿泊所によって異なりますが、それぞれの客室へ夕食を運ぶという形式をとっている旅館は少なくありません。この場合、Dinner will be ready after 5:30p.m.（夕食は5時半以降にご用意できます）、We'll bring dinner to your room.（夕食はお部屋の方へお持ちいたします）と説明を加えたうえで、客の希望する夕食時間を確認することが求められます。

- What time would you like to have dinner?（夕食は何時にいたしましょうか。）
- What time do you want us to bring dinner to your room?
（夕食は何時に部屋の方へお持ちいたしましょうか。）

■ might as well あるいは may as well は、「〜する方がよい」「〜してもいいね」という意味合いの控えめな提案をする言い回しです。

- We have final exams next week. Should we study in the library?
（来週は期末試験だ。図書館で勉強すべき？）
——Might as well.（まあ、そうしてもいいね。）

- We may as well go for a drive in the country. The weather is nice today.
（郊外をドライブするのもいいね。今日は天気がいいし。）

 Exercise　Prepare を答えた後、枠内のパターンを用いて質問と応答の練習をしましょう。

A: I don't know what to call things in Japanese, but in many cases pictograms can help me.
B: Then, do you know what the number 《one, two, ...》 pictogram represents?
A: It's easy. [or It's hard.] It means ＿＿＿＿＿＿＿＿ .
B: That's right. [or That's not right. Try again!]

Prepare

次の標識は何を表しますか。続く A〜J から選び、記入しなさい。

1. (　　)　2. (　　)　3. (　　)　4. (　　)　5. (　　)

6. (　　)　7. (　　)　8. (　　)　9. (　　)　10. (　　)

(A) Bar　　　　　　　(B) Room service　　　(C) Information Center
(D) Restaurant　　　　(E) Swimming room　　(F) Hot spring
(G) Laundry service　(H) Parking　　　　　　(I) Shrine
(J) Barber

Tips:

~~~~ To our guests ~~~~
お客様へ

Our check-in times : from 3 p.m. to 7 p.m. on the day of arrival.
チェックイン時間：到着日の午後3時から7時まで。
Check-out　　　 : up to 10 a.m. on the day of departure.
チェックアウト：出発日の午前10時まで。
※ If you wish to check out later than 10 a.m., please contact reception.
午前10以降にチェックアウトしたい場合、受付までご連絡ください。

Hours of Operation
運営時間
Breakfast buffet time: 7:00 a.m. − 9:30 a.m.
朝食バイキング　　 ：午前7時−午前9時30分
Dinner time: 6:00 p.m. − 9:00 p.m.
夕食時間 ：午後6時−午後9時

Bathing time for the large communal bath
大浴場の入浴時間
　　Morning: 5:00 a.m. − 10:00 a.m.
　　朝　 ：午前5時−午前10時
　　Evening: 5:00 p.m. − 12:00 a.m. /midnight
　　夜　 ：午後5時−午前0時

The main entrance is closed from 12:00 a.m. to 5:30 a.m. for guest and staff safety late at night. When entering the inn after 12:00 a.m., guests can unlock the door using their room key.
深夜の安全を確実にするために正面入り口は午前0時から午前5時30分まで閉められます。
午前0時以降に入館する際は、お客様の部屋鍵で正面入り口の錠を開けることができます。

Thank you for your cooperation and understanding.
ご協力とご理解に感謝申し上げます。

~~~~ About *Yukata* ~~~~
浴衣について

ꙮ The *yukata* is a Japanese-style bathrobe. You can also wear a *yukata* as loungewear and nightwear. It's perfectly okay to go outside your room wearing a *yukata*.
浴衣は日本式バスローブです。また、浴衣は部屋着や寝間着としてご利用いただけます。浴衣を着て、部屋の外を歩くこともまったく問題ありません。

~~~ Bathing Etiquette ~~~
入浴エチケット

ꙮ When using the large communal bath, please bring the bath towel and hand towel from your room. Shampoo, hair conditioner, and soap are provided there.
大浴場をご使用時には、部屋のバスタオルと手ぬぐいを持参してください。大浴場には、シャンプー、リンス、石鹸が用意されています。

ꙮ Please do not put the hand towel into the bath.
手ぬぐいを浴槽に入れないでください。

ꙮ Please use the soap outside the bath.
石鹸は浴槽の外でご使用ください。

ꙮ You can get into the bath after you have washed.
体を洗ってから浴槽にお入りください。

ꙮ Please do not swim in the bath so as not to trouble other users.
他のお客様のご迷惑になりますので、浴槽では泳がないでください。

ꙮ We alternate the men and the women's bath times during the day, so please confirm which bath to use before going into the large communal bath.
時間帯によって男湯と女湯が入れ替わります。大浴場をご使用の際はご確認ください。

We would appreciate it if you observe the bathing etiquette.
ご協力に感謝申し上げます。

（参考資料：群馬県温泉協会「上州温泉入浴10訓」）

Onsen and Accommodations

4

温泉・宿泊編

4-6 泉質と効能について説明する

Explaining the *onsen* quality and its effects

Guest: Excuse me. <u>What does this signboard say?</u>

Staff: It says "*Gensen Kakenagashi.*"

Guest: <u>What does that mean?</u>

Staff: "*Gensen Kakenagashi*" means *onsen* water coming directly from a hot spring.

Guest: You mean 100% [one hundred percent] free-flowing hot-spring water without any added cold water?

Staff: You got it.

Guest: <u>What's this *onsen* water good for?</u>

Staff: The quality of our *onsen* is characterized by a chloride spring. <u>Simply speaking</u>, the *onsen* water contains sodium, which is good for curing neuralgia, rheumatism, and skin diseases.

Guest: Sounds great!

Vocabulary

quality	泉質	effect	効能、効果
signboard	看板		
say	(新聞・本・看板などが) ~を述べている、~と書いてある		
free-flowing	掛け流し		
added	加えられた	※ add	~を加える、~を追加する
characterize	特徴づける	chloride	塩化物
simply speaking	簡単に言うと	contain	~を含む
sodium	ナトリウム	cure	~を治癒する
neuralgia	神経痛	rheumatism	リウマチ
skin disease	皮膚病		

English Points

- say には、「言う、話す」だけでなく「～と書いてある」の意味も含まれます。この動詞の意味範囲を把握すれば、What does this signboard say?（この看板に何と書いてあるのですか）の表現も容易に理解できます。

  ・There is a sign saying "No smoking."（「禁煙」と書かれた標識がありますよ。）
  ・The newspaper says a fire broke out at a chemical plant in *Kawasaki* City early Tuesday morning.
  （火曜日の早朝、川崎市の化学工場で火災が発生したと新聞に書いてあります。）

- What does that mean?（それはどういう意味ですか）の表現は、that の指すものについての説明を求める疑問文として使われます。これに対して、It means～（それは～を意味します）と説明します。

- 温泉に関する泉質や効能についてスタッフが説明できるに越したことはありませんが、しばしば専門用語が用いられ、説明は容易ではありません。人目につく場所に主要な言語での説明文を掲げるといった工夫が求められます。

  ・What's this *onsen* water good for?（ここの温泉は何に効きますか。）
  ——Please look at the signboard over there. It explains about spring water quality and the effects.
  （そこの看板をご覧ください。泉質と効能について説明しています。）

- ○○ speaking の決まり文句を発言文の冒頭に置くことで、話をまとめる効果があります。

  ・Simply speaking, *bonsai* are potted miniature trees.
  （簡単に言うと、盆栽は鉢植えのミニチュア樹木です。）

  ・Generally speaking, the people of *Gunma* love their hometown.
  （一般的に言えば、群馬の人々は郷土愛が強い。）

  ・Frankly speaking, you're not working efficiently.
  （率直に言うと、あなたは効率的に仕事をしていない。）

  ・Honestly speaking, I forgot about the matter.
  （正直に言うと、その件について忘れていました。）

  ・Theoretically speaking, brain death means death.
  （理論的に言えば、脳死は死亡を意味します。）

  ・Positively speaking, that guy is thrifty.（良く言えば、あの人は倹約家です。）

  ・Negatively speaking, that guy is stingy.（悪く言えば、あの人はケチです。）

Exercise Prepare を答えた後、枠内のパターンを用いて質問と応答の練習をしましょう。

> A: What does _____ mean?
> B: It means _____ .

Prepare

次の説明内容と合致する日本語表現を枠の中から選び、かっこに記入しなさい。

(1) (　　　　) It means "What a waste!" or "Do not waste!" in English.
(2) (　　　　) It means sunlight that comes through the leaves of the trees.
(3) (　　　　) It means someone who enjoys gourmet meals and goes broke.
(4) (　　　　) It means a father who is positively participating in childcare.
(5) (　　　　) It means to treasure every meeting, because it never reoccurs.
(6) (　　　　) It means the ability to understand each other without words.
(7) (　　　　) It means the beauty of nature, such as flowers, birds, wind, and the moon.
(8) (　　　　) It means someone who stays home for days isolated from others.

ichigo-ichie（一期一会）	*ishin-denshin*（以心伝心）	*mottainai*（もったいない）
komore-bi（木漏れ日）	*ikumen*（イクメン）	*kacho-fugetsu*（花鳥風月）
hikikomori（引きこもり）	*kuidaore*（食い倒れ）	

Tips:

- For the Japanese, a bath is not only a place for washing but also a place to enjoy a relaxing, good time while soaking in hot water. The Japanese believe that bathing in hot springs, called *onsen*, is more refreshing and enjoyable than bathing at home.
  日本人にとって、お風呂は単に体をきれいにする場所というだけでなく、湯につかりながらリラックスする時間を楽しむ場所でもあります。そして、温泉に入ることは、自家のお風呂に入るよりも爽快で楽しいと捉えています。

- An open-air bath is called "*roten-buro*" or "*soto-yu*" in Japanese. As it is set in natural surroundings, such as by a river or in a garden, people can enjoy the nature and scenery while bathing.
  屋外の温泉は、露天風呂もしくは外湯と呼ばれます。川や庭などの自然環境に設置されているので、入浴しながら自然や景色を楽しむことができます。

- There are more than 450 hot springs, and about 100 hot-spring resorts (with accommodation) in *Gunma* Prefecture.
  群馬県には450以上の源泉があり、宿泊施設のある温泉地が100カ所ほどあります。

- The *onsen* quality in *Gunma* varies depending on the region. *Onsens* are believed to be effective in curing neuralgia, muscle pain, joint pain, fatigue, skin disease, wounds, high blood pressure, digestive organ disorders, and so on.
  群馬の温泉の泉質は地域によって様々です。温泉は、神経痛、筋肉痛、関節炎、疲労、皮膚炎、傷、高血圧、消化器疾患などに効能があると言われています。

Spring quality and the effects（泉質と効能）

Isobe Onsen 磯部温泉	chloride spring 塩化物泉	heat retention 保温効果
Shimonita Onsen 下仁田温泉	hydrogen carbonate spring 炭酸水素塩泉（重曹泉）	fair skin effect 美肌効果
	carbon dioxide spring 二酸化炭素泉（炭酸泉）	high blood pressure, heart disease 高血圧　　　　　　心臓病
Ikaho Onsen 伊香保温泉	sulfate spring 硫酸塩泉	heat retention, high blood pressure, 保温効果　　　高血圧 arteriosclerosis 動脈硬化
Kusatsu Onsen 草津温泉	sulfur spring 硫黄泉	skin disease, high blood pressure, 皮膚病　　　　高血圧 heart disease 心臓病
	acid spring 酸性泉	chronic dermatological disorders (e.g., atopic dermatitis) 慢性皮膚病（アトピーなど）
	※ It has the effect of killing viruses.（殺菌効果がある。）	
Minakami Onsen 水上温泉	simple hot spring 単純泉	recuperation after illness or surgery 病後・手術後の静養
※ A simple hot spring refers to a hot spring that has no dominant ingredient. As it is mild, it can be used by elderly people and infants. 　（単純泉は、含有成分量が一定量に達していないものを指す。刺激の少ない温泉であるため、高齢者や乳幼児も入ることができる。）		

（参考資料：「群馬県内泉質別温泉一覧」群馬県ホームページ・他）

4-7 問題を処理する——部屋が寒すぎる

Handling a problem: The room is too cold

Front clerk: Hello, front desk. How may I help you?

Guest: Hello, this is Mr. Jones staying in *Hagi-no-ma*. It's a little cold in here. What should I do?

Front clerk: Is there a remote control for the air conditioner in the room?

Guest: Yes. I'm holding it, but I don't understand how to use it.

Front clerk: One of the staff will come to check. Please wait a while.

Guest: All right.

《Afterwards》

Staff: <u>Hi</u>. May I come in?

Guest: Sure. Come on in. It's a little cold in here. Can you adjust the temperature?

Staff: Certainly. Where is the remote control for the air conditioner?

Guest: It's on the table.

Staff: With the remote control pointing toward the air-conditioner unit, you press this button. The temperature increases when you press the upper button. When you want to lower the temperature, you press the lower button.

Guest: I just need these two buttons. <u>I'll keep that in mind</u>.

Staff: I have just set the room temperature to 26 degrees, which is what most people feel comfortable with. Please adjust the temperature as you like.

Guest: Okay. Thank you.

Vocabulary

handle	〜を処理する、〜に対処する
remote control	遠隔操作、リモコン
adjust	〜を調節する
temperature	温度
point toward	〜に向ける、〜を指す
press	〜を押す
increase	〜を上げる、〜を増大する
upper	上の、上の方の
lower	〜を下げる
	※（形容詞）lower［low の比較級］下の方の、下段の
keep that in mind	そのことを覚えておく、心に留める
feel comfortable with	〜を心地よく感じる

👉 English Points

■ リモコンやエアコンなどの短縮語は、日本語になったカタカナ英語です。カタカナ英語では通じないため、縮めずに発音することがポイントです。

- ・パソコン　⇒　personal computer
- ・リストラ　⇒　restructuring
- ・デモ　　　⇒　demonstration
- ・ロリコン　⇒　Lolita complex
- ・コネ　　　⇒　connection
- ・スマホ　　⇒　smartphone

■ 他者の部屋に入るとき、「失礼します」という日本の礼儀を表す感覚で Excuse me は用いません。こういう場合、英語では、Hello. や Good morning [afternoon, evening]. が一般的です。Excuse me は、会議中の部屋や相手が作業中の部屋に入る場合など、活動を中断させて「失礼します」というニュアンスで使用します。

■ keep something in mind もしくは keep in mind は、〈心に（何かを）保存する、持ち続ける〉という直訳で、「覚えておく」の意です。

- ・Thanks for your kind advice. I'll keep that in mind.
  （親切なアドバイスをありがとう。心に留めておきます。）
- ・You shoud keep it in mind that pedestrians walk on the right side of the road while cars drive on the left in Japan.
  （日本では歩行者は道路の右側を歩き、車は左側を走行することを覚えておくべきです。）
- ・Please keep in mind that you need to take care of this within a week.
  （1週間以内にこれを処理する必要があることを覚えておいてください。）

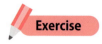 **Exercise** Prepare を答えた後、枠内のパターンを用いて質問と応答の練習をしましょう。

Example: A: What's *hotto kēki* called in English? I don't know the word.
B: Let's see. I think it's called pancake in English.

> A: What's _____ called in English? I don't know the word.
> B: Let's see. I think it's called _____ in English.

Prepare

次の英語が指し示すものを下の枠から選び記しなさい。

(1) iced tea   (   )
(2) corn dog   (   )
(3) hot chocolate   (   )
(4) creamed puff   (   )
(5) strawberry sponge cake (   )
(6) soft serve   (   )
(7) buffet   (   )
(8) custard pudding (   )
(9) bell pepper   (   )
(10) pancake   (   )
(11) french fries   (   )

和製英語：ココア	バイキング	ショートケーキ
フライドポテト	ソフトクリーム	アイスティー
シュークリーム	プリン	ホットケーキ
ピーマン	アメリカンドッグ	

Tips:

■ Japanese-English word（和製英語）とは、日本人の創作による英語のことで、通じないカタカナ英語を指します。カタカナ表示のため、英語であると思い込んで使用する日本人は少なくなく、混乱の一要因として留意しなくてはなりません。

食べ物に関する和製英語	
アメリカンドッグ	corn dog
ココア	hot chocolate
ショートケーキ	strawberry sponge cake
ソフトクリーム	soft serve / soft-serve ice cream
バイキング	buffet
プリン	creme caramel / custard pudding
ピーマン	bell pepper
ホットケーキ	pancake
フライドポテト	french fries（米）　potato chips（英）
テイクアウト	to go
モーニングサービス	breakfast special

道具・生活用品に関する和製英語

クーラー	air conditioner
コンセント	outlet（米）　　socket（英）
シール	sticker
シャーペン	mechanical pencil
ストーブ	heater
ダンボール	cardboard
電子レンジ	microwave oven
ドライバー	screwdriver
ドライヤー	hair dryer
ノートパソコン	laptop computer
ビニール袋	plastic bag
ベビーカー	baby carriage（米）　　stroller（英）
フライパン	pan
フローリング	wooden floor
ペットボトル	plastic bottle
ボールペン	ball point pen
ホッチキス	stapler
マンション	apartment

衣類に関する和製英語

ジャンパー	jacket
チャック／ファスナー	zipper
トレーナー	sweat shirt
パーカー	hooded sweatshirt / hoody / hoodie
ワイシャツ	shirt
ワンピース	dress

職業に関する和製英語

OL／サラリーマン	office worker
ガードマン	guard

その他

テーマ	topic
スマート	slim
ナイーブ	sensitive
メリット	advantage
パーキング	parking lot（米）　　car park（英）
ガソリンスタンド	gas station / service station（米） filling station / petrol station（英）

（参考資料：『和製英語と日本人』／「和製英語・カタカナ英語辞典」）

※カタカナ語は英語のみならず、他の言語に由来するものも少なくなく、例えば「パン」はポルトガル語、「アルバイト」はドイツ語です。英語では、bread（パン）と part-time job（アルバイト）というように、別の呼び方になることに留意する必要があります。

4-8 給仕をする──〔1〕

Waiting on tables：〔1〕

Staff: It's about time for dinner. Is it okay if we bring your dinner here?

Guest: Sure. After bathing, I'm thirsty and hungry now.

Staff: Would you like to have a drink with your meal?

Guest: I'll have (a) beer.

Staff: Draft or bottled beer?

Guest: I like draft beer.

Staff: One draft beer. I'll bring it right away.

《Several minutes later》

Staff: Here you are, a draft beer and the dishes.

Guest: The arrangement of food on the dishes is beautiful!

Staff: These are simmered assorted vegetables, and these are tuna, sweet shrimp, and salmon *sashimi*. The soy sauce is over there. I hope you enjoy your meal.

Guest: These look delicious!

Vocabulary

wait on tables	（飲食店で）給仕をする		
thirsty	喉が渇いた		
draft beer	生ビール	※ bottled beer	瓶ビール
arrangement	配置、配列		
simmered	煮た、炊いた	※ simmer	煮込む
assorted	盛り合わせた	※ assort	盛り合わせる

🖝 English Points

■ 「お待たせしました」は給仕人の決まり文句ですが、英語においては、本当に客を待たせた場合のみに、(I'm) Sorry to have kept you waiting. がお詫びの表現として用いられます。

■ 「いただきます」「ご馳走さま」の日本語表現に、厳密な意味で該当する英語表現は見当たりませんが、Let's eat!（食べましょう）や I'm all set.（十分にいただきました）が類似表現になります。

100

4-9 給仕をする──〔2〕

Waiting on tables：〔2〕

Staff: Are you finished with your meal? May I clear the table?

Guest: Yes, please. All the dishes were good.

Staff: I'm glad to hear that.

　　　《Clearing the table》

Staff: I'll come to make your bed later.

Guest: At what time? Because I want to go out and look around the *onsen* resort area.

Staff: Sure, you can go out anytime. We'll prepare your bed while you're out.

Guest: Oh, okay.

Vocabulary

be finished with	～を終えている
clear	～をきれいにする
make a [one's] bed	布団を敷く
prepare	～を準備する

English Points

■ 食事のペースや時間のかけ方に関しては文化的に多様です。「お食事はお済みですか」「お皿をお下げしてもよろしいですか」と確認することも、おもてなしのあり方です。

　・Have you finished?（お済みですか。）
　・Are you done eating?（お食事はお済みですか。）

　・May I take the dishes away?（お皿をお下げしてもよろしいですか。）
　・Is it okay to clear the table now?（テーブルを片付けてもよろしいですか。）

■ May I take your plate(s)?（お皿をお下げしてもよろしいですか）に対する応答は…

食べ終わっている場合	（まだ食べていて）下げてほしくない場合
・Sure.	・Still working.
・Yes, please.	・No, I'm still working on it.
・Of course.	・No, not yet.

Onsen and Accommodations

4

温泉・宿泊編

4-10 朝食の時間を確認する

Confirming breakfast time

Staff: What time would you like to have breakfast tomorrow morning?

Guest: When is breakfast?

Staff: It starts at 6 a.m. and finishes at 9.

Guest: Well, I'd like it at 8:30. I want to get up a little bit later tomorrow morning.

Staff: That's fine. Then I'll be here to fold up the futon about 10 minutes before breakfast.

Guest: All right. Can you give me a wake-up call at 8:15?

Staff: Sure. I'll tell the front desk clerk.

Vocabulary

breakfast	朝食
get up	起床する
fold up	～を折りたたむ
wake-up call	モーニングコール

English Points

■ get up の代わりに wake up を用いることもできますが、ニュアンスの違いを心得て使う必要があります。get up が体を起こして「起床する」ことを表すのに対して、wake up は「目が覚める」ことですから、体は寝ている状態でも使える表現ということです。

- I woke up at 6 o'clock this morning, but I stayed in bed as the room was cold. I finally got up at 7 o'clock.（今朝は 6 時に目が覚めましたが、部屋が寒かったのでベットの中にいました。7 時にようやく起床しました。）

■ 「モーニングコール」は和製英語です。wake-up call が本来の呼び方です（第 4 章、4-7.：Tips 欄を参照）。加えて、相手または自分のどちらに視点を置くか（＝主語を you または I のどちらにするか）によって、「モーニングコールをいただけますか」の表現が異なります。

- Can you give me a wake-up call at 6:30?
- Can I have a wake-up call at 6:30?

4-11 朝食バイキング
Breakfast buffet

> *Staff:* We serve a buffet breakfast that has various types of food. It's quite popular with guests.
>
> *Guest:* Is it all Japanese food?
>
> *Staff:* Not really. Some guests prefer bread to rice, so we provide a Western-style breakfast, too, such as pancakes, sausages, and scrambled eggs.
>
> *Guest:* Sounds good. I've been eating Japanese food since I came to Japan. I've missed bacon and eggs for breakfast.
>
> *Staff:* The buffet breakfast is served from 7 until 9:30 in the restaurant on the first floor.
>
> *Guest:* Will it be crowded?
>
> *Staff:* No, it won't be crowded. We have a few guests on package tours on weekdays.
>
> *Guest:* All right. I'll definitely be there.

Vocabulary

buffet breakfast	バイキング形式の朝食	prefer A to B	B よりも A を好む
provide	～を供給する、用意する		
miss	～がなくて寂しく思う		
crowded	混み合った		
package tour	パック旅行、(旅程・費用が設定された、旅行会社提供の) 団体旅行		
weekdays	平日	definitely	絶対に、確実に

English Points

■ 「食べ放題」の意味で「○○バイキング」と呼ばれていますが、これは和製英語ですから通じません。正しくは、all-you-can-eat for 3,000 yen（3,000円で食べ放題）、all-you-can-drink for 2,000 yen（2,000円で飲み放題）と言い表します。

■ 「バイキング料理」と呼ぶようになったのは、帝国ホテルに1958年に開業したレストランが、店名を「インペリアル・バイキング」と名付け、食べ放題の形式を始めたことに由来します。当時のアメリカ映画「バイキング」の中の食べ放題のシーンから創案され、名付けられたと言われています（参考資料：「コトバンク」）。

■ 英語では buffet（ビュッフェ）が一般的ですが、その定義は「好きな料理を好きだけ自分でとって立食する」ですから、バイキングとは多少意味内容が異なります。日本では、セルフサービス形式の食事を「ビュッフェ」と呼んでいますが、立食だけでなく、椅子に座って食べる場合も含まれます。

Onsen and Accommodations

4

温泉・宿泊編

■ have/has been V-ing 〜.（ずっと〜をしている、続けている）の表現には、〈これからも続くだろう〉のニュアンスが含まれます。

- It's been raining since last night.
  （昨夜からずっと雨が降り続いています。〈今後も降るだろう〉）
- I've been learning Spanish for 10 years.
  （10年間ずっとスペイン語を学んでいます。〈これからも学び続けるだろう〉）

対して、have/has V-ed 〜.（〜を完了する）では、現時点での現象や動作の終了・完了に着眼点が置かれます。

- It's rained since last night, but the weather is changing for the better.
  （昨夜からずっと雨が降り続きましたが、天気は次第によくなりつつあります。）
- I've learned Spanish for 10 years.（10年間スペイン語を学んできました。）

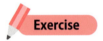 **Exercise**　Prepare を答えた後、枠内のパターンを用いて質問と応答の練習をしましょう。

```
A:  ___《date》___ is ___《name》___. What's it called in English / Japanese?
B:  It is called _____ .
```

Prepare

日本の祝日を枠の中から選び、かっこ内に記入しなさい。また、その祝日を言い表している英語とマッチングさせなさい。

	Japanese Name	Date of holiday	What's it called in English?
(1)	(正月（元旦))	January 1	· Children's Day
(2)	( )	The 2nd Monday in January	· New Year's Day
(3)	( )	February 3	· Culture Day
(4)	( )	March 3	· Labor Day
(5)	( )	May 3	· Health-Sports Day
(6)	( )	May 5	· Respect-for-the-Aged Day
(7)	( )	July 7	· The day before the beginning of spring
(8)	( )	The 3rd Monday in September	· Doll [Girls'] Festival
(9)	( )	The 2nd Monday in October	· Constitution Day
(10)	( )	November 3	· Coming-of-Age Day
(11)	( )	November 15	· Star Festival
(12)	( )	November 23	· The festival day for children of seven, five and three years of age

七夕	憲法記念日	節分	正月（元旦）	七五三	勤労感謝の日
成人の日	文化の日	ひな祭り	敬老の日	子どもの日	体育の日

4-12 フロントで部屋の鍵を預かる

Keeping the room key at the front desk

Guest: I'm going out now. Would you keep my room key?

Front clerk: Certainly, sir.

Guest: Is this neighborhood safe at night?

Front clerk: Oh, yes. It's safe at night so that even a woman can go out alone. But you should be careful because there are some <u>drunkards</u> in the *onsen* resort.

Guest: <u>You can say that again.</u> <u>I'm slightly drunk</u>, too.

Front clerk: After 8 o'clock, <u>everyone is tipsy</u>.

Guest: <u>The night is still young.</u> I'd like to enjoy the atmosphere in the *onsen* resort before going to bed.

Front clerk: Sure. Enjoy yourself. Please come back by twelve o'clock. That's our closing time.

Guest: Got it.

Vocabulary

keep	〜を保管する	neighborhood	近所、近隣
drunkard	泥酔者、酔っ払い	slightly	少し、わずか
drunk	酔っている	tipsy	ほろ酔い気分の
The night is young.	宵の口です。	atmosphere	雰囲気

English Points

■ ホテルの場合、門限を設けていないケースが一般的です。他方、旅館はというと、それぞれの営業形態によって様々です。門限が設定されている旅館の場合は、その旨を明示する、あるいは口頭で伝える、といった配慮が必要です。

■ a drunk (person), a drunken person, a drunkard は、どれも「酔っ払い、酔っている人」を指し、否定的なイメージを伴うため、当人に対して Are you a drunk (person)? では失礼な言い方になってしまいますが、Are you drunk?（酔っていますか）と状態を尋ねる表現であれば、一般的に使われます。答え方は、酔いの程度によって次のようになります。

・Are you drunk?（酔っていますか。）
——I'm | sober.　（しらふです。）
| tipsy.　（ほろ酔い気分です。）
| buzzed.　（ほろ酔い気分です。）
| drunk.　（酔っています。）
| wasted.　（泥酔しています。）

■ You can say that again.（もう一回言うことができます⇒全くその通りです）は、相手の発言に強く同調する表現です。

■ The night is young.（夜は若い⇒宵の口です）は、夜を人間にたとえた表現です。夜に関する表現はというと…

・The night is still young.（まだ宵の口です。）
・The night has just started.（夜は始まったばかりです。）
・It's late at night.（夜もおそいです。）
・The night wore on.（夜が更けました。）
・The night was far advanced.（夜がすっかり更けました。）

4-13 宿泊客に情報を提供する

Providing a hotel guest with information

Guest: Hi. I'd like to have lunch. <u>Do you know any good restaurants in this neighborhood?</u>

Staff: Yes, I know several. May I ask what you want to eat?

Guest: I'd like to have something which I can eat only in this region. What do you recommend?

Staff: <u>Let me see...</u> I recommend *okkirikomi*. It's thick *udon* noodles simmered with vegetables. I'll search for a picture on the internet.

Guest: Visual information is always helpful.

Staff: Here is a picture of *okkirikomi*. *Gunma* Prefecture is a wheat-producing area, so good pasta is made here. *Okkirikomi* is comfort food for *Gunma* locals.

Guest: Okay. I'll have *okkirikomi* for lunch. <u>The picture has made me hungry.</u> Could you tell me where the restaurant is?

Staff: Please look at the guide map of this area. ⟨Pointing to the places on the map⟩ We are here now. And the restaurant is here. It's about a ten-minute walk from here.

Guest: I might as well walk there. Thank you for your advice.

Staff: You're welcome, anytime.

Vocabulary

provide A with B	A に B を提供する
search for	～を検索する
visual	視覚的な
helpful	助けになる、役立つ
wheat-producing area	小麦生産地域
○○-minute walk	徒歩で○○分

👉 English Points

■ Do you know～?（～をご存知ですか）の代わりに Is there a～? / Are there any～? （～はありますか）の表現を用いることもできます。

Onsen and Accommodations

4 温泉・宿泊編

- Are there any good restaurants around here?
  （この辺によいレストランはありますか。）
- Is there a bank nearby? （近くに銀行はありますか。）
- Is there a drugstore [pharmacy] near here? （この近くに薬局はありますか。）

■ Let me see. （えーと、そうですねぇー）は、会話ですぐに答えが出てこないとき
のつなぎ表現です。

- Let's see... [=Let us see...]…………えーと…
- well... ………………………………えーと…
- ahh... …………………………………えー
- umm... / hmm...……………………うーん…
- uh-huh / ah-ha ………………………うんうん、アハーン
- yeah ……………………………………うん　　　※ yes のくだけた表現

　　※ ahh, umm, uh-huh などは、相づち表現または周辺言語と呼ばれ、会話をつ
　　　なぐだけでなく、相手に同調したり、また会話を盛り上げたり、といった
　　　機能も認められます。相づち表現は多種多様です（続く Tips 欄を参照）。

■ The picture has made me hungry. の make（〜に〜をさせる）は、使役動詞と呼
ばれます。主な使役動詞として make, have, let などがあげられますが、これらの
動詞には強制力の強弱に違いが認められ（第 5 章、5-9.：pp.146-147 を参照）、
make は最も強制力のある使役動詞として位置付けられます。make の使い方は次
の通り。

（1）make ＋ 人 ＋ 形容詞
- I often make my mother angry. （私はしばしば母親を怒らせます。）
- The news made us happy.
  （その知らせは私たちを喜ばせました⇒その知らせを聞いて私たちはうれしくな
  りました。）
- His speech made me sleepy.
  （彼のスピーチは私を眠くさせました⇒彼のスピーチを聞いて私は眠くなりまし
  た。）

（2）make ＋ 人 ＋ to なし不定詞
- Your joke always makes me laugh. （あなたの冗談はいつも私を笑わせます。）
- No one can make Ken do anything. He's stubborn.
  （誰もケンに何かを強制することはできないですね。彼は頑固ですから。）

（3）make ＋ 人 ＋ 名詞
- We'd like to know what made you a good leader.
  （何があなたを優れたリーダーにしたのかを知りたいのですが。）
- I hear that the movie made her a star.
  （その映画が彼女をスターにしたと聞いています。）

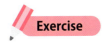 **Exercise** Prepareを答えた後、枠内のパターンを用いて質問と応答の練習をしましょう。

A: Hi. Do you know any good restaurants in this neighborhood?

B: Yes, I know several. May I ask what kind of food you want to eat?

A: Well, I'd like to have _____ .

B: Let me see... I recommend _____《*Name of shop or restaurant*》_____ .
   I'll search for the place on the internet to show you how to get there.

A: Thank you.

Prepare
次の飲食店について、高崎市もしくはあなたの地域における情報を調べてください。

Kind of food	Name of shop or restaurant
(1) *soba* noodle	(*Eki-soba, Fujimi-soba,*)
(2) *udon* noodle	( )
(3) *yakiniku*	( )
(4) *ramen* noodle	( )
(5) *okonomiyaki*	( )
(6) Italian food	( )
(7) French food	( )
(8) Mexican food	( )
(9) Chinese food	( )
(10) Korean food	( )

Tips:

Back-channeling expressions
(相づち表現)

|相手の言うことを理解したときの相づち|

I see. ……………………………………… わかった
Got it. / I got it. / I got you. / *Gotcha. ……… わかった
   *I got you. を省略した俗語
All right. ………………………………… 了解しました
That makes sense. ……………………… 理にかなっている

同意・賛同するときの相づち

Uh-huh. / Ah-ha. .... うんうん、アハーン
Sure. / I know. / I agree. .... そうだね
Absolutely. / Definitely. / Exactly. / Indeed.… 全くその通りです
That's right [true]. .... その通りです
You said it. .... おっしゃる通りです
That sounds good [great]. .... それはいいね
Good for you. .... 良かったね

驚くときの相づち

Wow! .... うわー!
Come on! .... ちょっと待ってよ!、冗談はやめろよ!
Give me a break! .... 〃
No kidding! .... 冗談だろう!
No way! / Oh no! / You don't say! .... まさか!
Oh my goodness. / Oh my god. .... なんということ!、大変だ!
Cool! / Amazing! / Great! / *Awesome! ……… すごい!
　　　　　*(畏敬の念を起こさせるくらい)すごいいい!
That's amazing! .... そりゃすごい!
That's incredible [unbelievable]! .... 信じられない!

驚くと同時に聞き返す相づち

Really? .... 本当ですか?
Is that so? .... そうなの?
Seriously? / Are you serious? .... マジで?
Are you kidding (me)? .... 冗談でしょう?

嘆くときの相づち

Uh-oh. .... あらら
Oh boy [man]. .... あら、まあ
Geez. / Jeez. / Gee. / Gosh. .... まったく、やれやれ、なんてこった
　　　　　　　　　　　　　　※ Jesus (Christ)! (ちくしょう!) の婉曲表現
That's terrible [awful]. .... それはひどい
That's too bad. / What a pity. / Poor thing. … お気の毒に

不確かなときの相づち

Huh? .... はぁ?
Oh? .... そうなの?
Kind of. .... まあね
Probably. / Maybe. / Could be. .... 多分ね
I guess so. .... そうみたいね

(参考資料:「間投詞・Interjection」ASPEC ホームページ・他)

4-14 チェックアウト
Check-out

Guest: I'd like to check out, please. My room is *Hagi-no-ma*, and here's my room key.

Front clerk: Certainly, sir. One moment, please.

《Calculating the rate》

Front clerk: <u>Your bill</u> is 32,000 [thirty-two thousand] yen. Here's the bill statement.

Guest: ⟨Looking through the bill statement⟩ 4,000 [four thousand] yen is added here. <u>Could you explain what this charge is for?</u>

Front clerk: You had four draft beers with your dinners. This is the price.

Guest: Two draft beers with each dinner. Now I see. I'll pay by credit card.

Front clerk: That's fine. <u>Could you sign here, please?</u>

Guest: Sure.

Front clerk: Thank you very much. Here's your card and the receipt. Have a nice trip.

Guest: <u>Thanks for everything.</u> <u>I really enjoyed my stay.</u>

Front clerk: Thank you for staying with us. We hope to see you again.

Vocabulary

calculate	〜を計算する
bill	請求書
bill statement	明細書　　　※ itemized bill と同じ
look through	〜に目を通す
sign	署名する
receipt	領収書

Onsen and Accommodations

4

温泉・宿泊編

English Points

■ bill には多くの意味がありますが、ここでは「請求書、勘定書き」を指します。

・I received the	electricity bill	the other day. （電気料金の請求書を先日受け取りました。）
	water bill	（水道料金 〃 ）
	mobile bill	（携帯電話料金 〃 ）
	grocery bill	（食料品店 〃 ）

■ チェックアウトの際、客は請求明細書に目を通し、「問題ない」と判断する場合は、This looks fine.（大丈夫そうです）の応答が返ってきます。不明な料金がある場合は Could you explain what this charge is for?（何の料金でしょうか）といった質問が向けられますので、詳細について説明できることが肝要です。

・This is the price for 2 cans of beer and 1 bottle of mineral water from the mini-bar.
（こちらはミニバーの缶ビール2本とミネラルウォーター1本の料金です。）
・These are the charges for room service and dry cleaning.
（こちらはルームサービスとドライクリーニングの料金になります。）

■ 日本語では「ここにサインをお願いします」と言いますが、英語の sign（署名する）は動詞です。名詞で使う場合は signature（署名）になるので、注意を要します。

・Could you sign here, please?（ここに署名していただけますか。）
・I need your signature here.（ここにあなたの署名が必要です。）

Tips:

■ 請求明細書の確認においては、納得のいくまで質問が続くのが普通です。実際、海外においては間違いが記載されることは珍しくありません。そのため、請求額の確認は不可欠な行為であると考えられているからです。

■ 英語圏では、チェックアウトの際、客が "Thanks for everything. I really enjoyed my stay." などと一言お礼を言って立ち去るという習慣があります。しかし、お世辞を言うのではなく、実際に称賛に値すると評価した場合です。サービスを提供する側と受ける側が対等であるというルールに基づくマナーとして捉えることができます。

Kusatsu Onsen
（草津温泉）

■ The spas in *Kusatsu* are some of the oldest in Japan, having existed since the eighth century (the *Nara* era).
　草津温泉は8世紀（奈良時代）から存在し、日本で最も古い温泉の一つです。

- *Kusatsu Onsen* is one of the best three *onsens* in Japan; the others are the *Arima and Gero Onsens*.

  草津温泉は日本三名泉の一つです。他の二つは、有馬温泉と下呂温泉を指します。

- *Kusatsu Onsen* is ranked the highest in Japan in terms of the quantity of natural spring water; 32,300 liters of hot water, which is equivalent to 161 barrels, gush from underground every minute.

  草津温泉は自然湧水量日本一です。毎分３万2,300リットル、ドラム缶に換算すると161本の温水が湧き出しています。

- It is said that "*Kusatsu Onsen* cures all sorts of ailments and illnesses except lovesickness." In the old days people visited *Kusatsu* for a hot-spring cure called "*touji*." The healing effects of hot springs were useful when medicine was not developed.

  「草津の湯は恋の病以外の万病に効く」と言い伝えられています。かつて人々は湯治——温泉に入ることで病気やけがを治療すること——のために草津を訪れてきました。温泉の治癒効果は、医学の発達していない時代に人々に重宝されたのです。

- *Kusatsu Onsen* is strongly acidic, so it is known as having cleansing effects. In other words, the hot spring is effective against various skin diseases.

  草津温泉は強酸性で、殺菌効果のあることで知られています。言い換えると、温泉はいろいろな皮膚病に対して効果的です。

- The prominent effects of the *Kusatsu Onsen* came to be known throughout the world because of Erwin von Bälz, a German doctor employed by the *Meiji* government to teach at *Tokyo Igakko* (*Tokyo* Medical School; the current *Tokyo* University medical department). Information about Erwin von Bälz can be found in the Bälz Memorial Hall in *Kusatsu*.

  草津温泉の優れた効能は、エルヴィン・フォン・ベルツによって世界に知られるようになりました。彼は、東京医学校（現在の東京大学医学部）で教鞭をとるために明治政府によって雇われたドイツ人医師です。彼に関する情報は草津町の「ベルツ記念館」にあります。

- At about 50 degrees Celsius, the water temperature is high direct from the hot spring. It needs to be lowered to bathing temperature using a traditional method called "*yumomi*." The hot water is cooled by stirring with large wooden paddles. *Yumomi* is a better way than adding cold water as it retains the healing effects of the natural hot spring.

  源泉の温度は50℃程度と高いため、草津伝統の「湯もみ」という方法で入浴できる温度に下げます。高温の湯は、大きな木の板でかき回されて冷まされます。温泉の効能を損なわないためには、冷水を加えるよりも、湯もみの方が優れた方法であるわけです。

- *Yubatake*, one of the spring sources, is located in the heart of the town and is a landmark of the *Kusatsu Onsen*. It is a device for collecting hot-spring mineral deposits (including sulfur) from the water and can also be used to cool the high-temperature spring water. The hot-spring temperature is lowered as it goes through the wooden conduits, and then it is sent to the inns and communal baths in the surrounding area.

  源泉の一つである湯畑は町の中心部に位置し、草津温泉のランドマークです。それは、源泉から湯の花（硫黄を含む鉱物沈殿物）を採取するとともに、高温の源泉を冷却する装置です。木樋（もくひ）を通る間に温度が下がった源泉は、周辺の旅館や共同浴場へ送られます。

- There are nearly 20 communal bath houses in *Kusatsu* called "*soto-yu*," which the local people use, but tourists and visitors can also use them. Except for the three bath houses managed by the *Kusatsu* Town Hall tourism division (*Shirahata-no-yu*, *Chiyo-no-yu*, and *Jizou-no-yu*), all communal bath houses are managed and cleaned by local people. They are available to anyone at any time as long as he/she observes good bathing manners.

  草津には地元の人々が利用する「外湯」と呼ばれる共同浴場が20カ所近く存在し、観光客へ

も解放されています。草津町役場観光課が管理する3カ所（白旗の湯、千代の湯、地蔵の湯）を除いて、すべての共同浴場は地元の人々によって管理・清掃が行われていますが、入浴マナーを守れば、いつでもどなたでも利用できます。

（情報提供：草津温泉観光協会）

■ There are several "*ashi-yu*," or footbaths, in *Kusatsu*. Foot bathing is easy to try and is said to be good for the health. The blood circulation in the lower part of the body is accelerated by warming the feet, which improves the function of the internal organs, as well as preventing and/or assisting with poor circulation, swelling, and muscle pain.

草津には数カ所の足湯があります。足湯は手軽に楽しめて健康に良いと言われています。足を温めることで下半身の血液循環が促進され、冷え性、むくみ、筋肉痛に効果があるとともに、内臓の機能もよくなります。

（参考資料：「草津温泉」『群馬県の歴史散歩』pp.215-218.・他）

Ikaho Onsen
（伊香保温泉）

■ *Ikaho Onsen* is also a historic hot spring and is as representative of *Gunma* Prefecture as *Kusatsu Onsen*. Hot springs were used as spas for injured *samurai* warriors in the 16th century (the civil war period).

伊香保温泉の歴史は古く、草津温泉と並んで群馬県を代表する温泉です。16世紀（戦国時代）に、負傷した武士の湯治場として使われたという経緯です。

■ One of the characteristics of the *Ikaho Onsen* is a long, stone stairway called "*Ishidan-gai*." The stairway has 365 steps, and as it is the traditional main street, it is lined with *ryokans* and souvenir shops. When people finish climbing the stairs, the *Ikaho* Shrine appears. There are some hot springs around the shrine, with the hot-spring water being supplied to the inns. The *Ikaho rotenburo* (*Ikaho* Outdoor Bath), which is a ten-minute walk from the shrine, is a popular communal bath with many tourists.

伊香保温泉の特徴の一つは「石段街」と呼ばれる長い石段です。365段の石段は伝統あるメインストリートで、温泉宿や土産店が建ち並びます。石段を上りきると、伊香保神社が現れます。神社周辺にはいくつかの源泉があり、温泉は旅館へ供給されます。神社から徒歩で10分ほどのところにある伊香保露天風呂は、多くの観光客が利用する人気のある共同浴場です。

■ The *Ikaho Onsen* has a unique structure as the hot-spring water around *Ikaho* Shrine runs under the stone stairway. The hot-spring water is carried to each inn through the main stone canal under the stairway. *Masayuki Sanada*, who was known as a great warlord, managed the construction in 1576, the year after the battle of *Nagashino*, in compliance with an order given by his lord, *Katsuyori Takeda*. As *Takeda's* army suffered many deaths and injuries in the battle, the injured warriors needed large-scale spas; therefore, a device for distributing the hot-spring water to each spa was constructed and has been used ever since.

伊香保温泉は、伊香保神社周辺の源泉水が石段の下を流れ落ちるという独特のつくりです。温泉水は、石段の下の本線（石管）を通って各旅館へ運ばれています。優れた武将として知られる真田昌幸は、1576年（長篠の戦いの翌年）に、主君の武田勝頼の命でこの工事に着手したのです。長篠の戦いで、武田軍には大勢の戦死者と負傷者がでました。負傷した武将や兵のために、大規模な湯治場が必要になり、それぞれの湯治場へ源泉水を分配する仕組みがつくられたのです。これが現在においても使われ続けているのです。

（情報提供：渋川伊香保温泉観光協会）

■ A few kilometers southeast of *Ikaho*, there is *Mizusawa Kanzeon* (*Mizusawa* Temple), dedicated to *Kannon* (the Buddhist goddess of Mercy). It is believed that the goddess grants wishes, so many people visit and worship at the temple, and then they can eat *Mizusawa udon* noodles afterwards, which have been eaten there for more than 400 years.

伊香保から南東へ2、3kmのところに、観音（仏教の慈悲の女神）をまつった水澤観世音（水澤寺）があります。観音が願いをかなえると信じられており、多くの人々が参拝に訪れます。訪問者たちは参拝した後、400年以上にわたり食されてきた水沢うどんを楽しむことができます。

■ *Onsen manju* (brown buns stuffed with *azuki*-bean paste, steamed in hot-spring vapor) are sold in many hot-spring resorts in Japan nowadays; however, it is said that they originated in *Ikaho*. The dark brown color of the *Ikaho* hot spring is one of its features as this indicates that it is rich in iron. A local confectioner created the sweet buns based on an image of the hot springs in the *Meiji* era.

今日、温泉まんじゅう（温泉の蒸気で蒸し上げた、小豆餡の入った茶色い饅頭）は、日本各地の温泉地で売られていますが、その始まりは伊香保温泉であると言われています。伊香保温泉は鉄分を多く含むため、茶褐色の温泉水であることが特徴の一つです。明治時代に地元の菓子屋が、温泉水のイメージにちなんだまんじゅうをつくり出したのです。

（参考資料：「伊香保温泉」『群馬県の歴史散歩』2005年）pp.190-192.・他)

第5章　世界遺産の見学

【富岡製糸場編】

5-1 窓口で来場者に対応する
Responding to a visitor at the counter

Front view of the East cocoon warehouse * （東置繭所正面）

Front gate* （表門）

*（画像提供：富岡市）

Visitor: ⟨Talking to oneself⟩ <u>The admission fees</u> are written on the signboard. An adult admission fee is 1,000 [a thousand] yen.

Clerk at window: Next, please.

Visitor: One adult, please. And I'd like to use an audio guide. How much is <u>the rental fee</u>?

Clerk at window: It's 200 [two hundred] yen.

Visitor: And where do I pay for it?

Clerk at window: Here is fine. That'll be 1,200 [twelve hundred] yen in total.

Visitor: Okay. Here you are.

Clerk at window: Here is an admission ticket and an audio guide with an instruction manual.

Visitor: Sure. Is it easy to use this device that's shaped like a cell phone? <u>I'm not very good at operating any type of electronics.</u>

Clerk at window: It's easy. You dial a corresponding number on the device, which you'll find on each explanatory panel. Then, you can listen to the audio explanation.

Visitor: Let me see.

Clerk at window: <u>For instance</u>, when you visit the East cocoon warehouse, you'll find the number "1" on the first explanatory panel. So, you press the button for that same number, which is also "1," on your audio guide. The explanation will start in two seconds. A red button may be displayed at the end of the explanation. By pushing that button, you'll receive a more detailed explanation of the item.

Visitor: Now I understand. I appreciate your kind explanation.

Clerk at window: Not at all. I hope you enjoy your visit to the Silk Mill.

Vocabulary

respond to	～に対応する、～に応答する
admission fee	入場料
audio guide	オーディオ・ガイド、音声案内
rental fee	レンタル料金
instruction manual	取扱説明書
device	装置、機器
operate	～を操作する
electronics	電子機器
corresponding	一致する
explanatory panel	説明看板
explanation	説明　　　※ explain　説明する
cocoon	繭
warehouse	倉庫
detailed	詳細な
appreciate	～に感謝する

👉 English Points

■ 入場・入園料および報酬・謝礼金の場合は fee が用いられます（詳しくは、第 1 章、1-2. を参照）。

- ・admission fee 　　　（入場料）
- ・rental fee 　　　　　（レンタル料）
- ・medical [doctor's] fee 　（診察料）
- ・legal [attorney's] fee 　（弁護士費用、相談料）
- ・consulting fee 　　　（顧問料、コンサルタント料）

■ be (not) good at～（～が（不）得意です）の決まり文句には、名詞もしくは動名詞（V-ing）が続きます。

- ・I'm good at flower arrangement.（生け花が得意です。）

Tomioka Silk Mill

5

富岡製糸場編

- My friend *Akira* is good at driving a car.（友人のアキラは車の運転が上手です。）
- All the staff are not good at speaking English.
（スタッフ全員が英語を話すことが苦手です。）

■ for instance は for example と同じ「例えば」という意味ですが、使い方に関しては違いがあります。for example では、見本となるような例を並べるのに対して、for instance の場合は、身近な実例を引いて説明するという具合です。

- My family members like Japanese sweets, for example, *daifuku* and *yokan*.
（私の家族は、例えば、大福や羊かんのような和菓子が好きです。）
- My family members like Japanese sweets. For instance, my mother often buys *dorayaki* and *monaka*.
（私の家族は和菓子が好きです。例えば、母はどら焼きや最中を頻繁に購入します。）

■ appreciate は thank you と同じく謝意を表す際に使いますが、「人」ではなく「行為」に感謝するため、使い方に違いがあります。

- I appreciate it.（感謝いたします。）　※ I appreciate you. ではないことに注意
- I really appreciate your help.（ご助力にとても感謝いたします。）
- I really appreciate how much you have helped me since we met.
（お会いして以来、ずいぶん助けていただいたことに本当に感謝しています。）

Tips:

■ For overseas visitors, an audio guide is available for a fee. It is a palm-sized portable device and allows you to listen to explanations in Japanese, English, French, Chinese, and Korean. You can rent the device at the entrance desk.
海外からの来訪者のために、audio guide（オーディオ・ガイド）が有料で用意されています。手のひらサイズの携帯用機器で、日本語、英語、フランス語、中国語、韓国語で解説を聴くことができます。入場の際に窓口で借りることができます。

■ Virtual reality (VR) scopes are available for visitors to enjoy a better *Tomioka* Silk Mill tour experience. Smart glasses for the VR scope allow you to see vivid pictures of what the buildings look like in the form a 360-degree three-dimensional image, and what the female workers looked like back then. These images are created with computer graphics. At the same time, you can listen to the narration in either Japanese or English.
富岡製糸場内ツアーをより楽しむために、VR scope（VR [virtual reality] は「仮想現実」の意）が用意されています。そのスマートグラスを着用すると360度の立体的な画像で、当時の建物や工女たちの働く様子などを CG [Computer Graphics] 映像で観ることができます。同時に、日本語もしくは英語のどちらかでナレーションを聞くことができます。

Smart glasses for the VR scope
(CG 映像機器：スマートグラス)

- The Computer graphics (CG) guided tour is available by reservation for a group of up to thirty people. Participants wear smart glasses and tour the site with a commentator. Usage fees for smart glasses are included in the group rate.

    CG ガイドツアーは 1 団体30人まで、予約をすると利用可能です。参加者はスマートグラスを着用して、解説員とともに場内を見学します。スマートグラス使用料は団体料金に含まれます。

- VR scopes are available for 800 yen (without tax) at the souvenir shop on the grounds. Setting up a VR scope is easy. Also, an explanation of how to download to a personal smartphone is written on the VR scope. By using the VR scope, you can experience the tour beyond time and space.

    「VR scope：富岡製糸場 CG 映像ガイド」（税別800円）は場内の土産店で購入できます。VR scope の組み立ては簡単です。またそこに、個人のスマートフォンへのダウンロードの説明が記されています。VR scope の使用によって、時空を超える場内ツアーを体験できます。

Flat-pack, assemble-it-yourself smart glasses for the VR scope
(組み立て式 CG 映像機器)

5-2 初対面で自己紹介する
Introducing yourself in the first meeting

Profile of Ms. *Mayuko Kuwata*:

Ms. *Mayuko Kuwata* is a student volunteer from *Tomioka* City. She is majoring in sightseeing and community development at a university near *Tomioka* City. She volunteers here to learn about her local area as part of her university studies.

Her hobby is visiting various *onsens*. After graduation, she'd like to work in the travel industry in her local area. Her hometown is aiming at opening the city to the world. The purpose of doing this is to attract as many tourists as possible from not only Japan but also foreign countries. She studies English in order to be able to explain regional specialities and features to foreign visitors. She volunteers at the *Tomioka* Silk Mill as a way of improving her English communication skills.

As foreign visitors look around the *Tomioka* Silk Mill, they can listen to explanations given on the audio guides. However, they may also be glad to have an English-speaking volunteer guide whom they can ask questions. *Mayuko* is sure that being able to communicate in English is the finest form of hospitality that can be offered to foreign visitors. She shows these visitors the mill complex and other tourist attractions in the surrounding area.

桑田まゆ子さんのプロフィール

　桑田まゆ子さんは、富岡市出身の学生ボランティアです。彼女は近隣の大学で観光まちづくりを専攻しています。彼女は大学での勉強の一環として郷土について学ぶために、ボランティアに参加しています。

　彼女の趣味は温泉巡りです。卒業後は、地元で観光産業に携わりたいと考えています。彼女の郷土は世界に開かれた街を目指しています。その目的は、国内だけでなく海外からもできるだけ多くの観光客に訪れていただきたいからです。彼女は、地元の特産や特徴を外国人訪問者に伝えるために、英語を勉強しています。そして英語コミュニケーション力をつけるために、富岡製糸場でボランティアをしています。

　外国人訪問者はオーディオ・ガイドを片手に製糸場を見学することができます。しかし、英語で質問に対応することのできるボランティア・ガイドがいれば、訪問者にとってはうれしい限りでしょう。まゆ子さんは言葉が通じるということが、外国人訪問者に対する最高のホスピタリティーであると確信しています。彼女が訪問者たちに製糸場およびその周辺の観光スポットを案内します。

Mayuko: Hello. I'm *Mayuko Kuwata*, your volunteer guide for today. <u>Nice to meet you</u>.

Visitor: Hi, <u>nice to meet you, too.</u> I'm Andrew Jones from Sacramento, California. I'm visiting Japan on business. A Japanese man I met on business was from *Gunma*, and he recommended that I go and see the *Tomioka* Silk Mill and visit an *onsen*. <u>I am taking a short excursion</u> before returning to my country. What do you do?

Mayuko: I'm a junior at a nearby university. I'd like to work in the travel industry in this area after graduation. I volunteer because I think that being an English guide is a great opportunity to improve my English speaking skills. Please ask any questions you might have. I don't have a lot of experience yet, but I'll do my best.

Visitor: Thanks, I will.

Mayuko: First, we are allowed to go into the East cocoon warehouse and the Silk-reeling plant at the *Tomioka* Silk Mill, but we cannot go into any of the other buildings.

Visitor: Why? Is it because of the deterioration of the buildings?

Mayuko: Uh-huh. They were built 140 [one hundred forty] years ago, so some of them are seriously damaged due to deterioration. And over the years, some of the rooms were remodeled because their purpose changed.

Visitor: Okay. How long does it take to look around?

Mayuko: About forty minutes. It won't take more than an hour. So, let's get started!

Vocabulary

introduce oneself	自己紹介する
volunteer	ボランティア　　　※（動詞）　進んで引き受ける
on business	商用で、仕事で
take an excursion	遠出する、小旅行する
junior	大学3年生
	※ freshman（1年生）、sophomore（2年生）、senior（4年生）
travel industry	観光産業

graduation	卒業
opportunity	機会
improve	～を向上させる
skill	技能、腕前
experience	経験、体験
do one's best	最善を尽くす
allow	～を許す、許可する
Silk-reeling plant	繰糸所
deterioration	老朽化　　　※ deteriorate　　朽ちる
damage	損傷を与える
remodel	～を改造する
purpose	目的

💬 English Points

■ 初対面でのあいさつとして、How do you do?（初めまして）がよく知られていますが、フォーマルな場面で使われる堅い表現のため、カジュアルな場面では使われない傾向にあります。むしろ、(It's) Nice to meet you.（お会いできて嬉しいです）をはじめ、次の表現が一般的です。

・(It's) Nice to meet you.
　　——Nice to meet you, **too**.
　　※最後の too を強く発音することで、「こちらこそ、お会いできてうれしいです」の意になります。ちなみに、(It was) Nice meeting you.（お会いできたことをうれしく思います）は、会話の最後に使う表現なので注意を要します。

・It's a pleasure to meet you.（お会いできてうれしいです。）
・(I'm) Pleased to meet you.（　　　　　〃　　　　　）
・I'm so glad to meet you.（　　　　　〃　　　　　）

■ ニュアンスの違いはありますが、「旅行する」の表現はいくつかあります。travel は動詞ですが、an excursion, a trip, a tour は名詞ですから、take や make の動詞とともに用います。

・I'll	travel	in Hokkaido next week.（来週、北海道を旅行します。）
	take　a trip	to　　〃
	go on　a tour	to　　〃
	*make　a journey	to　　〃
	an excursion	to　　〃

※ trip（比較的短い旅）、tour（視察・観光の往復旅行）、journey（主に陸路の長い旅行）、excursion（遠足や遠出などの小旅行）というニュアンスの違いがあります。

※「旅行する」の一般的な表現は、go on a trip または take a trip です。make a trip の場合は、「（ある目的のために）旅行する」という使い方になります。

・I took a trip to *Osaka* to see my best friend.
（親友に会うために大阪へ旅行しました。）

Tips:

■ Japan's isolation policy ended after the *Edo* era, and then the *Meiji* people turned their eyes to Europe and America. The *Meiji* government introduced a lot of knowledge and techniques related to, for example, education, culture, society, law, sciences, medicine, and the arts, from America and European countries to promote the modernization of Japan.
　鎖国政策は江戸時代とともに終わり、明治の人々の目は欧米に向けられました。明治政府は日本の近代化のために、欧米諸国から教育、文化、社会、法律、科学、医学、芸術などに関する多くの知識や技術を導入しました。

■ When Japan opened its doors to the outside world at the end of the *Edo* era, the Industrial Revolution had already occurred in Europe and America. To catch up with those countries, the *Meiji* government proposed a policy of "the promotion of modern industry."
　江戸時代の終わり、日本が開国したとき、欧米では既に産業革命が起こっていました。欧米諸国に追い付くため、明治政府は「殖産興業」の政策を打ち出しました。

■ Today, Japan is known as an industrial country, and its Industrial Revolution started in *Tomioka*.
　現在、日本は工業国として世界に知られていますが、日本の産業革命は富岡から始まったのです。

■ The *Tomioka* Silk Mill was established by the *Meiji* government in 1872 (at the beginning of the *Meiji* era).
　富岡製糸場は1872年（明治5）に明治政府によって設立されました。

■ The *Tomioka* Silk Mill is the only factory that is still in near-perfect condition among the government-controlled factories at that time.
　富岡製糸場は、当時の官営工場の中でほぼ完全な状態で残っている唯一の工場です。

■ The *Meiji* government intended to raise funds through the export of raw silk.
　明治政府は生糸の輸出で資金を調達することを企てました。

■ The *Tomioka* Silk Mill was the first model silk-reeling factory established during the modernization of Japan.
　富岡製糸場は、日本の近代化における最初の模範器械繰糸場です。

■ Before that, raw silk was spun from cocoons by hand. Mass production was difficult.
　それ以前、生糸は繭から手作業で紡がれていました。大量生産が難しかったのです。

■ To mass-produce high-quality raw silk, the *Meiji* government determined that it needed to set up a modern factory and introduce efficient spinning machines from Western countries.
　高品質の生糸を大量生産するために、明治政府は近代的な工場を設置し、西洋から効率の良い繰糸器を導入することを決断しました。

■ The *Meiji* government thought that the fastest way to achieve technical improvement in each field was to hire an expert and an engineer. In those days, many foreigners were employed as directors, and Paul Brunat was one of them.
　明治政府は各分野の技術向上のために、専門家や技術者を雇うことが一番の近道であると考

125

えました。当時は多く外国人が指導者として雇われ、ポール・ブリュナもそういった一人でした。

■ Paul Brunat, a Frenchman commissioned by the *Meiji* government, chose *Tomioka* as the location for the construction of a mill complex for the following reasons.
明治政府に委託されたフランス人、ポール・ブリュナは次の理由から富岡を工場建設地に選びました。

① Sericulture flourished in this region, and cocoons were plentiful.
この地域は養蚕が盛んで、十分な繭が供給された。　　※ sericulture（養蚕文化）

② A nearby river supplied water, which is necessary for silk reeling.
繰糸に必要な水が近くの川から確保できた。

③ A large plot of land was available for the mill complex.
工場用の広い敷地があった。

④ Coal as a fuel for steam engines was mined in nearby towns.
蒸気エンジンの燃料となる石炭が近くで採れた。

⑤ Local residents accepted the construction of a mill complex.
地元住人が工場建設を受け入れた。

※ An additional reason is that, from the perspective of trade and transportation, *Tomioka* was close to *Tokyo* and the *Yokohama* Port.
さらなる理由として、貿易と輸送の観点から、富岡は東京並びに横浜港に近いということがあげられます。

(参考資料：「富岡製糸場ができるまで」『世界文化遺産　富岡製糸場』pp.24-41.／
『世界へはばたけ！　富岡製糸場　まゆみとココのふしぎな旅』／『富岡製糸場事典』)

Eiichi Shibusawa
（渋沢栄一）

■ *Eiichi Shibusawa* was born in what is currently called *Fukaya City, Saitama*, in 1840, and became a government official for the Shogunate. After the *Meiji* Restoration, he was entrusted with the construction of the *Tomioka* Silk Mill by the *Meiji* government.
渋沢栄一は1840年に現在の埼玉県深谷市に生まれ、幕府の役人になりました。明治維新後、彼は明治政府から富岡製糸場建設を一任されました。

■ *Eiichi Shibusawa* was key in the construction of the *Tomioka* Silk Mill due to the recruiting of capable personnel, such as Paul Brunat, a French engineer, and *Junchu Odaka*. *Shibusawa* was introduced to Brunat by a Frenchman, who was a legal adviser for the government. As *Shibusawa* was convinced of Brunat's ability, he signed a contract with Brunat regarding the construction of a mill complex. *Shibusawa* also appointed *Junchu Odaka* as the first head manager of the *Tomioka* Silk Mill.
渋沢栄一は、フランス人技師のポール・ブリュナと尾高惇忠の有能な人材の登用を行った、富岡製糸場建設における中心人物でした。渋沢は、政府の法律顧問を担当していたフランス人からブリュナを紹介されました。彼はブリュナの有能さを認め、工場建設について契約を交わしました。また渋沢は、尾高惇忠を富岡製糸場初代場長に任命しました。

■ *Eiichi Shibusawa* resigned from his position at the Ministry of Finance the year after the establishment of the *Tomioka* Silk Mill, and then he established a bank that same year. He played an active part as a businessman. *Shibusawa* was a businessman who participated in the establishment of many companies engaged in the modernization of Japan and is called the Father of the Modern Japanese Economy or the Father of Japanese Capitalism.

渋沢栄一は富岡製糸場設立の翌年に大蔵省を辞任し、同年に銀行を設立し、その後は実業家として活躍しました。渋沢は、日本の産業基盤に携わる多くの会社の設立に関与した実業家であり、近代日本経済の父、もしくは日本資本主義の父と称されています。

(参考資料：「絹の街、絹の里、深谷　埼玉県深谷市」『世界文化遺産　富岡製糸場』pp.87-89.／
「渋沢栄一」『富岡製糸場事典』pp.120-121.)

Junchu Odaka
お だか じゅん ちゅう
(尾高 惇 忠)

■ *Junchu Odaka* was another key member in the construction of the *Tomioka* Silk Mill. He was a cousin of *Eiichi Shibusawa* and the person who affected young *Shibusawa* in terms of teaching the Analects of Confucius.

尾高惇忠は富岡製糸場の建設のもう一人の要人でした。彼は渋沢栄一の従兄弟であり、また『論語』の師でもあり、若き渋沢に影響を与えた人物でした。

■ *Junchu Odaka* was appointed by *Eiichi Shibusawa*, to construct the *Tomioka* Silk Mill. He chose the site, persuaded the local people to accept the plan, arranged for the supply of building materials, and oversaw the construction. Later, he became the first head manager of the *Tomioka* Silk Mill.

尾高惇忠は富岡製糸場設立のために渋沢栄一に登用されました。敷地の選択、地元の人々の説得、建築資材の調達、建設工事の指揮に尽力し、後に初代場長に就任しました。

■ The recruitment of female workers was difficult at the time because the Japanese were unfamiliar with foreigners, misunderstood their foreign customs, and generally afraid of them. To deny the rumors, *Odaka* made his daughter, *Yuu*, a female worker. At the age of 14, *Yuu* became the first female worker.

当時の日本人は外国人に馴染みがなく、彼らの習慣を誤解し恐れたために、工女募集は難航しました。尾高は風評を打ち消すために、自分の娘である勇を工女にしたのです。14歳の勇は、最初の工女になったのです。

(参考文献：「絹の街、絹の里、深谷　埼玉県深谷市」『世界文化遺産　富岡製糸場』pp.87-89.／
「尾高惇忠」「尾高勇」『富岡製糸場事典』pp.122-123, pp.134-135.)

5-3 瓦職人、煉瓦を焼く
Roof tile craftsmen made bricks

Keystone of the East cocoon warehouse
（東置繭所のキーストーン）

Bricks laid in French style
*（フランス式で積まれた煉瓦）

Company name engraved in brick
*（煉瓦刻印「ヤマニ」）
*（画像提供：富岡市）

Visitor: The Western-style brick buildings were modern for the Japanese in those days, I guess.

Mayuko: They represented Japan's modernization.

Visitor: Who designed these Western-style brick buildings?

Mayuko: Paul Brunat, the director of the *Tomioka* Silk Mill, planned the design of the mill complex, and Auguste Bastien completed the design drawings. He was a French draftsman that Brunat employed.

Visitor: So, French craftsmen built these buildings?

Mayuko: No. Japanese craftsmen did the actual construction. But at the time, no one knew how to make bricks in Japan, so Brunat and a French architect taught the roof tile craftsmen how to produce bricks. Kilns were built in *Fukushima, Kanra-machi*, near the *Tomioka* Silk Mill, where the bricks were baked, but they were of low quality.

Visitor: They showed great craftsmanship.

Mayuko: The Japanese people of the *Meiji* period were high-spirited.

Visitor: Is that the *Meiji* spirit or the Japanese spirit?

Mayuko: I'm deeply moved by your words.

Vocabulary

roof tile craftsman	屋根瓦（かわら）職人	brick	煉瓦（れんが）
those days	当時 ⇔ these days　最近		
modernization	近代化　※ modern　近代的な		
design	設計　※ design drawing　設計図		
mill complex	（関係する）工場群	complete	〜を完成させる
draftsman	製図技師	employ	〜を雇う、雇用する
construction	建設工事、建設作業	architect	建築技師、建築家
kiln	（煉瓦を焼く）窯（かま）	quality	品質
craftsmanship	職人気質	high-spirited	気概のある
spirit	精神、魂	be moved by	〜に感動する

English Points

■ Kilns were made.（窯がつくられた）や The bricks were baked.（煉瓦が焼かれた）は、受動態（be 動詞 ＋ 動詞の過去分詞）と呼ばれる表現です。第 3 章（3-2. : p.61）で既習していますが、ここでは「行為をする人」について説明を加えます。「行為をする人」は受動態の文では by の後に続きますが、行為をする人が不明な場合や言い表す必要のない場合は、「by ＋ 行為をする人」は省かれます。

・That song is loved by many people.
（あの曲は多くの人によって愛されています。）
・*Thousand Cranes* was written by *Yasunari Kawabata*.
（『千羽鶴』は川端康成によって書かれました。）

・English is spoken in many countries.（英語は多くの国で話されています。）
・This house was built a hundred years ago.（この家は百年前に建てられました。）

■ 英語での感情表現には、しばしば受動態が使われます。これは、感情が外部要因によって引き起こされると捉えるためです。

・I was moved by her kindness.（彼女の親切に感動しました。）
・He's so excited about participating in the festival.
（彼は祭りに参加することにとても興奮しています。）

be amazed at [with]〜 …………	〜に驚く
be bored with〜 ………………	〜に退屈する
be confused by [with]〜 …………	〜に混乱する
be delighted at [with]〜 ………	〜に喜んでいる
be depressed by〜 ………………	〜に憂鬱である
be disappointed in [with]〜 ……	〜にがっかりする
be excited at [about]〜 …………	〜に興奮する
be frustrated by [with]〜 ………	〜にいら立つ
be interested in〜 ………………	〜に興味を持つ
be satisfied with〜 ……………	〜に満足する

be scared of〜	·················	〜におびえる
be shocked at〜	·················	〜に衝撃を受ける
be surprised at〜	·················	〜に驚く

■ 感情表現のもう一つの特徴は、「be ＋ 形容詞」の文型に確認できます。基本的な
喜怒哀楽の感情を整理すると…

〔喜び〕	I'm He/She's You/They're	happy. glad. grateful.	（幸せです） （うれしい） （感謝している）
〔楽しい〕	〃	pleasant. delightful. calm. comfortable.	（楽しい） （愉快な） （落ち着いている） （快適だ）
〔怒り〕	〃	angry. mad. upset. furious. grumpy. sour.	（怒っている） （怒っている） （腹を立てている） （激怒している） （機嫌が悪い） （機嫌が悪い）
〔哀しい／悲しい〕	〃	sad. lonely. unhappy. homesick.	（悲しい） （寂しい） （不幸な） （ホームシックになる）
〔その他〕	〃	nervous. （緊張している、神経質になっている） anxious. sick (of it). jealous. envious. proud. respectful. curious.	 （心配している） （嫌気がさしている） （うらやましい） （ねたましい） （誇りに思う） （敬意を表する） （好奇心が強い）

5-4 東置繭所で
At the East cocoon warehouse

East cocoon warehouse*（東置繭所）

Meeting place for guided tour
（ガイドツアー出発場所）

*（画像提供：富岡市）

Mayuko: This large building is the East cocoon warehouse. It was made out of wood and brick, so it's called "timber-framed, constructed of bricks." It's a European-style building with the technology used by the Japanese in wooden buildings. In other words, it combines European and Japanese traditions.

Visitor: According to the guide map, there is a warehouse that's the same size on the west side, too. I wonder why they built two large warehouses.

Mayuko: The sericulture in this area was carried out only once a year at that time. This is because a silkworm only forms a cocoon once a year. Big warehouses were necessary to store the large number of cocoons that were bought.

Visitor: While a silkworm was in storage at the warehouse, didn't it hatch to become a moth?

Mayuko: Cocoons that were collected were dried before they were stored in the warehouse.

Visitor: I see ...

Mayuko: Next, we'll take a look at the Silk-reeling plant.

Vocabulary

timber-framed, constructed of bricks	木骨煉瓦造		
European-style	洋風の、欧風の、洋式の	technology	技術
in other words	言い換えると		
combine	〜を結合する、融合する	tradition	伝統

carry out	～を実施する		silkworm	蚕（かいこ）
form	～を形づくる			
store	～を貯蔵する	※ storage	貯蔵	
hatch	孵化（ふか）する		moth	蛾（が）
collect	～を集める			

👉 English Points

■ I wonder～（～なのだろう、～なのかしら）は、確証の持てない場合の表現です。疑問詞（why, who, what, where, when, how）を伴って、次のように用いられます。

・I wonder
why he is late for work.（なぜ彼は仕事に遅れているのかしら。）
who is in charge of the new project.
（誰が新プロジェクトを担当するのだろう。）
what she plans on my birthday.
（彼女は僕の誕生日に何を計画しているのだろう。）
where they want to live.（彼らはどこに住みたいのだろう。）
when this building will be completed.
（この建物はいつ完成するのかしら。）
how to use this cooking utensil.
（この調理用具はどうやって使うのかしら。）

■ This [That] is because～（それは～だからです）は、理由を説明する表現です。

・I have to cancel my reservation for tonight. That is because bad weather is preventing the plane from taking off.
（今晩の予約をキャンセルしなくてはなりません。それは悪天候で飛行機が出ないからです。）

対して、This[That] is why～（だから～です）は、結論・結果を述べる表現になります。

・Bad weather prevents a plane from taking off. That's why I have to cancel my reservation for tonight.
（悪天候で飛行機が出ません。だから今晩の予約をキャンセルしなくてはならないのです。）

5-5 繰糸所で
At the Silk-reeling plant

Silk-reeling plant
（繰糸所）

Exterior view of the building
*（繰糸所外観）
*（画像提供：富岡市）

Mayuko: Here's the Silk-reeling plant. It's the place where the threads from cocoons were wound into raw silk.

Visitor: What a long building this is!

Mayuko: It's approximately 140 [one hundred forty] meters long. <u>This is the longest building in the entire *Tomioka* Silk Mill complex.</u>

Visitor: The building has many windows.

Mayuko: Natural sunlight was indispensable. There were no electric lights in those days. Another feature of the building is that it doesn't have any center pillars because the truss construction supports the roof. You'll find a large workspace inside.

Visitor: Okay, let's look around inside!

Mayuko: Sure!

Vocabulary

thread	糸	
wind	巻き取る	※ wind–wound–wound
indispensable	必要不可欠な	
electric light	電灯	
feature	特徴、形体	
pillar	柱	
truss construction	トラス構造（三角形の集合体を用いた構造骨組の一種）	
support	〜を支える	

English Points

- 最上級のつくり方は、短い形容詞の場合は the ○○ -est の形をつくり、長いものは the most を前置します。「短い・長い」語と判断するのは音節数によってです（第2章、2-5.: p.40を参照）。

    - The number of driver's license holders in *Gunma* Prefecture is <u>the largest</u> in Japan.
      （群馬県の運転免許保有者数は日本で最も多いです。）
    - This is <u>the most valuable</u> painting in this museum's collection.
      （これはこの美術館の収集の中で最も価値のある絵画です。）

Exercise Prepare を答えた後、枠内のパターンを用いて質問と応答の練習をしましょう。

Example: A: Why is *Gunma* Prefecture known as the best in Japan?
         B: The amount of hot spring water is extraordinary. It is the largest amount in Japan.

A: Why is *Gunma* Prefecture known as the best in Japan?
B: _____ . It is the _____ in Japan.

Provide information

(1) The amount of hot-spring water is extraordinary.
(2) About 900,000 [nine hundred thousand] *Daruma* dolls are produced every year.
(3) The production of the *konnyaku* potato accounts for more than 90% [ninety percent] of that in the whole country.
(4) The percentage of people with driver's licenses is 83.1% [eighty-three point one percent].
(5) There is a greater number of noodle shops (*udon*, *soba*, *ramen*, and so forth) per citizen than in any other prefectures.
(6) The staircase at *Doai* Station on the *JR Joetsu* line has 486 [four hundred (and) eighty-six] steps. For a staircase at a station, that number of steps is outrageous.

Prepare

続く形容詞を比較級と最上級に変化させなさい。

(1) 規則的に変化する形容詞

原級の和訳	原　　級	比　較　級	最　上　級
	high		
	short		
	old		
	small		
	exciting		
	heavy		
	interesting		

原級の和訳	原　級	比　較　級	最　上　級
	fast		
	young		
	important		
	early		
	difficult		

（2）不規則に変化する形容詞

原級の和訳	原　級	比　較　級	最　上　級
	many		
	much		
	little		
	good		
	well		
	bad		

5-6 繰糸所内で──〔1〕
In the Silk-reeling plant：〔1〕

Truss construction
*(トラス構造)

Automatic silk-reeling machines
(自動繰糸機)
*(画像提供：富岡市)

Visitor: Wow, these are silk-reeling machines. <u>If these machines were moving all at once, it would be spectacular.</u>

Mayuko: I'm sure it was. Now, please look at this photograph of a panel. You'll see the first silk-reeling machines used at this plant. There is something like a pot sitting on a stand. This was a pot for boiling cocoons. The number of pots showed the scale of the factory's production, and there were three hundred pots here. Considering that factories in other countries were equipped with no more than one hundred fifty pots at that time, <u>it can be said that</u> this was one of the largest silk mills in the world.

Visitor: That means, there were up to three hundred women working here in those days?

Mayuko: More than that. <u>According to the records</u>, more than five hundred young women worked at this silk mill in 1873. Three hundred women were in charge of silk reeling, but besides that, there were various other tasks to be done in the factory. Female workers were recruited from all over Japan. They learned silk-reeling techniques with the machines and brought those techniques back to each of their hometowns, where they taught them to workers at newly established plants.

Visitor: So the female workers of the *Tomioka* Silk Mill spread the techniques for working with silk-reeling machines in Japan.

Mayuko: Okaya City in *Nagano* is a sister city of *Tomioka* for that very reason. And raw silk is still produced.

Vocabulary

silk-reeling machine	繰糸機	move	動く、作動する
all at once	一斉に、全部が同時に	spectacular	壮観な、壮大な
photograph	写真	plant	工場
pot	深なべ、釜	boil	〜を煮る、茹でる
scale	規模		
equip	〜を装備する、備え付ける		
be in charge of	〜を担当している	female worker	工女
various tasks	様々な仕事	recruit	〜を募集する
spread	〜を広める	carry out	〜を実行する

English Points

■ If〜（もし〜）の表現には、実現可能な「直説法」と現実に反する「仮定法」があります。直説法では時制のズレがないのに対して、仮定法においては、現在の事実に反することを「仮定法過去」、そして過去の事実に反することを「仮定法過去完了」で表し、時制のズレが文法的特徴として認められます。

(1) 直説法：現実に起こり得る（可能性が五分五分の）ことを表す。

> If 主語 + 動詞［時制のズレなし］〜, 主語 + 動詞［時制のズレなし］〜.

- If Mr. *Sugihara* is home, I would like to talk with him.
  （杉原氏が在宅なら、彼とお話をさせていただきたい。）
- Let's have a barbecue in the garden if it's nice tomorrow.
  （明日天気がよければ、庭でバーベキューをしよう。）
- If you felt sick, why didn't you go to the doctor?
  （もし気分が悪かったのなら、なぜあなたは医者に診てもらわなかったのですか。）

(2) 仮定法過去：現実に反すること、可能性がほとんどないことについて表す。

> If 主語 + 動詞［過去形］〜, 主語 + would [could, could] + 動詞［原型］〜.

- If I had two million yen, I would buy that land.
  （もし私に200万円があれば、あの土地を買うだろうに。）
- If I knew her phone number, I could make a phone call.
  （彼女の電話番号を知っていれば、電話をかけられるのだが。）
- If I were a bird, I would fly to you.　　※ was ではなく were を用いる。
  （もし私が鳥なら、あなたのもとへ飛んで行くだろうに。）

（3）仮定法過去完了：過去の事実に反することを言い表す。

> If 主語 + had + 動詞［過去分詞］～, 主語 + would [could, could] + have +
> 動詞［過去分詞］～.

- If I had had two million yen at that time, I would have bought that land.
  （もしあの時、私に200万円があったなら、あの土地を買っただろうに。）
- If I had known her phone number, I would have called her.
  （もし私が彼女の電話番号を知っていたら、私は彼女に電話したでしょう。）
- If I had been a bird, I could have flown to you.
  （もし私が鳥だったなら、あなたのもとへ飛んで行けただろうに。）

■ It is said that～（～と言われている）や、It can be said that～（～と言うことができる）の言い回しは、客観的な見解を示す際に使われます。

- It is said that women in *Gunma* are hard workers.
  （群馬の女性たちは働き者だと言われています。）
- It can be said that working women are economically independent.
  （働く女性たちは経済的に自立していると言うことができます。）

■ According to the newspaper [the weather forecast, what I heard...]（新聞［天気予報、聞いたところ…］によると）というように、情報源を示す際の表現です。

- According to the guidebook, the festival has been held for three hundred years.
  （ガイドブックによれば、そのお祭りは300年間行われてきました。）
- According to the weather forecast, it will rain this afternoon.
  （天気予報によれば、今日の午後は雨になるだろう。）

5-7 繰糸所内で──〔2〕
In the Silk-reeling plant：〔2〕

Filature device
（座繰り器、糸繰り装置）

Mayuko: Look at this photograph. <u>This is called</u> a *zaguri-ki*, which is a traditional Japanese filature device. Women removed the threads from cocoons in this way in their own homes before this silk mill was established.

Visitor: I bet they needed a lot of patience.

Mayuko: You're right. That's why the introduction of the silk-reeling machines was an epoch-making event for the silk industry. Mass production of high-quality raw silk was born.

Visitor: I can imagine. <u>Even though silk was a luxury in the past,</u> it's available even for the average person nowadays. My grandmother used to wear her silk blouse on special days.

Mayuko: Various silk goods are displayed at the gift shop. They make good souvenirs.

Visitor: Let me check on that later.

Mayuko: Let's go on to the next one.

Vocabulary

traditional	伝統的な、古くからの
remove	～を移す
patience	根気、忍耐
introduction	導入、紹介
epoch-making	画期的な
mass production	大量生産
imagine	想像する
luxury	ぜいたく
grandmother	祖母

📢 English Points

■ This [That, It] is called〜（これ［あれ、それ］は〜と呼ばれている）は、前に示されたものの呼び名を紹介する表現です。

- A dry wind blows in this area during the winter. It is called *karakkaze*.
  （冬の間、この地域に乾いた風が吹きます。それは空っ風と呼ばれています。）
- *Gunma* Prefecture is the name that it took after the *Meiji* era. In the old days, it was called *Joshu*.（群馬県は明治時代以降の名称です。昔は上州と呼ばれていました。）

■ (even) though（〜だけれども）は、逆説を表す接続詞です。接続詞は文と文をつなぐ役割を果たしますが、二つの文の内容が相反する場合、逆説の接続詞が用いられます。although は though よりもフォーマルで、however に関しては文語的な表現です。

カジュアル ◀━━━━━━━━━━━━━━━━━━▶ フォーマル
but（しかし）　though（〜だけれども）　although（〜だけれども）　however（しかしながら）

- My father is busy, <u>but</u> he is often my best counselor.
  （父は忙しいが、しばしば私のよき相談相手です。）

- I like to play badminton, <u>even though</u> I'm not very good at it.
  （あまりうまくないけれど、私はバトミントをするのが好きです。）

- <u>Although</u> he is an excellent singer, he is a failure as an actor.
  （彼はすばらしい歌手だけれど、役者としては落第です。）

- Typhoons cause damage. <u>However</u>, they solve the problem of a water shortage.
  （台風は被害をもたらします。しかしながら、水不足の問題は解消します。）

5-8 ブリュナ館で——〔1〕
At the Brunat House : 〔1〕

Inspector's house
*（検査人館）

Brunat House
（ブリュナ館）

Dormitory for French female instructors *（女工館）

*（画像提供：富岡市）

Mayuko: Here we are. We are in front of the Brunat House. Let me tell you about it from here, because we're not allowed to go inside the building.

Visitor: That's too bad. Because I wanted to see the people's lifestyle.

Mayuko: I'm hoping that the house will open soon, but let me tell you about Paul Brunat. He was a Frenchman who inspected raw silk for a French trading firm in *Yokohama*. He was commissioned by the *Meiji* government in 1870. So, he was in charge of setting up, directing, and managing the *Tomioka* Silk Mill.

Visitor: He certainly had a lot of knowledge about raw silk.

Mayuko: He imported silk-reeling machines from France. He employed several French engineers and instructors. They stayed in the dormitories, which you can see on your left. Later, a dormitory for the French male engineers was used as an inspector's house, but the dormitory for the French female instructors remained like it was.

Visitor: Their life in Japan must have been difficult.

Mayuko: Yes, I guess so. However, it was reported that they were treated well in terms of the salaries they earned. Brunat, as the director of the silk mill, received almost the same salary as a minister at that time. He lived in this big house with his family.

Visitor: It is a European-style building with a veranda around it, which looks like the Glover House in *Nagasaki*.

Mayuko: That's right. It is a colonial-style house. It has a veranda and a raised floor for shade from the sun and ventilation.

Visitor: It must have been hot for foreigners during the summer in Japan.

Mayuko: Oh, you can say that again. The summer in Japan is very hot and humid. It's difficult even for Japanese people.

Vocabulary

inspect	～を検査する ※ inspector 検査人
trading firm	貿易会社
commission	（権限）を委託する、～を委任する
set up	～を設立する
direct	～を指導する ※ director 指導者
manage	（会社など）を管理・運営する
knowledge	知識
import	～を輸入する
engineer	技術者、技師
instructor	指導員
dormitory	宿舎
male	男（性） ※ female 女（性）
remain	残る
treat	～を扱う
in terms of	～に関して、～の点から
minister	大臣
colonial	植民地の ※ colonial-style house: 植民地の気候・風土に合わせた欧州様式の建物
ventilation	風通し、通気
humid	湿度の高い、蒸し蒸しする

👉 English Points

- That's too bad.（それは残念だ、気の毒に）は、よくない出来事や知らせに対して使われる表現です。

  ・The outdoor concert was canceled due to the typhoon.
  （野外コンサートは台風で中止になりました。）
  ——That's too bad. We were looking forward to it.
  （それは残念ですね。楽しみにしていたのに。）

  ・I'm afraid my son will be absent from classes for a few days due to influenza.
  （息子はインフルエンザのために数日間、授業を欠席いたします。）
  ——That's too bad. I hope he'll get well soon.
  （お気の毒に。早くよくなることを願っています。）

- 「助動詞 + 完了形（have + 動詞の過去分詞）」は、過去の出来事を言い表します。助動詞を過去形にするのではなく、完了形を後に置くことがポイントです（助動詞の働きと種類については、続く Tips 欄を参照）。

  ・I cannot find my bicycle. It <u>might have been stolen</u>.
  （自転車が見当たらない。盗まれたかもしれない。）
  ・I have been waiting for him for half an hour. He <u>must have forgotten</u> his appointment with me.
  （30分彼を待っています。彼は私と会う約束を忘れているに違いない。）
  ・I <u>should have asked</u> her out on a date at that time.
  （あの時、僕は彼女にデートを申し込むべきでした。）

Tips:

- 助動詞とは、文字通りに「動詞を助ける語」という意味です。その働きは、動詞が表しきれない微妙な意味合いやニュアンスを付け加えることで、人間味のある表現にしてくれるというものです。助動詞の種類は多様ですが、主語によって変化することもないので、使い方は容易です。

助動詞に関する文法上の注意

・助動詞の後には動詞（原形）が続く
　He can <u>play</u> the guitar well.

・主語が何人称でも、助動詞は変わらない（ -s/-es は付かない）
　He <u>plays</u> the guitar well.　vs.　He <u>can</u> play the guitar well.

・疑問文の場合、助動詞を文頭に移動する
　<u>Can</u> he play the guitar well?

・否定文の場合、助動詞の後に not を置く
　He <u>can't [can not, cannot]</u> play the guitar well.

Tomioka Silk Mill

5

富岡製糸場編

助動詞の種類と働き

助動詞	意 味	例　文
will	意志	We will eat out tonight. （今晩、私たちは外食します。）
	未来	My daughter will be twenty years old next year. （来年、娘は20歳になります。）
can	可能	He can dance like Michael Jackson. （彼はマイケル・ジャクソンのように踊ることができます。）
cannot	推量	She cannot be late for work. （彼女が仕事に遅れるはずがない。）
must	義務	You must submit your report by the end of this month. （あなたは今月末までにレポートを提出しなくてはなりません。）
	忠告	You must stay in bed until your fever goes down. （あなたは熱が下がるまで安静にしていなくてはなりません。）
	推量	The couple over there must be Mr. and Mrs. Brown. （あそこのカップルは、ブラウン夫妻にちがいありません。）
must not	禁止	Children must not stay up late. （子どもたちは夜ふかししてはいけません。）
have/has to	必要	It's getting dark. I have to leave soon. （暗くなってきました。私はそろそろお暇しなくてはなりません。）
don't/doesn't have to	不必要	You don't have to tell me about that if you don't want to. （そのことについて話したくなければ、私に話す必要はありません。）
may	許可	You may use my car tonight. Drive safely. （今晩、私の車を使ってもいいです。気を付けて運転してください。）
	推量	This may be a real diamond. （これは本物のダイヤモンドかもしれない。）
might	推量	This might be a real diamond. （ひょっとしたらこれは本物のダイヤモンドかもしれない。） ※ might は may よりも確信度合いが低い。
should	忠告	You should eat vegetables every day. （野菜を毎日食べるべきです。）
	義務	We should always keep our promise. （私たちはいつも約束を守るべきです。）
had better	忠告	We had better stay healthy and live longer. （私たちは健康で長生きした方がいい。）
will/can	依頼	Will [Can] you help me carry this box? （この箱を運ぶのを手伝ってもらえますか。）
would/could	丁寧な依頼	Would [Could] you give me a ride to the station? （駅まで乗せていただけますか。）
used to	過去の状態	There used to be a public telephone here. （以前はここに公衆電話がありました。）
used to/ would	過去の習慣	I used to [would] play soccer in this park when I was a child. （子どもの頃にこの公園でサッカーをしていたものだった。）

（参考資料：小野（監修）『English Quest Basic—CD-ROM で学ぶ英語の基礎：初級編』pp.31-35.）

5-9 ブリュナ館で──〔2〕

At the Brunat House：〔2〕

Mayuko: Brunat lived in this house as the director of the *Tomioka* Silk Mill from 1873 to 1875. After he left, the Brunat House was used as a night school for the female workers.

Visitor: It's a big house, isn't it?

Mayuko: Uh-huh. There are brick storerooms in the basement, and it is thought that food and wine were stored there.

Visitor: For the French, wine is a daily necessity. I can see that Brunat had an elegant life here.

Mayuko: There is an interesting story about the French. They could not get any female workers when the mill was first established because a rumor had spread that the French drank the blood of living people. The Japanese people feared that the French would drink their blood. The Japanese at that time mistook red wine for blood, so there were problems recruiting female workers.

Visitor: That's an interesting story, but it also teaches us that cross-cultural understanding is not easy. When I saw *nori* for the first time, I did not think the black paper was edible. But I cannot live without *sushi* now.

Mayuko: That makes me laugh. By the way, to deny the unsavory rumor, *Junchu Odaka*, the first manager of the *Tomioka* Silk Mill, made his daughter work at the plant. *Yuu Odaka*, a fourteen-year-old girl, became the first female worker at the *Tomioka* Silk Mill.

Visitor: Was the daughter's opinion respected? I mean, did she want to work there?

Mayuko: *Yuu* respected her father's wishes, and she eagerly learned the techniques. It is reported that she became a first-class female worker.

Visitor: She was a strong, capable woman.

Mayuko: Uh-huh, I have heard that women from the *Meiji* period were strong.

Vocabulary

night school	夜間学校		
store	貯蔵する	※ storeroom	貯蔵室
basement	地下	daily necessity	生活必需品
elegant	優雅な	rumor	噂
blood	血	fear	〜を恐れる
mistake A for B	AをBと間違える		
recruit	〜を募集する、〜を採用する		
cross-cultural understanding	異文化理解		
edible	食べられる、食用になる		
deny	〜を否定する、〜を打ち消す		
daughter	娘	opinion	意見、考え
respect	〜を尊重する	eagerly	熱心に
capable	能力のある		

👉 English Points

■ mistake A for B（AをBと間違える）の使い方は…

・I made a sweet curry because I mistook the sugar for the salt.
（私が砂糖を塩と間違えたため、甘いカレーに仕上がりました。）
・Children have a strong imagination and often mistake fantasy for reality.
（子どもたちはたくましい想像力で、しばしば空想を現実と間違えます。）
・Japanese people mistake a tattooed foreigner for a gangster.
（日本人は刺青をした外国人を暴力団員と取り違えます。）

■ 否定表現に関して、日本語の場合は「〜では<u>ない</u>と思う」または「〜だとは思わ<u>ない</u>」というようにどちらの言い回しも可能です。他方、英語においては続く例文の通り、後者が一般的であることに注意を要します。

・「黒い紙は食べられないと思った」⇒「黒い紙が食べられるとは思わなかった」
× I thought (that) black paper wasn't edible.
○ I did not think (that) black paper was edible.

・「彼は正直ではないと思う」⇒「彼が正直だとは思わない」
× I think he is not honest.
○ I do not think he is honest

■ 使役動詞の文法上の特徴（to なし不定詞が続く）については、第 4 章（4-13.：p.108）で既習しています。ここでは、主な使役動詞 make（〜させる）、have（〜してもらう）、let（〜させてやる）を紹介します。強制力の最も強い make に対して、have や let は緩い使役動詞です。ニュアンスの違いを踏まえて使い分けることがポイントです。

- Your story <u>makes</u> me laugh. （あなたの話は私を笑わせます。）
- I <u>made</u> my little sister organize her bookshelf. （妹に本棚の整理をさせました。）

- I <u>had</u> my brother John fix my bicycle.
  （ジョン兄さんに自転車を修理してもらいました。）
- I'll <u>have</u> my father sign this document tonight.
  （今夜、父にこの書類に署名してもらいます。）

- You seem to be in a hurry. I'll <u>let</u> you go.
  （急いでいるようですね。行かせてあげましょう。）
- I'll <u>let</u> you drive the car. Please drive safely.
  （あなたに車の運転させてあげます。安全運転でお願いしますよ。）

■ I mean ... は、I mean to say ...（私が言おうとしているのは…）の 省略形で、「つまり」「というか」の意味合いで、説明を加えたり、より適切に言い直したり、誤りを訂正したりするときに使われます。

- Do you have any plans for this weekend? I mean, would you like to go to a movie with me this weekend?
  （今週末、何か予定が入っていますか。つまり、この週末に僕と映画に行きませんか。）
- *Nobu* is good at cooking. I mean, he is the chef of a Japanese restaurant.
  （ノブは料理がうまいです。というか、彼は日本料理店の板前です。）

さらに、I mean it. という場合は、「冗談ではなく、本気で言っている」の意になります。

- She lied to me again. Our friendship is over. I mean it.
  （彼女はまた私に嘘をついたし、私たちの友情は終わりです。本気で言っています。）

Tomioka Silk Mill

5

富岡製糸場編

5-10 寄宿舎で
At the Dormitories for female workers

Dormitories for female workers
(寄宿舎)

Mayuko: The two buildings <u>in a row</u> that you can see in front of you are dormitories for female workers.

Visitor: What was their life like there?

Mayuko: They had a simple, well-regulated life. Their working hours were from sunrise to sunset because that was the time when there were no lights. In other words, they worked from 7 a.m. to 4:30 p.m. with one break besides lunchtime. They worked six days a week and were off on Sundays.

Visitor: <u>The system of one day off a week</u> doesn't sound too good to me. Were they paid well?

Mayuko: Their net income was small, but there was no charge for boarding, and medical care was free. So, calculating the meal expenses as a part of their salary, roughly speaking, they made half the amount of a carpenter's pay at that time.

Visitor: They must have worked hard because Japan became one of the world's industrial powers in a short period of one hundred years. I can see that the women working in the silk industry built its foundation.

Mayuko: It is often said that the Japanese work too much, but I can understand why, when I have a glimpse at such history.

Visitor: But work is not everything. We should realize the idea of a work-life balance, you know.

Mayuko: That's a good point.

Vocabulary

dormitory	寄宿舎
well-regulated	規則正しい
from sunrise to sunset	日の出から日没まで
break	休憩
be off	休む
net income	純収入、手取り
boarding	（食事付きの）寄宿
medical care	医療
calculate	～を計算［算出］する
meal expense	食費
roughly saying	大まかに言うと
carpenter	大工
industrial power	工業大国
foundation	基礎、基盤
have [get] a glimpse	垣間見る、ちらりと見る　　※ =have a look
realize	～に気付く、～をはっきり理解する
work-life balance	ワーク・ライフ・バランス（仕事と生活の調和）

👉 English Points

■ in a row は「一列に、連続で」の意で、次のように用います。

・The chairs were lined up in a row.（椅子は一列に並べられていた。）
・We'll have three days off in a row next month.（来月に3日連休があります。）

■ the system of one day off a week は「週休1日制」の意です。「週休2日制」の場合は…

・Due to the system of two days off a week, the post office is not open on Saturdays and Sundays in Japan.
（週休2日制のため、日本では郵便局は土・日曜日は開いていません。）
・Although our company has the system of two days off a week, there is no guarantee of a weekend off.
（弊社は週休2日制を敷いていますが、週末の休日という保証はありません。）

Tomioka Silk Mill

5

富岡製糸場編

Tip:

Women workers at the *Tomioka* Silk Mill
(富岡製糸場の工女たち)

Regarding the women workers of the silk-reeling plant of the *Meiji* era, many Japanese have the image that they led unhappy lives, according to the documentary literature: *Jokou Aishi* [Sad stories of factory girls] (*Wakizo Hosoi,* 1925) and *Ah, Nomugi Touge* [*Nomugi* Pass] (*Shigemi Yamamoto,* 1968). Because *Ah, Nomugi Touge* was made into a movie, many Japanese believe the storyline: The women workers had to work for long hours, under severe conditions, and away from home due to poverty, and they ended up dying of an illness.

However, the labor circumstances of the women workers at the *Tomioka* Silk Mill contradict those stories. At *Tomioka,* considering the circumstances of the hot and humid temperature in the silk-reeling plant, the break for the midsummer period was extended, and the vacation systems for the summer and at the beginning and the end of the year were introduced, with consideration for the health of women workers and the efficiency of silk production. Also, the lives of the women workers in those days were written about in the *Tomioka Diary* by *Ei Wada,* who was one of them. In a time when it was uncommon for women to have a profession, the women workers were leading an economically independent life.

　明治期の製糸場で働いた工女たちについては、『女工哀史』（細井和喜蔵著、1925年）や『あゝ野麦峠』（山本茂実著、1968年）の記録文学から、不幸な人生を送ったというイメージを抱いている日本人が多いようです。後者については映画化もされましたから、工女たちの貧しい生い立ちから出稼ぎに行かざるを得なかった事情や、厳しい監視下で長時間労働をさせられ、病死するという工女たちの悲しい物語が多くの日本人に共有されています。

　しかしながら、富岡製糸場の工女の労働環境は、これらの物語とは一線を画します。そこでは蒸し暑い繰糸所内の事情を考慮し、盛夏期の休憩時間が延長されており、夏休みや年末年始の休暇制度も導入されており、能率増進とともに工女たちの健康管理への配慮がうかがえます。また、当時の工女たちの暮らしぶりは、工女の一人、和田英の『富岡日記』に書き記されています。女性が職業を持つことは当たり前でない時代に、工女たちは経済的に自立した生活を送っていたのです。

（参考資料：「工女寄宿舎」「会食所（食堂）と賄所（調理場）」「工女の暮らし編」
『富岡製糸場事典』pp.54-55, pp.56-57, pp.145-171.）

5-11 工女たちの作業着
Work clothes of female workers

Female worker of the *Tomioka* Silk Mill wearing a *hakama*
（袴をはいた富岡製糸場の工女）

Visitor: According to a photograph in the panel, which I saw a little while ago, female workers wore a *kimono* with a Japanese hairstyle. What is the wide skirt called?

Mayuko: It is called a *hakama*. People usually wear it on a formal occasion, and it is easy to move in it because it's a type of divided skirt. That is why female workers wore it when working, I think.

Visitor: Kendo players also put on a *hakama*. *Hakamas* are cool!

Mayuko: Yeah, I think so, too. A person looks very dignified in it.

Visitor: Very! I might want to get one for myself.

Vocabulary

work clothes	作業着
a little while ago	少し前に、先ほど
Japanese hairstyle	日本髪
on a formal occasion	改まった席で、正式な場で
divided skirt	キュロットスカート　※ divided　分かれた
dignified	威厳のある、凛とした

English Points

■ What is [are] ○○ called?（○○は何て呼ぶのですか）は、How do you say this? と同様に呼び方を尋ねる表現です。

・What is an electric heating table covered by a blanket called?
（電気の暖房テーブルで毛布で覆われているものは、何と呼ばれますか。）
——It is called a "*kotatsu*," a traditional Japanese heating appliance.
（「こたつ」と呼ばれます。日本の伝統的な暖房器具です。）

5-12 見解を示す

Expressing one's opinion

Visitor: Today, <u>I think I learned a lot about the *Meiji* period in Japan.</u>

Mayuko: Good! People of the *Meiji* era steadily adopted new techniques from Western countries and used them in their own way.

Visitor: I think the reason why Japan succeeded in modernizing in only one hundred years has to do with the *Meiji* spirit.

Mayuko: Ha-ha. Though it was an uneasy time <u>from a historical perspective</u>, it was a time that was full of energy.

Visitor: I also understand that women played a major role in Japanese modernization.

Mayuko: Very well done!

Vocabulary

express one's opinion	意見を述べる
steadily	着々と、どんどん
adopt	〜を取り入れる
in one's own way	自分なりの方法［やり方］で
succeed in	〜に成功する、うまくいく
modernize	近代化する
have to do with	〜と関係［関連］がある
from a historical perspective	歴史的見地［観点］から
be full of energy	活気がある、気迫に満ちている
play a major role	大役を果たす

English Points

■ 「主語 ＋ 一般動詞 ＋ that …」の文型において、that は続く文（従属節と呼ばれる）を導く接続詞として機能します。同時に、that は省略されることもあります。

・People believe (that) gods' spirits dwell in that big tree.
（人々はあの大木に神が宿ると信じています。）
・I'm surprised (that) he can make buckwheat noodles.
（彼が蕎麦を打てるとは驚きです。）
・My boss always says (that) I should have more confidence.
（私はもっと自信を持つべきだと、上司がいつも言うんです。）

※ that の前文（主文と呼ばれる）の動詞としてよく使われるのが、think（思う）、know（知っている）、hope（希望する）、feel（感じる）、say（言う）、explain（説明する）、admit（認める）など。

■ from a(n) ～ perspective（～の観点から）の決まり文句は、これに続く発言を方向付ける表現です。同時に、聞き手の理解を助ける役割を果たします。

・I'm writing a report on the silk industry in *Gunma* <u>from a historical perspective</u>.
（群馬の絹産業について歴史的な観点からレポートを書いています。）

※ historical と historic は、どちらも「歴史的な」という意味ですが、historical が歴史に関する事実を言い表すのに対して、historic は特に重要な歴史上の出来事について述べる場合に用いられます。例えば、
The *Tokyo* Olympic Games in 1964 represented a <u>historic</u> event for the Japanese at the time.
（1964年の東京オリンピックは当時の日本人にとって歴史的な出来事でした。）

・<u>From a medical perspective</u>, the efficacy of hot springs has been pointed out.
（医学的な見地から、温泉の効能は指摘されてきました。）
・<u>From an objective perspective</u>, *Gunma* Prefecture is blessed with tourism resources, but people do not seem to notice it.
（客観的に見て、群馬県は観光資源に恵まれていますが、人々はそれに気付いてないようです。）

同種の決まり文句として、from a(n) ～ viewpoint, from ～ point of view（～の観点から）も有用です。

・They discussed this matter <u>from a different viewpoint</u>.
（彼らは異なる観点から、この問題について議論しました。）
・<u>From my point of view</u>, the people in *Gunma* are conservative.
（私の観点から、群馬の人々は保守的です。）

Tomioka Silk Mill

5

富岡製糸場編

5-13 養蚕と群馬の女性
Sericulture and women in *Gunma*

Mayuko: And one more thing. <u>I want you to be aware of</u> the significance of the sericulture for women in *Gunma*.

Visitor: All right.

Mayuko: The sericulture assured women's income in *Gunma*. <u>In other words</u>, women were able to gain a stable income by reeling silk from cocoons or weaving cloth with a machine at home. Women in *Gunma* were hard workers as well.

Visitor: <u>That means that</u> women in *Gunma* had a strong financial influence because of the sericulture.

Mayuko: As expressed in the saying "*Joshu no kakaadenka to karakkaze*," which is translated as "bossy wives and cold dry wind in *Gunma*," *Gunma* has been well-known for its strong women and strong wind.

Visitor: That's interesting. A husband is supposed to be the boss of his family in Japan.

Mayuko: Well, *Gunma* was an exception. Women were strong and tough due to the sericulture. They were able to support their family financially.

Visitor: It sounds like women are very independent in *Gunma*. You should be proud of yourself for being one of them.

Mayuko: But strong-minded women are rather disliked in Japan.

Visitor: Things change as time passes.

Vocabulary

be aware of	～に気付く	significance	意義、重要性
assure	～を保証する	in other words	言い換えると
stable income	安定した収入	weave cloth	布を織る
financial influence	経済的な影響	※ financially	経済的に
be translated as	～と訳される		
bossy	いばりたがる、親分ぶる	※ boss	親分、上司
be known for	～で知られている	※ be known as	～として知られている

be supposed to	〜であるはずである		
exception	例外	tough	たくましい、タフな
independent	自立した	be proud of	〜を誇りに思う
strong-minded	意思の強い	dislike	〜を嫌う

📖 English Points

■ want someone to do something（誰かに何かをしてもらいたいと思う）は、ある人に to に続く動詞（原型）の動作・行為をしてもらいたいという願望を表します。

・I want you to come with me.（あなたに一緒に来てほしいの。）
・They want me to join the band, but I'm busy working part-time.
　（彼らは僕にバンドに入ってほしいと思っているけど、僕はバイトで忙しい。）

この文型で使える動詞には、want の他に ask, tell, expect, advise, urge などがあります。

・I asked my English teacher to pronounce the word again.
　（英語の先生にその単語をもう一度発音するようにお願いしました。）
・The doctor told me to rest for a few days.
　（医者は私に２、３日安静にするように言いました。）
・My parents expect me to become a civil servant.
　（両親は私に公務員になることを期待しています。）
・She advised me not to go on a shopping spree.
　（彼女は私に爆買いしないように忠告しました。）
・He urged me to buy stock in that company.
　（彼は私にあの会社の株を買うようにしきりにすすめました。）

■ in other words（言い換えると）は、わかりやすく説明を加える際に用いる慣用句です。

・Bob lacks motivation. In other words, he is lazy.
　（ボブはやる気がない。別の言い方をすると、彼は怠け者です。）
・Naomi often gets lost. In other words, she has no sense of direction.
　（ナオミはしばしば道に迷います。言い換えれば、彼女は方向音痴です。）

■ This/That means that〜（これ／それは〜を意味する）は、「つまり」の説明を導く表現です。

・It has rained every day, with few hours of sunshine. This means that the price of vegetables will rise.
　（このところ雨続きで日照時間が少ない。このことは野菜の価格が上がることを意味します。）
・It has been snowing since this morning. This means that the traffic will soon start to become paralyzed.
　（今朝から雪が降り続いています。これは、すぐに交通がマヒすることを意味します。）

5-14 お手洗いの場所を説明する

Explaining a restroom's location

Visitor: Excuse me, but I need to go to the restroom. Could you tell me where it is?

Mayuko: There is one near the infirmary. Go back to the Brunat House, and it will be on your right.

Visitor: The problem is, there was a long line a while ago, wasn't there?

Mayuko: If there is a crowd, please use the restroom next to the Silk-reeling plant.

Visitor: Thanks. I'll do so.

Vocabulary

restroom	お手洗い、トイレ
infirmary	診療所
a while ago	ちょっと前に
crowd	人混み、群衆

English Points

■ toilet（トイレ）は直接的な言葉なので、restroom または bathroom が婉曲表現として一般的です。加えて、「トイレをお借りできますか」は、May I <u>use</u> the bathroom? と表現します。つまり、トイレは使わせてもらうものという認識です。borrow は、持ち運び可能なものを借りる場合です。例えば、Can I borrow your pen?（あなたのペンをお借りできますか）のように用います。

第6章　おすすめパワースポット

【周辺観光編】

Sightseeing Spots

6-1 貫前神社はユニーク！
The *Nukisaki* Shrine is unique!

Tower gate of the *Nukisaki* Shrine
(貫前神社楼門)

Main hall
(本殿)

Mayuko: Are you interested in *Shinto* shrines and Buddhist temples?

Visitor: Of course. It's one of the reasons for my trips to see them. Are there any shrines or temples near here?

Mayuko: Sure. There are many shrines and temples scattered around *Tomioka* City and its surroundings. The people in this area have worshiped at them since ancient times. They are the heart and soul of the Japanese people.

Visitor: I don't belong to those religions, but I like seeing *Shinto* shrines and Buddhist temples. They make me feel calm.

Mayuko: Then, you may be interested in visiting the *Nukisaki* Shrine in *Tomioka* City. It's an old *Shinto* shrine with a long history, and it's near here.

Visitor: How do I get there?

Mayuko: You get off at *Joshu Ichinomiya* Station, which is the third stop from *Joshu Tomioka* Station. Then, it takes about fifteen minutes on foot.

Visitor: Sounds easy. But it may take time because the trains don't come very often on that line.

Mayuko: The easiest way is to hail a taxi. It takes around ten minutes to get there.

Visitor: I'm sure that the train fare is more reasonable, but I can save time if I take a taxi.

Mayuko: You can get to the outer gate by taxi. From there, go down the stairs to the tower gate, and you can visit the main hall through the tower gate, <u>which is an unusual form of worship</u>.

Visitor: Now, I want to visit that shrine. Where is the taxi stand?

Mayuko: This way. If there are no taxis, I can call one on the phone.

Visitor: Thank you for your help.

Mayuko: Sure, anytime.

Vocabulary

unique	独特な、珍しい
be interested in	～に興味を持つ
(Shinto) shrines	（神道）神社
(Buddhist) temples	（仏教）寺院
(be) scattered around	～に散在している
surrounding	周辺、周囲
worship	参拝する　（名詞）参拝
since ancient times	昔から、太古より
heart and soul	心の拠り所
belong to	～に所属する
religion	宗教
feel calm	（心が）落ち着く
hail a taxi	タクシーを呼び止める
save time	時間を節約する
outer gate	総門
tower gate	楼門
taxi stand	タクシー乗り場

👉 English Points

■ The people in this area have worshiped at them since ancient times.（地域の人々は昔からそれらに参拝してきました）は、過去から現在までの状態の継続を表す現在完了形（have[has] ＋ 動詞の過去分詞）の文です。

・Sarah has been ill in bed for two weeks.
（サラは 2 週間ずっと病気で寝込んでいます。）
・I have known *Isamu* since we were children.
（子どもの頃からずっとイサムを知っています。）

現在完了形は、上述の「継続」の他に、過去から行ってきた動作の「完了または結果」と現在までの「経験」を言い表します。

・We have just finished breakfast. （ちょうど朝食を終えたところです。）
・He has gone to Italy to study architecture.
（彼は建築の勉強のためにイタリアへ行ってしまいました。）

・Mr. *Kimura* has donated blood several times.
（木村さんは何回も献血しています。）
・Have you ever done a bungee jump?
（バンジージャンプをやったことはありますか。）

■ 非制限用法（〜, which〜）における関係代名詞 which は、前文全体を先行詞として受けることが特徴です。

・Annie tried to chase Tony on the sandy beach, which she found difficult.
（アニーは砂浜でトニーを追いかけようとしましたが、難しいとわかりました。）
・I bake bread every Sunday, which I enjoy as a pastime.
（毎週日曜日にはパンを焼きますが、私はそれを余暇として楽しみます。）

Tips:

■ The *Ichinomiya Nukisaki* Shrine is about ten minutes by car from the World Heritage Site the *Tomioka* Silk Mill, and it's distinguished by being more than fourteen hundred years old.
一之宮貫前神社は世界遺産・富岡製糸場から車で約10分の地点にあって、1400年以上の歴史を有する由緒ある神社です。

■ As people enter the approach road, a long staircase continues, and they can see a big *torii gate*. A *torii* is a gate to a shrine and also a symbol of the division between worldly and sacred places. As people go through the *torii*, they realize that they become naturally sacred through the majestic atmosphere in the precincts.
参道へ入ると長い階段が続き、大きな鳥居が見えてきます。鳥居は神社の入り口であり、また俗世と聖地をわける象徴でもあります。人々は鳥居をくぐると、境内の荘厳な雰囲気により、おのずと神聖な気持ちになっていくのを実感します。

- The main hall and some other buildings of the *Nukisaki* Shrine are cultural properties of national importance.
  貫前神社の本殿と他のいくつかの建物は国の重要文化財（国指定重要文化財）です。

- The *Nukisaki* Shrine is dedicated to two gods. One of the gods has been referred to as a guardian deity of the local sericulture.
  貫前神社は二人の神様を祭っています。その一人はその土地の養蚕の守護神です。

- Huge trees estimated to be one thousand years old grow around the shrine, which creates splendid scenes.
  神社の周囲には、推定樹齢千年の巨木が立ち茂り、すばらしい景観をつくり出しています。

- An admission fee is charged when you visit the treasure hall, called the *Houbutsu-kan*, at the shrine, but you can appreciate the national cultural assets.
  境内の「宝物館」は有料ですが、国の文化財を鑑賞することができます。

（参考資料：「貫前神社」『群馬県の歴史散歩』pp.95-96.・他）

6-2 城下町小幡はカッコイイ！
Castle town *Obata* is cool!

Rakusan-en
（楽山園）

The cemetery of the *Oda* clan
（織田宗家七代の墓）

Irrigation canal
（かんがい用水路）

Mayuko: One of my favorite spots is the castle town *Obata* in *Kanra-machi*, a town neighboring *Tomioka* City.

Visitor: Because a castle is there?

Mayuko: The castle is not there anymore, but the ruins of the castle and a splendid Japanese garden called *Rakusan-en* remain. I can enjoy a tea break there. A staff member serves tea that is prepared in the same way as in the Japanese tea ceremony.

Visitor: Are the admission and the tea free?

Mayuko: There is a charge for both, but it's reasonable.

Visitor: Hmm. A *samurai* lord would enjoy the garden while enjoying a tea ceremony, I guess. It's not bad to experience such a feeling, is it?

Mayuko: Sure, why not? It is a place where anyone can feel very relaxed. Also, in the area around the garden, Japanese-style buildings of that period are preserved by the community.

Visitor: You mean the buildings remain in which the *samurai* lived?

Mayuko: Oh, yes. You can look around *samurai* residences and gardens <u>that</u> have been maintained by their descendants.

Visitor: That's cool.

Mayuko: I really like the atmosphere of the *Edo* era in the district. The streets are lined with stylish houses, which takes me back in time.

Visitor: It seems to <u>be worth a visit.</u> And it's near here ...

Mayuko: I'm sure you'll like that.

Vocabulary

castle town	城下町
favorite	お気に入りの
neighbor	～に隣接する
ruin	（建物の）跡、廃墟
splendid	立派な、壮麗な
remain	残存する
tea ceremony	茶道
samurai lord	殿様
experience	経験する
feel relaxed	ゆったりした気分になる
preserve	～を保存する
samurai residences	武家屋敷
maintain	～を維持する
descendant	子孫
district	地区
stylish	粋な、かっこいい
worth	～の価値がある

English Points

■ It's not bad to experience such a feeling, is it?（そういう気分を味わうのも悪くないですよね）は、念を押す、または確認を取る表現で、付加疑問文と呼ばれます。

・You <u>like</u> sweets, <u>don't you</u>? （甘いものはお好きですよね。）
　　　　　　　　　　➡ 前節が肯定なら否定が続く

Sightseeing Spots

6

周辺観光編

- Mr. *Tanabe* <u>is</u> such a gentleman, <u>isn't he</u>?　（田辺氏はかなりの紳士ですよね。）
　　　　　　　　　➡ 前節が肯定なら否定が続く

- You<u>'re not</u> busy now, <u>are you</u>?　（今、あなたは忙しくないですよね。）
　　　　　　　　➡ 前節が否定なら肯定が続く

- The children <u>didn't go out</u> last night, <u>did they</u>?　（子どもたちは昨夜は外出
　　　　　　　　　　　　　　　　　　　　　しませんでしたよね。）
　　　　　　　　➡ 前節が否定なら肯定が続く

■　It is ～ that [where, who, which...]～.（～なのは～です）は、強調構文と呼ばれ、that の前の語句を強調します。例えば、*Satoko* visited *Kamakura* with *Ichiro* last Saturday. のどの部分を強調するのかによって、次の（下線部を強調する）構文をつくることができます。

- It was *Satoko* that [who] visited *Kamakura* with *Ichiro* last Saturday.
（先週土曜日に一郎と鎌倉を訪れたのはさと子でした。）

- It was *Kamakura* that [where] *Satoko* visited with *Ichiro* last Saturday.
（先週土曜日にさと子が一郎と訪れたのは鎌倉でした。）

- It was *Ichiro* that [whom] *Satoko* visited *Kamakura* with last Saturday.
（先週土曜日にさと子がともに鎌倉を訪れたのは一郎でした。）

- It was <u>last Saturday</u> that [when] *Satoko* visited *Kamakura* with *Ichiro*.
（さと子が一郎と鎌倉を訪れたのは先週土曜日でした。）

■　関係代名詞は先行詞と格によって決まります。which は先行詞がモノの場合に用いられる関係代名詞です。先行詞とは、関係代名詞の前にくる名詞です。先行詞が関係代名詞に導かれる節でどのような働き（主語、所有代名詞、目的語）をするのかによって関係代名詞の格が決まります（先行詞が人の場合の who/whom については、次節 6-3. を参照）。

先行詞	主　格		所有格	目的格	
人	who	that	whose	whom [who]	that
物・動物	which		whose [of which]	which	

- This is the pearl necklace <u>which</u> was given to me by my parents on my twentieth birthday.
（これは私の20歳の誕生日に両親によって贈られた真珠のネックレスです。）

・This is the pearl necklace *(which) my parents gave me on my twentieth birthday.
（これは私の20歳の誕生日に両親が贈ってくれた真珠のネックレスです。）
　　*目的格の場合、関係代名詞は省略可能

■ 前置詞はしばしば関係代名詞の前に移動し、in/at ＋ which は where（関係副詞）に置き換えることができます。

・This is a river <u>in which</u> [=where] my father and I used to fish.
（ここは父と私がかつて釣りをした川です。）

・The supermarket <u>at which</u> [=where] my mother often shops is near the station.
（母がよく買い物をするスーパーは駅の近くにあります。）

■ （be) worth a visit は「一度は訪れる価値がある」の意です。加えて、（be) worth V-ing（～する価値がある）は、見解や判断を伝える際の決まり文句です。

・This book was a bit difficult for me, but it was worth reading.
（この本は私にとっては少々難しかったですが、読む価値がありました。）

・Since this scale also shows body fat, muscle rate, and bone quantity, it is worth buying for health management.
（この体重計は、体脂肪・筋肉率・骨量も表示しますから、健康管理のために購入する価値があります。）

・Considering the risk of passive smoke, I don't think it's worth discussing the rights of smokers.
（受動喫煙のリスクを考えると、喫煙者の権利について議論する価値はないと私は考えます。）

Tips:

■ *Obata* was ruled by the *Oda* clan for approximately 150 years, from the first *Nobukatsu* to the eighth generation *Nobukuni*. *Nobukatsu* was the second son of *Nobunaga Oda*, who aimed to reunify Japan but harmed himself at the *Honnō-ji* Temple. The graves from *Nobukatsu* to the seventh generation *Nobuyoshi* remain as "the cemetery of the *Oda* clan" in the *Sofuku-ji* Temple.
小幡（おばた）は、初代信雄（のぶかつ）から八代目の信邦（のぶくに）まで約150年にわたり、織田氏によって治められました。信雄は、天下統一を目指しながらも本能寺の変で自害した織田信長の次男です。信雄から七代目の信富（のぶよし）までの墓が、「織田宗家七代の墓」として崇福寺に残っています。

■ *Rakusan-en*, a fine landscape garden, was constructed by the *Oda* clan in the early *Edo* era. The garden has the same features as the *Katsura Rikyu* in *Kyoto*, such as arranged ponds and teahouses, and was made by employing the surrounding mountains as a landscape.
洗練された庭園、楽山園は江戸時代初期に織田氏によってつくられました。その庭園は池や茶屋を配するなど、京都の桂離宮と同じ特色を有し、また周囲の山々を借景として取り込む

方式でつくられています。

- Irrigation canals are set up around the castle town *Obata* to draw water from the *Ogawa* channel, which shows the people's great technical skills and technological know-how at the time.
  城下町小幡には、雄川堰（おがわぜき）から水を引くための用水路が張り巡らされており、当時の高度な技術をうかがい知ることができます。

- At the *Kanra-machi* History and Folklore Museum, historic materials and artifacts conveying the sericulture are displayed.
  甘楽町歴史民俗資料館には、養蚕を伝える史料や遺物が展示されています。

(参考資料：「小幡陣屋」『群馬県の歴史散歩』pp.91-93.・他)

6-3 群馬県立自然史博物館
The *Gunma* Museum of Natural History

The *Gunma* Museum of Natural History
（群馬県立自然史博物館）

Full-size model of a Tyrannosaurus
（ティランノサウルス実物大模型）

Skeleton of a Camarasaurus
（カマラサウルス全身骨格）

Mayuko: The *Gunma* Museum of Natural History is a wonderful place for someone who is interested in Earth, nature, or life.

Visitor: Well, who isn't? These are eternal themes for humans.

Mayuko: In particular, it is a good place for children to learn while having fun. Their displays are really exciting, even for adults.

Visitor: For example?

Mayuko: Well, a full-sized Tyrannosaurus raises its head and makes a loud noise.

Visitor: A Tyrannosaurus … you mean a dinosaur?

Mayuko: Of course it's a model, but it looks so real and powerful. I heard that some kids burst into tears.

Visitor: I would be scared, too, if a full-sized Tyrannosaurus glared at me.

Mayuko: Hahaha. Also, the whole body frame of a Camarasaurus is displayed there. According to the museum staff, there are few museums in the world that have a skeleton of a Camarasaurus in a nearly complete state.

Visitor: That's great!

Mayuko: Don't miss it.

Vocabulary

Earth	地球
nature	自然
eternal theme	永遠のテーマ
humans	人類、人間
in particular	特に
exciting	刺激的な、興奮する
full-sized Tyrannosaurus	実物大の *ティランノサウルス　*ティラノサウルスの学名
raise one's head	頭をもたげる
make a loud noise	大きな鳴き声を上げる
dinosaur	恐竜
burst into tears	泣き出す
be scared	怯える
glare at	～をにらみ付ける
whole body frame of a Camarasaurus	カマラサウルスの全身骨格
in the world	世界中で
skeleton	骨格、骸骨

English Points

■ 先行詞が人の場合は who, whom, that の関係代名詞が用いられます。who（主格）に対して、whom [who]（目的格）は省略される傾向にあります。

- Mr. *Oyama* is our coworker <u>who</u> is trusted the most in the office.
（大山さんは職場で最も信頼されている私たちの同僚です。）
- Mr. *Oyama* is our coworker (whom [who]) we trust the most in the office.
（大山さんは私たちが職場で最も信頼する同僚です。）

■ 従位接続詞 while（～する間に、～しながら、一方で）に導かれる節は、主節を補足する役目を担います。

- *Wataru* empties his mind while (he is) jogging.
（ジョギングしている間、ワタルは無心です。）
- I enjoyed the conversation we had while (we were) taking a walk.
（私は散歩をしながら会話を楽しみました。）
- I appreciated their kindness, while I felt it burdensome.
（私は彼らの親切に感謝する一方で、負担にも感じました。）

Tips:

- The *Gunma* Museum of Natural History is exciting for someone who is interested in the Earth, nature, or life. Natural history includes the history of the Earth and the evolution of life. You can follow the Earth's history for 4.6 [four point six] billion years and its formation to the present, and you can see the evolutionary processes of life. You can also discover that *Gunma* has a lot of nature.

  地球・自然・生命に興味のある方には、群馬県立自然史博物館は胸が高なります。自然史とは、地球の歴史や生命の進化の歩みのことです。地球誕生から現在まで、46億年の歴史をたどり、生命の進化を見て取ることができます。また、群馬の自然の豊かさを発見するでしょう。

- In addition to the exhibition that recreates the nature of *Gunma* in the hall, the *Gunma* Museum of Natural History has unparalleled exhibits, such as the complete real skeleton of a Camarasaurus and a moving model of a full-sized Tyrannosaurus. The whole body frame of a dinosaur measuring fifteen meters in length stimulates visitors' imagination, and the appearance of a full-sized dinosaur raising its head is so lifelike that it makes children take a step back.

  群馬県立自然史博物館は、群馬の自然を館内に再現する展示に加え、カマラサウルスの実物全身骨格やティランノサウルスの実物大の動く模型など、他に類を見ない展示が行われています。全長15mの恐竜の全身骨格標本は、想像力を刺激しますし、実物大の恐竜が頭をもたげる姿は子どもたちを後ずさりさせるほど迫力があります。

- An old bone from an animal was discovered on the grounds of *Kamikuroiwa*, *Tomioka* City, in 1797. Later, it was determined to be a fossil of the large-antlered elk (Sinomegaceros yabei). This fossil is said to be the oldest fossil discovery in Japan. In other words, modern archaeology in Japan began in *Kamikuroiwa*. That is why the *Gunma* Museum of Natural History was built at that location.

  1797年に富岡市上黒岩の地で、動物の古い骨が発見されました。その後の研究によって、ヤベオオツノジカの化石であることがわかりました。これが日本最古の化石発掘であると言われています。言い換えると、日本における近代考古学が上黒岩から始まったということです。その経緯で、その地に群馬県立自然史博物館が建設されたのです。

- When visiting the *Gunma* Museum of Natural History, the nearest station is *Joshu Nanokaichi* Station on the *Joshin* line. The trip to the museum, located in *Momijidaira Sougou* Park, from the station takes about twenty-five minutes on foot and fifteen minutes by taxi from *Joshu Tomioka* Station (taxies are not available at *Joshu Nanokaichi* Station).

  群馬県立自然史博物館へ行く場合、最寄り駅は上信線の上州七日市駅です。もみじ平総合公園内にある博物館へは、駅から徒歩で約25分、また上州富岡駅からタクシーで15分程度です（上州七日市駅ではタクシーは利用できません）。

(参考資料：『群馬県立自然史博物館　総合案内』／『群馬県立自然史博物館　展示ガイドブック』)

6-4 アドバイスをする――〔1〕
Giving advice：〔1〕

Isobe Onsen
（磯部温泉）

Japan's oldest *onsen* mark
（日本最古の温泉記号）

Ryokan
（旅館）

Isobe senbei
（磯部せんべい）

Visitor: Mayuko, may I ask you one more question?

Mayuko: Sure. I'll be happy to answer as many questions as you have.

Visitor: I think I mentioned this before. Another reason for my visit to *Gunma* is to experience *onsen*. <u>Do you happen to know</u> any good *onsen* resorts?

Mayuko: Gunma is well-known for its *onsens*, so there are many of these types of resorts. <u>What type of *onsen* resort do you prefer?</u> A famous one even if it's far away, or one that is near here?

Visitor: Let me see...

Mayuko: Well, *Ikaho*, *Kusatsu*, and *Shima* are well-known *onsen* resorts. But those are located in the central and northern parts of *Gunma*. I mean, it takes time to get there.

Visitor: How long does it take?

Mayuko: It takes <u>around</u> two hours to get to *Ikaho*, and three hours to *Kusatsu* from here.

Visitor: That may be a little far for me.

Mayuko: Then, I'd recommend the *Shimonita Onsen* or the *Isobe Onsen* in *Annaka* City near *Tomioka*. If you like a quiet atmosphere with rustic charm, these *onsen* resorts may suit you.

Visitor: Sounds great.

Mayuko: To visit the *Shimonita Onsen*, the nearest station is *Shimonita* Station, which is the last stop on the *Joshin* line. The trip takes <u>approximately</u> thirty minutes by train. From there, you can take a taxi to the *onsen*.

Visitor: That's not bad.

Mayuko: And the *Isobe Onsen* is located in *Annaka* City. The nearest station is *Isobe* Station. The trip takes <u>about</u> ten minutes on the JR *Shin-etsu* line from *Takasaki* Station.

Visitor: That's not bad, either. Which one do I want to visit?

Mayuko: It's an important decision to make. <u>Why don't you check them out on your smartphone?</u>

Visitor: That's a good idea! Let's see ...

Vocabulary

be happy to V	喜んで〜します
mention	〜をちょっと言う、〜に言及する
rustic charm	田舎の魅力、ひなびた趣き
suit	〜に合う、〜に適合する
important	重要な
decision	決断　　※ make a decision　　決断をする

English Points

■ Do you happen to know 〜?（もしかして［ひょっとして］、〜をご存知ですか）は、情報を求める言い回しです。Do you know 〜? よりも丁寧な表現として使われます。

- Do you happen to know where there is a good Japanese restaurant around here?
  （ひょっとして、この辺のおいしい和食のレストランを知っていますか。）
- Do you happen to know anyone who can teach flower arrangement?
  （もしかして、どなたか生け花を教えられる方をご存知ですか。）

■ What type [kind, sort] of 〜 do you prefer? は、相手の好みを確認する表現です。レンタカー店・レストラン・土産店などで有用な言い回しです。

- What type of car do you prefer?（どのようなタイプの車をお望みですか。）
  —— I prefer a *Toyota* Corolla.（トヨタ・カローラが好みです。）

- What kind of dressing would you like?
  （どのような種類のドレッシングがお好きですか。）
  —— I'd like Italian.（イタリアンをお願いします。）

- What sort of souvenir are you looking for?
  （どのような種類のお土産をお探しですか。）
  —— I'm looking for something to remember my trip by.
    （旅の記念になるものを探しています。）

■ about, around, approximately（大体、おおよそ、約）は、わずかなニュアンスの違いはあるものの、意味を同じくする語です。about と around は交換可能ですし、approximately に関しては、少し改まった言い方をする際に用います。

■ Why don't you 〜?（〜してはいかがでしょうか）は、提案をする際の表現です。

- Why don't you try on that jacket?
  （そのジャケットを試着してみてはいかがですか。）
- Why don't you taste a sample and decide if you want to buy it or not?
  （試食をしてみて、買うか否かを決めるのはいかがでしょうか。）

  Why don't we 〜? の場合は、「（自分も含めて）〜してはいかがでしょうか」の意味合いになります。

- Why don't we try eel *kabayaki* for lunch?
  （昼食にウナギのかば焼きに挑戦してみるのはいかがでしょうか。）
- It's already 8 o'clock. Why don't we call it a day?
  （すでに 8 時が過ぎています。今日はこれで終わりにしてはいかがでしょうか。）

Tips:

- *Isobe Onsen* has no bustling area; instead, it is a hideaway *onsen* resort blessed with high-quality hot spring water. *Isobe* is the birthplace of Japan's oldest *onsen* mark (♨), and it is said to be the birthplace of a Japanese classic story, "The Tongue-cut Sparrow." This chidren's story is widely known in Japan.

  磯部（いそべ）にはにぎやかな温泉街はありませんが、効能の高い温泉水に恵まれた、隠れ家的な温泉地です。磯部は日本最古の温泉記号（♨）発祥の地であり、また「舌切り雀」伝説発祥の地であるとされています。「舌切り雀」は日本では広く知られているおとぎ話です。

- Although it is called *Isobe senbei* (rice cracker in English), rice is not a raw material. It is a thin, grilled cracker with the taste of a hot spring, made by adding mineral water to wheat flour and sugar and baking them individually. It is a confection with a simple flavor that has been handed down since the end of the *Edo* era, and the crispy texture is still popular today.

  磯部せんべいと呼ばれているものの、お米が原料ではありません。小麦粉と砂糖に鉱泉水を加えて、一枚ずつ焼き上げる方法でつくられる、温泉の味がする薄焼きせんべいです。江戸末期から伝わる、素朴な味わいの菓子ですが、サクサクの食感は今日も人気です。

（参考資料：「あんなか観光ガイド」）

6-5 アドバイスをする——〔2〕
Giving advice：〔2〕

Shimonita Station
（下仁田駅）

Arafune cold storage
（荒船風穴）

Kouzu dairy farm
（神津牧場）

Visitor: All these photographs are nice. I can't make up my mind. <u>Which one do you think is better?</u>

Mayuko: If you are interested in seeing the oldest Japanese *onsen* symbol, it's in *Isobe Onsen*.

Visitor: The oldest Japanese *onsen* symbol?

Mayuko: Haven't you seen the symbol of steam rising from a bowl? 〈Drawing the symbol (♨) on a piece of scratch paper〉 It looks like this …

Visitor: To me, <u>this symbol seems to represent a restaurant</u> that serves hot food.

Mayuko: Foreigners may misinterpret the symbol as a restaurant, but it is the *onsen* symbol, and it has been used for more than three hundred and fifty years, since the *Edo* era.

Visitor: That means, I can see the oldest one if I visit *Isobe Onsen*?

Mayuko: That's right. And you can also enjoy the *onsen* that is known as the birthplace of the symbol.

Visitor: Mmm.

Mayuko: You don't seem to be impressed. In that case, I recommend *Shimonita Onsen*, because it takes only five minutes by taxi from *Shimonita* Station, and *Arafune-fūketsu* is located in *Shimonita*, too.

Visitor: *Arafune* ...? What's that?

Mayuko: It's a cold storage facility where they kept silkworm eggs. It is a place where natural cold air comes through the crevices of the rocks. By making use of the cold air, they were able to delay the hatching of the eggs. Increasing the number of hatching times increased the production of raw silk.

Visitor: Now I remember, it's one of the sites related to the *Tomioka* Silk Mill.

Mayuko: That's right. Would you like to visit the *Arafune* cold storage facility and enjoy a local *onsen*?

Visitor: Sounds good! How do I get there?

Mayuko: You can take a shared taxi from *Shimonita* Station. The taxi fare should be reasonable. You need to make a reservation, though. I'll help you with that if you want me to.

Visitor: I'd really appreciate that.

Mayuko: There is a cattle farm near the *Arafune* cold storage facility. It's the *Kouzu* dairy farm, one of the oldest Western-style farms in Japan. You can rest there, have fresh soft-serve ice cream, and see a cow parade.

Visitor: A cow parade?

Mayuko: Yeah. The cattle that were put out to pasture are gathered together and led to the barns in the afternoon, which is really like a parade.

Visitor: It could be worth visiting *Shimonita*.

Vocabulary

make up one's mind	決断する	scratch paper	メモ用紙
misinterpret	～を間違って解釈する、～を誤解する		
be impressed	感銘を受ける、感動する		
storage facility	貯蔵施設、倉庫	crevice	裂け目、割れ目
make use of	～を利用する	delay	～を遅らせる
increase	～を増やす	cattle farm	牧場
dairy farm	酪農場	take a rest	休憩する
put cattle out to pasture	牛を放牧する	lead to	～へ導く
barn	納屋、牛小屋		

English Points

■ Which one do you think is better?（あなたはどちらがよいと思いますか）は、2 つを比較して相手に意見を求める際の表現です。Which one is better?（どちらが いいですか）に do you think が挿入された言い回しです。

・You can visit the *Gunma* Safari Park and try dishes with crocodile meat and/or ostrich meat. Or you can go to *Konnyaku* Park and enjoy a free buffet with all types of *konnyaku* dishes. Which one do you think is better?
（群馬サファリパークを訪れて、ワニ肉やダチョウ肉の料理を試すことができま す。あるいは、こんにゃくパークへ行くと、あらゆる種類のこんにゃく料理バ イキングを無料で楽しめます。どちらがよいと思いますか。）

3つ以上を比較して意見を求める場合は、Which one do you think is the best [most]?（あなたはどれが一番いいと思いますか）の言い回しを使います。

・Seeing a *Kabuki* play, making pottery with a wheel, enjoying *hanami* and the tea ceremony, taking a *Toyosu* tour, and so forth. Which one [activity] do you think is the best?
（歌舞伎見物、ろくろを使った陶芸、お花見茶会、豊洲ツアーなど、あなたはど れ［どの活動］が一番いいと思いますか。）

■ seem の使い方については、第1章（1-8.: p.21）で既習していますが、ここでは sound, look との違いについて説明を加えます。どれも、「～らしい」の意味で断 定しない柔らかな言い回しとして使用されますが、厳密にはそれぞれニュアンス が異なります。

・He <u>sounds</u> like a nice person.（彼はいい人らしいです。）
　　※聴覚的な要素（言葉遣い、口調など）から判断

・He <u>looks</u> like a nice person.（彼はいい人みたいです。）
　　※視覚的な要素から判断

・He <u>seems</u> like a nice person.（彼はいい人らしいです。）
　　※総合的な要素から判断した個人的な印象、主観性の強い表現

6-6 高崎のバス観光をすすめる──〔1〕
Recommending a bus tour in *Takasaki*:〔1〕

Takasaki Byakue Dai-kannon
（高崎白衣大観音）

Main hall of *Jigen-in*
（慈眼院本堂）

Mayuko: There are many sightseeing spots and tourist attractions in *Takasaki* City. Since bullet trains make stops at *Takasaki* Station, it might be a good idea to visit some of those places. You can go to some of those places by bus.

Visitor: That reminds me, when I came to *Takasaki*, I saw a <u>huge</u> white statue from the window of the bullet train. I was wondering what it was.

Mayuko: That <u>giant</u> white statue is the symbol of *Takasaki* City. The official name is *Takasaki Byakue Dai-kannon*, but it's called *Kannon-sama* in the region. It was created in the hope of peace and prosperity for *Takasaki* City in 1936.

Visitor: Is it a Buddha statue?

Mayuko: Uh-huh. *Kannon*, which is translated as "Goddess of Mercy" in English, is one of the saints of Buddhism who saves people and all living creatures.

Visitor: <u>How tall is it?</u>

Mayuko: The statue is 41.8 [forty-one point eight] meters high, and made from reinforced concrete. A visitor can go inside the statue.

Visitor: It's taller than the Great Buddha of *Nara*!

Mayuko: The Great Buddha of *Nara* is approximately fifteen meters tall, so the *Takasaki Byakue Dai-kannon* is a lot taller than that.

Visitor: That huge? I think I'd be interested in taking a closer look. How do I get there?

Mayuko: The *Kannon* statue is at the top of *Kannon-yama*. You take the number 13 or 14 *Gururin* bus at the west exit of *Takasaki* Station. It goes to *Kannon-yama*. The trip takes twenty-five minutes by bus.

Visitor: The number 13 or 14 *Gururin* bus ...

Mayuko: Uh-huh. *Gururin* buses stand out because of their colorful illustrations on the sides. The bus fare is 200 [two hundred] yen, a flat rate.

Visitor: I pay 200 [two hundred] yen no matter where I go. That's great!

Mayuko: You'll feel calm with the gentle figure of *Kannon-sama* watching over the region. In addition, at the top of *Kannon-yama*, you can view the entire area of *Takasaki* City.

Visitor: It must be one of the scenic spots.

Mayuko: *Kannon-yama* is spectacular with the cherry blossoms in the spring and the leaves changing color in the autumn. It has a superb view year-round.

Vocabulary

tourist attraction	観光名所
bullet train	新幹線　　※直訳すると弾丸（のように速い）列車
remind	〜に思い出させる
official name	正式名称
Buddha statue	仏像
saint	聖人
Buddhism	仏教
living creature	生命体、生き物
reinforced concrete	鉄筋コンクリート
take a close look	近くで見る、もっとよく見る
stand out	目立つ

scenic spot	絶景スポット
cherry blossoms	桜の花
superb	素晴らしい、飛び切り上等な
year-round	一年中、一年を通して

🗣 English Points

■ 「大きい」を表す語彙は、いくつかあります。極端に大きいものを指す場合、huge, enormous, giant が用いられ、grand には「りっぱな、雄大な」のニュアンスが加わります。

big	…………	数量・形状・規模などの物理的サイズ。存在・功績、重要度。
		※ fat（太った）、overweight（肥満の）、obese（太りすぎの）といったネガティブな表現を避けたい時などにも、big が使われる。
large	………	数量・形状・規模などの物理的サイズ。big よりもフォーマルな語。
great	………	数量・形状・規模などの物理的サイズ。存在・功績。驚きや感嘆を含む。
grand	………	物理的に大きく、りっぱな、壮大な。
huge	………	物理的にとても大きい、巨大な。
enormous	…	巨大な、程度や規模が並外れて大きい。
giant	………	巨大な、けた外れに大きな。 ※名詞の場合は「巨人」の意
gigantic	……	巨大な、けた外れに大きな。 ※ giant よりも口語的
massive	……	巨大な、非常に重い。
immense	…	莫大な、計り知れない。
vast	…………	広大な、広漠とした、膨大な。

- Godzilla is a huge [gigantic] monster. （ゴジラは巨大な怪物です。）
- There is a huge [vast] park in the middle of New York City.
  （ニューヨーク市のど真ん中に広大な公園があります。）

■ How tall 〜? は、身長を尋ねる際の表現です。tall は〈下から上まで〉の「高さ」を意識した語です。これに対して、How high 〜? という場合、high は〈空間的な位置〉の「高さ」を意味します。

〈高い〉 〈低い〉　　　　　　　　　　　　　　 *印は、どちらでも表現可能
tall ⇔ short： 身長、樹木、像、*建物、*山など。
high ⇔ low ： *建物、*山、空、価格、レベルなど。

- How tall is your brother? （お兄さんの身長はどのくらいですか。）
- How tall [high] is Mount *Akagi*? （赤城山はどれくらい高いですか。）
- How tall [high] is *Tokyo* Skytree? （東京スカイツリーはどれくらい高いですか。）
- The sky is high in the autumn. （秋は空が高い。）
- *Takasaki* City Hall is 102.5 (one hundred and two point five) meters high and has twenty-one stories.
  （高崎市庁舎は102.5mの高さで、21階建てです。）

- The prefectural office building located in *Maebashi* is the tallest building in *Gunma* Prefecture.
  （前橋に位置する群馬県庁舎は、群馬県で一番高い建物です。）
- *Kurobe* Dam, located in a hidden part of *Toyama* Prefecture, is the highest dam in Japan (186 meters), and it has a striking view.
  （富山県秘境に建設された黒部ダムは、日本一の高さ（186m）を誇り、その壮大な景観に目を奪われます。）

Tips:

■ The *Jigen-in* Temple, which has a long history, manages *Takasaki Byakue Dai-kannon*, located at the top of *Kannon-yama*. The giant white statue stands at the place where visitors cross over an arched bridge from the main hall of the *Jigen-in*.
古い歴史を持つ慈眼院が、観音山の頂上に位置する高崎白衣大観音を管理しています。慈眼院本堂から太鼓橋を渡ったところに、白い巨象がそびえ立ちます。

■ The *Takasaki Byakue Dai-kannon* was built by *Yasusaburo Inoue* (a businessman in *Takasaki*) in 1936. The statue of *konnon* (Goddess of Mercy) was constructed based on his hope that it would comfort the spirits of the war dead, save people and all living creatures, and help *Takasaki* City prosper and develop. *Inoue*'s bronze statue also stands on the premises of *Jigen-in* Temple, which is a little ways away from the giant *konnon* statue.
高崎白衣大観音は、1936年に井上保三郎（高崎の実業家）により建設されました。その観世音菩薩像が戦没者の霊を慰め、人々および万物を救い、高崎市を繁栄・発展させるだろうという彼の願いのもとに建立されました。井上氏の銅像もまた大観音像から少し離れた慈眼院の敷地内に立っています。

■ The *Takasaki Byakue Dai-kannon* was designated as a registered tangible cultural property of Japan in 2000.
高崎白衣大観音は2000年に国の登録有形文化財に指定されました。

（参考資料：「白衣大観音」『群馬県の歴史散歩』p.58.・他）

6-7 高崎のバス観光をすすめる——〔2〕
Recommending a bus tour in *Takasaki*：〔2〕

Shorinzan Daruma-ji
(少林山達磨寺)

Senshin-tei
(洗心亭)

Mayuko: The *Shorinzan Daruma-ji* is one of the tourist attractions in *Takasaki* City and is accessible by bus. *Daruma-ji* means "Dharma Temple" in English. The temple is the birthplace of the *Daruma* doll.

Visitor: Isn't that a round mascot? I've been wondering why the doll has no hands and feet since the first time I saw it at the store.

Mayuko: Daruma was a great priest of Buddhism. He was known to be a person who meditated for many years. However, because his arms and legs were hidden under his clothes, he looked like a round shape when he meditated.

Visitor: Now, I see.

Mayuko: But people believe that the round doll brings good luck because it straightens itself into an upright position immediately when it falls down.

Visitor: The *Daruma* doll teaches us not to give up, right?

Mayuko: You're right. There is a Japanese proverb that says, "Fall down seven times, get up eight," and the *Daruma* doll symbolizes that "never-give-up attitude."

Visitor: I'd better keep that in mind, because life is full of ups and downs. By the way, please tell me the way to the temple.

Mayuko: You take the number 1 *Gururin* bus at the west exit of *Takasaki* Station and get off at the entrance of *Shorinzan*. The trip takes about twenty minutes. The outer gate of the *Daruma-ji* is near the bus stop.

Visitor: Can I experience *Zen* meditation there?

Mayuko: I'm not sure <u>whether or not</u> it's open to all visitors. Why don't you ask the chief priest about it directly? Even if he says "no" at first, keep asking, and he may finally say "yes." Remember the "never-give-up attitude!"

Visitor: Okay. It's really challenging to practice my never-give-up attitude at *Daruma* Temple, isn't it?

Mayuko: <u>You said it!</u> By the way, <u>don't forget to take</u> the number 2 *Gururin* bus when you return to the station.

Visitor: I won't. Thanks.

Vocabulary

accessible	行きやすい	straighten	〜を真っすぐにする
upright position	直立位置	immediately	すぐに
proverb	ことわざ	symbolize	象徴する
never-give-up attitude	諦めない態度		
keep 〜 in mind	〜を心にとどめておく、忘れずに覚えておく		
chief priest	住職	practice	〜を実践する、〜を実行する

English Points

■ whether <u>or not</u>〜（〜か否か）は、不確実な状況や情報を述べる表現です。下線部の or not は文の末尾に置くことも可能ですし、省略することもできます。

・I have no idea <u>whether or not</u> she will attend the party.
（彼女がパーティーに出席するか否かわかりません。）

・I'm not sure <u>whether</u> your decision is right <u>or not</u>, but I think that you have to trust yourself.
（あなたの決断が正しいか否かわからないけど、自分を信じなくてはならないと思います。）

・Please let us know about <u>whether</u> you will extend your stay <u>(or not)</u>.
（お客様の滞在を延長されるのか否かについてお知らせください。）

■ You said it.（その通りです）は、相手の言ったことに強く同意する表現として使われます（第4章、4-13. Tips 欄：相づち表現を参照）。

・ "This TV drama is boring." "You said it!"
（このテレビドラマは退屈だね。）（まったく、そうだね。）

・ "Our dreams will come true, but we need time and patience." "You said it."
（私たちの夢は実現します。時間と忍耐を要しますが。）（その通りです。）

■ forget to V と forget V-ing とでは、意味が異なります。つまり、不定詞（to V）が続く場合、未来の〈これから行う〉ことを忘れる、そして動名詞（V-ing）が続く場合は、過去の〈すでに行った〉ことを忘れるという意味になります。

・ Don't <u>forget to set</u> the alarm clock before going to bed.
（寝る前に目覚まし時計を設定することを忘れないでください。）

・ I <u>forgot setting</u> the alarm clock last night. I was surprised by the sound of the alarm and nearly fell out of bed this morning.
（昨夜、目覚まし時計を設定したことを忘れていて。今朝はアラームの音に驚いてベッドから落ちそうになりました。）

※多くの動詞は、like 動詞のように不定詞（to V）と 動名詞（V-ing）のどちらも用いることができますし、意味が異なることもありません。他方、不定詞のみをとる動詞、または動名詞のみをとる動詞、さらに上述の forget のようにどちらもとるが、意味が違ってしまう動詞があり、次の 4 パターンに分類されます。
・ I <u>like</u> to swim.（私は泳ぐことが好きです。）
・ I <u>like</u> swimming.（　　　　　〃　　　　　）

パターン	動　詞
動詞＋不定詞 （to V）のみ	want（欲しい）　decide（決める）　hope（望む） plan（計画する）　promise（約束する） expect（期待する）　prepare（準備する）　refuse（断る） agree（同意する）　intend（意図する）　wish（願う） arrange（手配する）
動詞＋動名詞 （V-ing）のみ	enjoy（楽しむ）　finish（終える）　mind（気にする） quit（やめる）　practice（練習する）　avoid（避ける） escape（逃げる）　keep (on)（続ける） give up（あきらめる、やめる） look forward to（楽しみにする）
動詞＋不定詞／動名詞 双方とも意味が同じ	like（好き）　love（愛する）　hate（嫌う） begin（始める）　start（始める）　continue（続ける）

Sightseeing Spots

6

周辺観光編

パターン	動　詞
動詞＋不定詞・動名詞 それぞれ意味が異なる	forget（忘れる）　remember（覚えている） regret（後悔する）　try（試みる） stop（やめる、立ち止まる）

Tips:

■ When the great famine occurred in the middle of the *Edo* era, *Tohgaku*, the ninth chief priest of the *Daruma-ji*, taught the farmers to make paper *Daruma* dolls to be sold at the fair on January 7, which was the origin of the *Takasaki Daruma* dolls. In this manner, the farmers were able to overcome their hardships.

江戸時代中期の大飢饉の折、達磨寺の9代目東嶽和尚は1月7日の七草大祭で売るための張り子だるまの作り方を農民たちに教えました。それが、高崎だるまの起源でした。これによって、農民たちは苦難を乗り越えることができたのです。

■ One of the largest *Daruma* markets in Japan is held on January 6 and 7 in the *Shorinzan Daruma-ji* Temple every year. Many worshipers visit this traditional event, which has been held since the *Edo* era, and buy a new *Daruma* doll. (An estimate is that approximately 300,000 people visit the temple during the two days.) Since 2017, the *Takasaki Daruma* market, sponsored by *Takasaki* City, has been held in front of the JR *Takasaki* Station west exit on January 1 and 2, in addition to the *Daruma* market that is sponsored by the *Daruma-ji*. Is this the start of a new history of the *Daruma* market?

日本で最も大きなだるま市の一つは、少林山達磨寺で毎年1月6、7日に開催されます。この江戸時代から続く伝統行事に、大勢の参拝者が訪れ、新しいだるまを買い求めます。（2日間で、およそ30万人が訪れると見積もられます。）2017年から、達磨寺の七草大祭だるま市とは別に、高崎市主催の高崎だるま市が1月1、2日にJR高崎駅西口駅前通りで開催されるようになりました。だるま市の新しい歴史の始まりでしょうか。

■ Many venders sell *Darumas* and haggle about the price at the market, which is quite lively. The eyes of a new *Daruma* doll are blank. People paint the left eye of the *Daruma* doll while making a wish. When the wish comes true, they paint the right eye. At the end of one year, they return the *Daruma* doll to the temple to be burned. The burning of the old dolls is part of a ceremony intended to return souls to the sky.

だるま市には多くの露天商が並び、販売や値引き交渉でにぎやかです。新しいだるまには両目が入っていません。人々は願いを込めながら、だるまの左目を入れます。願いがかなったら、右目を入れます。一年の終わりに、だるまは寺に戻されて、魂を天に戻すために焚かれます。

■ Bruno Taut, a German architect, stayed at the *Daruma-ji*. Taut left Germany with his partner (Erica Wittich) because he sensed imminent danger under the Nazi regime. They arrived in Japan about two months later and stayed there for three and a half years (May 1933─ October 1936). During most of their stay in Japan, they lived in the *Senshin-tei*, a villa located on the temple grounds of the *Daruma-ji*. Taut studied many of the Japanese structures and was deeply impressed by Japanese culture. Later, the books he wrote about Japan came to be considered important documents by Westerners in understanding Japanese culture. His works and photographs are displayed in a room at *Zuiunkaku* in the *Daruma-ji*.

ドイツの建築家、ブルーノ・タウトが達磨寺に滞在したことはよく知られています。彼はナチス政権下で身に迫る危険を感じ、パートナー（エリカ・ヴィッティヒ）とともにドイツを離れました。約2カ月後に日本に到着し、3年半（1933年5月−1936年10月）滞在すること

になります。日本滞在の大部分を達磨寺境内の洗心亭で過ごしました。タウトは日本建築を見て回り、日本文化に深く傾倒しました。彼が日本滞在中に書き残した書籍は、後に西洋の人々が日本文化を理解することにおいて貴重な資料になったと考えられています。タウトの著作物や写真は達磨寺境内の瑞雲閣の一室に展示されています。

■ In those days, the Japanese government was leaning toward militarism and had developed close relations with Nazi Germany. Taut, who had few opportunities to engage in architecture in Japan, accepted a position from Turkey's government. At his farewell party in Japan, he said that his health was failing and that he wanted to be buried in the *Shorinzan*. After working as an architect in Turkey for over two years, Taut passed away due to a cerebral hemorrhage. His body was laid to rest in Edirnekapi cemetery in Istanbul, but in keeping with his wishes, his death mask was brought to the *Daruma-ji* by his partner.

当時、軍国主義に向かう日本政府はナチスとの連携を深めつつあり、日本で建築に携わることがほとんどできなかったタウトは、トルコ政府からの仕事の依頼を受け入れました。日本での送別会の席で、彼は自分の健康に懸念を示し、遺骨を少林山に埋葬してほしいと言い残したのです。その後、タウトはトルコで2年余り建築に携わり、脳溢血で亡くなります。タウトの遺体はトルコのエディルネカピ墓地に埋葬されますが、彼の遺志を汲み、パートナーによってデス・マスクが達磨寺に納められました。

(参考資料:「少林山達磨寺」『群馬県の歴史散歩』pp.56-58.・他)

Column

History of *Daruma-ji*
(達磨寺の歴史)

In the *Genroku* period (circa.1697), *Shinetsu*, a Zen Priest from China, founded this temple. He was the mentor for *Tokugawa-Mitsukuni*, a high-ranking officer from the *Mito* lineage of the *Tokugawa* Family in the shogunnate in the *Edo* era. What *Shinetsu* brought with him was a holy statue called *Hokushin-chintaku Reifuson* that realizes the wishes of peace and happiness with the prayer for the polar star. His disciple and successor, the Japanese Zen Priest *Tenshu*, from *Mito*, became the second abbot, and built a shrine to house the *Reifuson*.

1697年(元禄10)、中国からの渡来僧 東皐心越禅師を開山に迎えてこのお寺が建てられました。心越禅師は天下の副将軍・水戸黄門こと徳川光圀公が心の師と仰いだ禅僧です。心越禅師はこの寺に中国から奉持された北極星信仰の守護神 北辰鎮宅霊符尊を、国家安穏平穏無事の祈りを込めて祀りました。そして心越禅師の高弟 天湫和尚が水戸からお越しになり、2代目の住職となって霊符尊をお祀りする本堂を建てられました。

【達磨寺より寄稿】

6-8 高崎のバス観光をすすめる──〔3〕
Recommending a bus tour in *Takasaki*：〔3〕

Souryu gate
（双龍門）

Main hall of *Haruna* Shrine
（榛名神社本殿）

Mayuko: It is a little far, but there is another tourist place you can go to by bus.

Visitor: Where is it?

Mayuko: It is the *Haruna* Shrine on the hillside of Mount *Haruna*. The *Shinto* shrine is part of a huge rock on Mount *Haruna*, which is totally unbelievable. It's a place where we can feel the power of nature.

Visitor: Hmmm, is that a spiritual hot spot?

Mayuko: Yes, it is. It's said to be one of the strong spiritual hot spots in the *Kanto* region.

Visitor: Can people receive good luck after they worship at the shrine?

Mayuko: You bet! The *Haruna* Shrine is dedicated to "the gods of fire and earth" that dwell on Mount *Haruna*. Those gods offer blessings for a good harvest, success, marriage... for almost everything, I hear.

Visitor: It sounds like a Japanese myth.

Mayuko: Exactly. It was founded in ancient times, so it can be explained only in a myth. It's one of the oldest *Shinto* shrines in Japan.

Visitor: It sounds like it's worth going there even if it's far. Can I get there by taking the *Gururin* bus?

Mayuko: No, you can't. Take a *Gunma* bus to Lake *Haruna* via *Hongo* at the west exit of *Takasaki* Station and get off in front of the *Haruna* Shrine. The trip takes about seventy or eighty minutes. From the bus stop, it's a fifteen-minute walk to the shrine.

Visitor: How often does the bus run?

Mayuko: It runs every hour.

Visitor: I see.

Vocabulary

hillside	山腹
unbelievable	信じられない
spiritual hot spot	パワースポット　※パワースポットは和製英語
dedicate to	～に捧げる
dwell	住む
offer	～を提供する
blessing	恩恵、天恵
harvest	収穫
myth	神話
found	～を設立する

English Points

■ You bet. は状況によって、「もちろん、いいですよ、その通り、どういたしまして…」などの意で使うことができるくだけた表現です。

　・Brian, can you babysit my kids this afternoon while I go shopping?
　（ブライアン、今日の午後、私が買い物に行く間、子どもたちのベビーシッターを頼める？）
　　——You bet!　※ Okay の意
　　（いいよ。）

　・Thank you for the concert ticket. This is exactly what I wanted.
　（コンサートのチケットをありがとう。まさに欲しかったものです。）
　　——Yeah, you bet.　※ You are welcome. はフォーマルな表現
　　（えぇ、どういたしまして）

■ one of the oldest *Shinto* shrines in Japan（日本で最も古い神社の１つ）という表現に違和感を抱く日本人は少なくないでしょう。日本語においては「最も、一番の」という場合、複数を指さないのが普通だからです。他方、英語では最上級を必ずしも１つ（人）のみと捉えない場合もあることから、このような「最上級＋名詞の複数形」を使用することができるのです。物理的に世界で最も高い山は１つだけですが、最も美しい山は複数あってもよいという捉え方が垣間見られます。

- Mount *Fuji* is one of the most beautiful mountains in the world.
  （富士山は世界で最も美しい山の１つです。）

- *Tokyo* is one of the most densely populated areas in the world.
  （東京は世界で最も人口密度の高い地域の１つです。）

- *Natto* is one of the smelliest foods, but it is also one of the healthiest foods.
  （納豆は最も臭い食べ物の１つですが、最も健康的な食べ物の１つでもあります。）

Tips:

■ An entry for the *Haruna* Shrine was made in a register called *Jinmyocho / Shinmeicho* (published in 927) during the *Heian* era. The register is a history book with the names of the main shrines throughout the country. Therefore, it can be confirmed that the *Haruna* Shrine was already established as a venerable shrine at that time.

　榛名神社は平安時代の台帳、『神名帳（じんみょうちょう／しんめいちょう）』（927年）に登録されています。その台帳は全国の主な神社名を搭載した歴史書です。これによって、榛名神社はその時すでに由緒正しい神社として成立していたことが確認されます。

■ The area of the *Haruna* Shrine is spacious and features many important buildings and cultural assets; additionally, a rich natural environment is preserved there. It is a comfortable space where many trees are lined up, and visitors can listen to the sounds of water flowing over waterfalls and the echoes of rivers.

　榛名神社の境内は広く、多くの重要な建物や文化財が保存されているだけでなく、豊かな自然環境が保たれています。多くの樹木が立ち並び、滝や川を流れる水の音が響き渡る心地よい空間です。

■ *Chozusha*, or *Chozuya*, is a place where visitors can purify themselves before visiting a shrine. It is equipped with a stone basin filled with water and dippers, so visitors can rinse their hands and mouth.

　手水舎は、神社に参拝する前に訪問者が身を清める場所です。そこには石造りの水盤と柄杓（ひしゃく）が装備されていて、参拝者は手を洗い、口をすすぐことができます。

■ The outstanding design of the *Souryu* gate attracts visitors' attention. The gate was built with huge rocks in the back, and its unique building overwhelms visitors. Moreover, the huge *Misugata-iwa,* located behind the main hall, is the holy rock where God appeared, as the name suggests, and the main hall has been built to honor that massive rock. So clearly, our ancestors found gods in the power and form of nature.

　ひときわ訪問者の目を引くのが、双龍門の佇まいです。巨大な岩を背負う形で建てられた門構えで、他に類を見ない建造物は訪問者を圧倒します。さらに、本殿の背後にそびえる巨大な御姿岩（みすがたいわ）は、呼び名のとおり〈神様の姿が現れた岩〉の意で、その巨岩を敬うように本殿が建てられています。先人たちが自然の力や造形の中に神々を見い出してきたことをうかがい知ることができます。

（参考資料：「榛名神社」『群馬県の歴史散歩』pp.76-78.・他）

6-9 吹割の滝で
At *Fukiware* Falls

Fukiware Falls
(吹割の滝)

Apple trees
(林檎の木)

Mayuko: I hear the sound of the waterfall. Please be careful because the road is narrow.

Visitor: I can see the waterfall ahead. I've never seen such a waterfall where the water flows into slits in the rocks. Splendid!

Mayuko: It's called the "Oriental Niagara Falls."

Visitor: The relative size is small, but it certainly has the same shape as Niagara Falls.

Mayuko: You can see that.

Visitor: There is a tourist taking a picture near the falls. Isn't that dangerous?

Mayuko: He will be safe <u>as long as</u> he stands behind the white warning line. The sign says, "Stay behind the white line."

Visitor: Very interesting!

Mayuko: I heard that accidents happened in the past. Some people crossed the white line and slipped and fell to the bottom of the waterfall.

Visitor: Were the guys who fell at this waterfall saved?

Mayuko: No, they weren't. Because the waterfall is very deep, even their bodies were difficult to find.

Visitor: I think they should do more to protect visitors' safety. Signs informing the public about the danger of falling don't seem to be enough.

Mayuko: I can understand that way of thinking, because one doesn't want to spoil the scenery. Above all, we should pay attention to the warning.

Vocabulary

falls / waterfall	滝　　※ falls は複数形で用いる
careful	注意深い
flow into	～に流れ込む
slit	切れ目
relative	比較上の、相対的な
take a picture	写真を撮る
dangerous	危険な　　※ danger　　危険
as long as	～する限り
warning	警告
stand behind / stay behind	（～を超えないで）とどまる、後ろに控えている
slip and fall	滑り落ちる
protect	～を守る、～を保護する
spoil	～を台なしにする
pay attention to	～に注意する、～に留意する

English Points

■ as long as と as far as はどちらも「～する限り」の意で、類似した決まり文句ですが、as long as は「条件」を、as far as は「範囲」を示す場合に使われます。

・As long as you continue to challenge yourself, your future will be bright.
（挑戦し続ける限り、君の未来は明るいでしょう。）
・As long as he is living with his parents, it will be difficult for him to develop a sense of independence, I think.
（彼が親と一緒に暮らしている限り、自立心を養うことは困難だと思います。）

・As far as I know, no major natural disasters have occurred in this area.
（私の知る限り、この地域にはこれまでに大きな自然災害が起こっていません。）
・As far as I'm concerned, she has not yet shown her ability.
（私の意見では、彼女はまだ実力を発揮していません。）

Tips:

■ *Fukiware* Falls is located in *Numata* City in northern *Gunma*. The falls is seven meters high, and thirty meters wide, and is called the "Oriental Niagara Falls" because its shape resembles Niagara Falls. Although it takes around fifty minutes to get from *Takasaki* to *Numata* by the JR *Joetsu* line, and approximately forty-five minutes from *Numata* Station to *Fukiware* Falls by a *Kan-etsu* bus, visitors can enjoy the scenery from the bus windows, and they won't be bored.

吹割の滝は、群馬県北部の沼田市に位置します。その滝は高さ 7 m、幅30mで、形状が似ているので とから東洋のナイヤガラと呼ばれています。高崎から JR 上越線で沼田駅まで約50分、沼田駅から関越バスで45分程度かかりますが、車窓からの景色を楽しむことができるので、退屈することはありません。

■ *Fukiware* Falls is a national natural treasure. The fast-moving water rushes into the basin of the waterfall, which is spectacular. In particular, from spring to early summer, it provides a powerful, magnificent impression with the increasing amount of water due to the snow thawing. In the autumn, the valley provides breathtaking scenery with the colored leaves.

吹割の滝は国指定の天然記念物です。水しぶきを上げながら、急流が滝つぼに流れ落ちていく光景は、壮観です。特に、春から初夏にかけては、雪解けで水量が増すため、迫力のある雄大な景観を見ることができます。秋は紅葉に彩られ、渓谷は息をのむ景観を見せてくれます。

■ To avoid spoiling the scenery, there are no handrails on the sidewalk near the waterfall. Additionally, the sidewalk is narrow, and two people can barely pass each other. Therefore, ideally, one should wear shoes with soles that do not slip and have consideration for others. Visitors need to make way for each other for safety's sake.

景観を損なわないため、滝の近くの歩道には手すりがありません。また、道幅も狭く、2 人がようやくすれちがうことのできる程度です。よって、滑らないシューズを履くことと、他者への配慮を要します。安全のために道を譲り合うことが求められます。

■ Visitors can enjoy being very close to falls. Of course, they must be careful because of the slippery rocks.

訪問客は、滝のすぐ近くまで接近することができます。もちろん、滑りやすい岩のため、十分な注意が必要です。

■ A rope is set up around the dangerous areas, and a visitor must not cross the rope to take photographs. It is almost impossible to rescue a person who slips and falls into the waterfall.

危険な場所にはロープが張り巡らされているので、ロープを越えて写真を撮るのは禁止です。足を滑らせて滝に落ちた場合、救助はほとんど不可能です。

■ Promenades exist around *Fukiware* valley, so that tourists can enjoy viewing the waterfall from various angles. It takes about one hour to go around the promenades. During winter, the promenades are closed because of the snow.

吹割渓谷の周囲には遊歩道がつくられていて、観光客は様々な角度から滝の眺めを楽しむことができます。遊歩道を一周するのに 1 時間程度を要します。冬の間、降雪のため遊歩道は閉鎖されます。

(参考資料：「城下町沼田をめぐる」『群馬県の歴史散歩』pp.226-239.・他)

Numata and the *Sanada* clan
（沼田と真田一族）

■ *Numata* City is located in the northern part of *Gunma* on a river terrace more than 250 meters above sea level overlooking the *Tone* River. It is surrounded by mountains and was the ideal landform for a fortress. Additionally, the road leading to each region (*Musashi*, *Shinano*, *Echigo*, *Kai*, *Aizu*) passed through *Numata*; thus, it was an important traffic point and a key strategic point for ruling the *Kanto* district. Warlords competed for possession of this land in the *Sengoku* period (1467-1568).

　　群馬県の北部に位置する沼田市は、利根川を見下ろす標高250m以上の河岸段丘の上にあり
ます。四方を山に囲まれており、要塞として理想的な地形でした。加えて、各地方（武蔵、
信濃、越後、甲斐、会津）へ向かう街道が通っていたことから、沼田は交通の要衝であると
ともに、関東を支配するのに重要な軍事拠点でした。戦国時代に武将たちはこの地の領有を
奪い合いました。

■ *Numata* was the *Sanadas'* territory from 1590 to 1681. *Nobuyuki Sanada* (the eldest son of *Masayuki Sanada*), the first feudal lord, irrigated with water from the *Usune* River in *Kawaba* to secure sufficient amont of water for the territory, which was on a plateau. It is called the *Kawaba* canal. His son, *Nobuyoshi*, carried out the large-scale construction of the *Joubori-gawa* canal, which joined the *Kawaba* canal to the existing *Shirasawa* canal. Approximately 100 irrigation canals of various sizes are still used for agriculture today.

　　沼田は1590年から91年間にわたり、真田家の領地でした。初代藩主の真田信之（真田昌幸の
長男）は、沼田が台地であるために不足しがちな水を確保するために、川場の薄根川から水
を引きました。それが川場用水です。その子信吉は川場用水を既存の白沢用水に合流させる
大規模な「城掘川」の工事を手がけました。大小合わせて100もの用水路がつくられ、現在も
農業用水として使われています。

（情報提供：沼田市観光案内所）

■ The crest of the *Sanada* family was *roku-mon-sen* [six *mon* coins]. The *mon* is an old currency unit. In the medieval period in Japan, it was believed that when a deceased person departed for next world, that person crossed a river called the *Sanzu-no-kawa*, which flowed between this world and the next. The fare for crossing the river was *roku-mon*; thus, there was a custom of giving a deceased person this money. In short, the crest of *roku-mon-sen* was expressed in the *Sanadas'* readiness as warriors. *Sanadas'* army flew flags with *roku-mon-sen*, which displayed bravery and strength.

　　真田家の家紋は、六文銭です。文は昔の通貨単位です。中世の日本においては、亡くなった
者があの世へ旅立つ際、三途の川を渡ると考えられていました。それは、この世とあの世を
分ける川です。その川を渡る船賃が六文であり、亡くなった者に持たせるという習慣があり
ました。つまり、六文銭の家紋は、武人としての覚悟を表したものなのです。真田軍は六文
銭の旗を掲げ、勇敢さと強さを示したのです。

■ *Yukimura Sanada*, the second son of *Masayuki Sanada*, is said to be one of the most popular warlords that the Japanese people like. He was a faithful and great warlord with a clever strategy who lived during the *Sengoku* period. It is reported that *Ieyasu Tokugawa* feared *Sanadas'* army the most because they were the strongest.

　　真田昌幸の次男である真田幸村は、日本人が最も好きな武将の一人です。義に厚く、戦国時
代を巧みに生き抜いた優れた武将でした。真田軍は最強で、徳川家康が最も恐れた軍団で
あったと伝えられています。

■ Today, the site of *Numata* Castle has been developed into a park, and stone statues of *Nobuyuki Sanada* and his wife, Princess *Komatsu*, stand in the park. The landscape of the surrounding peaceful countryside is spread out, so it is difficult to imagine that it was a battlefield in the old days. In this area, various farms cultivate crops such as rice, vegetables, and fruit. Apple cultivation is the most prosperous, and "*Numata* apples" are brand-name products.

今日、沼田城址は公園として整備され、真田信之とその妻の小松姫の石像が置かれています。その昔、戦場であったことを想像するのが難しいほど、のどかな田園風景が広がります。この地域では、米、野菜、果物などの様々な農産物が生産されています。中でもリンゴづくりが盛んで、「沼田のリンゴ」はブランド品です。

（参考資料：「沼田市」「川場村」真田街道ホームページ・他）

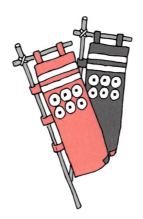

Fukiware Falls leads to *Ryugu-jo* ...

    Ryugu-jo, the underwater kingdom, is the place under the sea where *Urashima Taro*, a fisherman, was brought on the back of a turtle he saved from being bullied by some boys on the beach. The fairy tale of "*Urashima Taro*" is well-known among Japanese people. In the *Numata* area, it has been told that *Fukiware* Falls leads to *Ryugu-jo*.

吹割の滝は龍宮城に通じる…

    龍宮城は、漁師の浦島太郎が浜辺で男の子たちにいじめられていた亀を救い、その亀の背に乗って訪れた海の下の御殿です。「浦島太郎」は日本人の誰もが知っているおとぎ話です。沼田地域では、吹割の滝が龍宮城に通じていると語り伝えられて来ました。

An old tale in *Numata*,
"Wooden Bowls of *Ryugu*"

    As the summer festival was coming up, *Heisuke*, a farmer in the village, murmured beside *Fukiware* Falls that he had no wooden bowls for soup for his guests.
    Then, a girl appeared from the waterfall, and asked him, "How many wooden bowls do you need?" The princess of *Ryugu-jo* heard *Heisuke's* murmur and sent a girl to him.
"Three wooden bowls," he answered.
The girl disappeared. After several minutes, she appeared and said,
"I have a message from the princess of *Ryugu-jo*. Come back tomorrow morning. Three wooden bowls will be ready by then. But you must return them after the meal."

                                     — 1 —

    The next morning, *Heisuke* found three wooden bowls floating in *Fukiware* Falls. He brought them back to his house, and he treated his guests with them.
    After that, *Heisuke* thought he could keep one of the bowls just in case someone would be interested in seeing it, since he had boasted that the wooden bowls were from his ancestors. So he returned only two wooden bowls to *Fukiware* Falls. Then, a fire occurred in the village. As *Heisuke* went home hastily, his house was on fire. The princess was angry at his dishonesty and destroyed his house by fire, together with the wooden bowl. She also blocked up the hole of the waterfall leading to *Ryugu-jo*.

                                       — 2 —

沼田の昔話
「龍宮の椀」

    夏祭りがやってくるころ、村のお百姓の平助は、客をもてなすための膳椀がないことを吹割の滝の淵でつぶやきました。
    すると、滝の中から女の子が現れ、「何人前御用ですか」と平助に尋ねました。龍宮の乙姫様が平助のつぶやきを聞いて女の子を送ったのです。
    「三人前ほど」と平助が答えると、女の子は姿を消し、数分後にまた現れて言いました。
    「乙姫様からの伝言です。明日の朝、ここへおいでください。三人前の椀を用意して置きます。しかし、必ずお返しください。」

                                       — 1 —

    翌朝、平助は吹割の滝で三人前の膳椀が浮かんでいるのを見つけ、家へ持ち帰り、その椀で客をもてなしました。
    その後、平助は先祖からの膳椀だと客に自慢してしまった手前、誰かが見せてほしいと来たときのために一つを手元に置き、二つだけを滝へ返しました。
    その時、村で火事が起こり、平助が飛んで帰ると、自分の家が燃えていました。乙姫様は、平助の不正直に怒り、椀もろとも平助の家を焼失させたのでした。
    そして、龍宮に通じる滝の穴を塞いでしまったのです。

                                       — 2 —

（出典：小野忠孝、「龍宮の椀」『日本の民話20　上州の民話　第1集』pp.15-18.）

付 記

【会話：日本語訳】

会話（日本語訳）

第1章　上信電鉄でお出かけ【交通編】

1-1　高崎駅で——上信線乗り場への行き方

訪問者：すみません。世界遺産の富岡製糸場へ行きたいのですが、何線ですか。
通行人：上信線です。ゼロ番線で乗れます。その階段を下りると、上信線の入り口
　　　　があります。100mほど進むと、改札口があります。
訪問者：わかりました。どうもありがとう。
通行人：どういたしまして。切符販売機の使い方がJRとは異なるので、駅員に聞く
　　　　といいですよ。
訪問者：そうします。アドバイスをありがとうございます。
通行人：いいえ。楽しい旅行を。
訪問者：さようなら。

1-2　上信線乗り場で——切符の買い方を説明する

訪問者：すみません。自動販売機で切符を買うのを手伝っていただけますか。使い
　　　　方がわかりません。
　駅員：はい、ただいま。まず、行き先と料金を画面で確認してください。行き先
　　　　はどこですか。
訪問者：世界遺産の富岡製糸場です。最寄りの駅はどこですか。
　駅員：上州富岡駅行の切符を購入してください。〈画面上で〉行き先ボタンに駅名
　　　　がローマ字でも表示されています。それぞれの駅名の下に料金が表示され
　　　　ています。ここに上州富岡駅とあります。
訪問者：えぇ、790円とありますね。
　駅員：そしたら、投入口に料金を入れて、人数ボタンと到着駅ボタンを押してく
　　　　ださい。それだけです。
訪問者：使い方がJRの切符販売機とは少し違いますね。
　駅員：その通りです。でも、操作は簡単ですから、誰でも使えますよ。
訪問者：わかりました。ところで、何分ぐらいかかりますか。
　駅員：40分ぐらいです。13番目の駅、上州富岡で下車してください。
訪問者：承知しました。お手数をおかけしました。
　駅員：どういたしまして。ローカル線の景色を楽しんでください。

1-3　上州富岡駅で——乗客に対応する

訪問者：すみません。インフォメーション・センターはどこでしょうか。

196

駅員：改札口を出て、右側です。あそこに見えるのがそうです。
訪問者：案内スタッフはいますか。
駅員：いいえ、平日はいません。土、日にはボランティアの案内係が詰めているんですが。ご自由にお持ちいただける町の地図や小冊子がそこに置いてありますので。
訪問者：立ち寄って見てみます。ありがとう。
駅員：どういたしまして。

1-4　行き方を教える──〔1〕

〈上州富岡駅で〉
駅員：こんにちは。富岡製糸場への行き方の地図をどうぞ。
訪問者：どうも。これはいい。道順がわかりやすいし、「徒歩で15分」で行けますね。
駅員：タクシーに乗れば早いですが、歩ける距離です。
訪問者：街中を見物したいので歩きます。
駅員：それがいいですよ。よい一日を！
訪問者：ありがとう。あなたもね。

1-5　行き方を教える──〔2〕

《上州富岡駅を後に》
訪問者：〈独り言を言う〉あれ、道に迷ったかな。誰かに尋ねてみよう。
《辺りを見回す》
訪問者：すみません。富岡製糸場への行き方を教えていただけますか。
通行人：はい。この道路を1ブロックまっすぐ行ってください。そして右に曲がって1ブロックです。
訪問者：了解です。あとどれくらいかかりますか。地図に載ってる店をのぞきながら来たので、駅からどれくらい歩いたのかわかりません。
通行人：もう一息で着きますよ。この道を右に曲がると、前方に煉瓦造りの建物が見えてきます。すぐにわかりますよ。
訪問者：よかった！もう少しだ。ありがとうございました。
通行人：どういたしまして。

付記

1-6　客を乗せる

運転手：こんにちは。どちらまで。
旅客：雪見通りの梅乃井旅館までお願いできますか。
運転手：はい。荷物はありますか。
旅客：えぇ。スーツケースが1つ。
運転手：車に乗って、シートベルトを締めてください。スーツケースは私がトランクに入れますので。
旅客：旅館へはどれくらいで行きますか。

運転手：道が混んでいなければ、12分くらいです。
　　　　《しばらくして》
運転手：着きました。
　旅客：おいくらですか。
運転手：1,810円です。
　旅客：2,000円で。お釣りは取っといて。
運転手：ありがとうございました。よい一日を！
　旅客：どうも。あなたもね。

1-7　ぐるりんバスの乗り方を教える

　旅客：すみません。観音山へ行きたいのですが、何番のバスに乗ればいいですか。
運転手：13番または14番のバスを利用してください。あそこの８番のバス停から乗れます。
　旅客：ありがとうございます。
運転手：どういたしまして。
　　　　《バス運転手にルートを確認する》
　旅客：こんにちは。このバスは、観音山へ行きますか。
運転手：えぇ、行きますよ。行き先はどこですか。
　旅客：えーと、高崎白衣大観音の近くのバス停まで。時間はどれくらいですか。
運転手：もっとも近いバス停は「白衣観音前」ですね。約25分です。下車したい停留所がアナウンスされたら、ボタンを押してください。
　旅客：了解です。えーと、もう一つ質問が…、チケットはどこで買うのですか。
運転手：チケットは要りません。降りるとき、その機械に200円を入れるだけです。一律料金なんで。
　旅客：どこまで乗っても、200円。いいですね。
運転手：ところで、そろそろ出発の時間です。乗車してください。
　旅客：あぁ、そうします。情報をありがとうございました。
運転手：どういたしまして。

1-8　観光バスに関する情報を提供する

　ガイド：あのぉ…、高崎市は路線バスが発達しているので、バスで目的地へ行けますが、運行本数に関しては多いとはいえません。
　訪問者：地元の人たちは車で移動しているようですが、観光客は公共の交通手段に頼らなくてはならないでしょう。
　ガイド：確かに。そこで、耳寄りの情報があります。定期観光バスが週末出ています。たとえば、高崎駅発、榛名湖、榛名神社、達磨寺、高崎観音などの主な観光名所を訪れる定期観光バスは便利です。それらを一日で回れますから。
　訪問者：わくわくしてきた！料金はいくらですか。
　ガイド：手頃な料金だったと記憶しています。
　訪問者：これは、行くしかないね。
　ガイド：楽しんでください。

第2章　物産店でお土産を買う【買い物編】

2-1　土産店で──〔1〕

販売員：いらっしゃいませ。何かお探しですか。
　　客：見ているだけですので。
販売員：ごゆっくりご覧ください。何かございましたら、お声をお掛けください。
　　客：そうします。どうも。

2-2　土産店で──〔2〕

　　客：すみません、ちょっとお願いできますか。
販売員：はい、何でしょうか。
　　客：そこの商品棚にあるものを見たいのですが。
販売員：今、お取りします。どちらでしょうか。
　　客：左から2番目の手前のものです。
販売員：こちらですか。
　　客：はい、それです。
販売員：はい、どうぞ。こちらのご購入でよろしいですか。
　　客：気に入りました。これをいただきます。

2-3　土産店で──〔3〕

　　客：すみません。これ、いくらですか。
販売員：税込みで2,980円です。
　　客：値引きしていただけますか。
販売員：既に値引きされています。
　　客：他のお店で同じ商品が販売されていました。でも、こちらの方の色が私の
　　　　好みです。高級感もあるし。
販売員：とってもお買い得ですよ。
　　客：帰りにまた寄ります。気が変わらなければ購入します。
販売員：では、またお会いしましょう。

2-4　土産店で──〔4〕

　　客：すみません。この黒っぽいゼリー状のかたまりは何ですか。豆腐の一種で
　　　　すか。
販売員：いえ、それはヤム・ケーキ（芋を固めたもの）です。日本語でコンニャク
　　　　と言います。ゼリーのような食感で、煮ても焼いても食感は変わりません。
　　客：味はどうですか。
販売員：コンニャク自体に味はありませんから、使用される調味料によって味が
　　　　違ってきます。

客：無味な食品に魅力は感じないけど。

販売員：でも、コンニャクは食物繊維が豊富でカロリーがほとんどないので、ダイエット食品として人気があります。群馬の特産品ですよ。

客：へぇ、そうなの。

販売員：コンニャク芋は群馬県の特産品で、日本全国の９割が群馬県でつくられています。すき焼きに入れるしらたきもコンニャクですよ。

客：じゃぁ、コンニャクは食べたことがありますね。すき焼きは大好きです。たくさんしらたきを入れれば、すき焼きはダイエット料理になりますね。

販売員：よいアイデアですね。

2-5　土産店で——〔5〕

客：すみません、プラスチックカップに入った一口サイズのコンニャクゼリーを探しています。ここにありますか。

販売員：はい、ございます。そこのラックの上です。いくつか種類がありますので、お好きな味をお選びください。

客：どうも。レモン風味（のコンニャクゼリー）はありますか。

販売員：申し訳ございません。只今、在庫切れです。入荷まで数日かかってしまいます。グレープフルーツ風味はいかがですか。

客：人気商品なんですね。

販売員：パイナップル風味はとても人気があります。桃、リンゴ、マスカット風味も人気があります。どれもおすすめですよ。

客：では、それぞれの風味を一袋ずついただきます。

販売員：ご自宅用ですか、それとも贈り物ですか。ご希望により贈答用のラッピングも承ります。

客：ホームパーティー用なので、過剰な包装は不要です。これをデザートに出して、友人たちの受けを狙うんです。ダイエットに取りつかれている友人が多いので。

販売員：コンニャクゼリーはヤム芋が原料ですから、動物性のゼラチンゼリーよりも健康にいいですよ。

客：何と言っても、おいしいから買うんですけどね。

販売員：お友達も低カロリーのスィーツをきっと気に入ると思います。

客：そう願っています。

2-6　土産店で——〔6〕

客：すみません。このハッピを購入したいんですが、サイズ表記が見当たらないんです。

販売員：フリーサイズです。試着してみてください。

客：このサイズはピッタリです。でも、少し派手ですね。落ち着いた色合いのものが欲しいです。

販売員：ハッピはイベントを盛り上げるために着るので、目立つ柄が好まれるんです。

客：なるほどね。では、これにします。

販売員：お支払いはどうされますか。
　客：クレジットカードで支払えますか。
販売員：どこのカードですか。
　客：ビザ・カードです。
販売員：えぇ、ビザ・カードでしたらお受けします。

2−7　土産店で──〔7〕

　客：これは何ですか。触ってもいいですか。
販売員：どうぞ、手にとってごらんください。
　客：これ、どうやって使うんですか？
販売員：達磨は縁起物です。この置物は幸運をもたらすと信じられています。新年の初めに達磨を購入して、平和・健康・成功などを願うのです。
　客：いい風習ですね。でも、眼が空白なのはなぜですか。
販売員：左の眼を黒く塗って祈願します。願いがかなった際に右の眼を塗るんです。倒されても起き上がるので、必ず勝利するという縁起物です。
　客：達磨に手足がないのはどうして？
販売員：達磨は偉い僧侶でした。彼は何年もの長い間瞑想をした人物として知られていますが、瞑想をしているとき手足は衣に隠れて見えなかったことから、彼の姿は丸い形に見えたんですね。
　客：なるほど。この人形はけっして諦めるなと教えているんですね。
販売員：おっしゃる通りです。
　客：お土産にいいですね。1ついただきます。
販売員：承知しました。

2−8　土産店で──〔8〕

　客：あそこのゴジラプリントTシャツを見せていただけますか。
販売員：はい。サイズはいくつですか。
　客：ふつうはMサイズを着用しますが、ご覧の通り旅行者なので、この国のサイズ基準がわかりません。
販売員：Mサイズで間に合うと思います。試着してみてはいかがですか。
　客：そうしましょう。試着室はどちらですか。
販売員：こちらです。
　客：私にはちょっと小さいです。もう少し大きいサイズはありますか。
販売員：では、多分Lサイズがお客様に合いますね。
　客：そして、もう一つ、この色は私に似合わない。これと同じ品物で別の色はありますか。
販売員：はい、赤と青がございます。そうぞ、ご試着ください。
　客：こちらのサイズの方が合うし、青色の方が似合うと思う。この青いのをいただきます。
販売員：お買い上げありがとうございます。ただいま会計いたします。税込みで4,800円になります。
　客：このTシャツを着て、ゴジラ映画を見に行くつもりです。

販売員：いいですね。人生を楽しまなくては。

2-9　薬局で

薬剤師：こんにちは。ご用件を承ります。
　　客：どうも。風邪をひいてしまったようです。よく効く風邪薬を勧めていただけますか。
薬剤師：処方せんをお持ちですか。
　　客：いいえ。持っていません。
薬剤師：では、処方せんなしで買えるお薬をお勧めします。もう少し詳しい症状を教えていただけますか。
　　客：喉が痛いのと、鼻水が出ます。
薬剤師：わかりました。熱はありますか。
　　客：えぇ。微熱があります。
薬剤師：何か薬を常用していますか。
　　客：いいえ。
薬剤師：では、何か薬のアレルギーはありますか。
　　客：私の知る限りでは、ないと思います。
薬剤師：どうも。では、どの市販薬でも大丈夫です。
　　客：どこに置いてありますか。
薬剤師：この通路に沿って、右側の棚にあります。ご案内しましょう。
　　客：どうも。
　　　　《棚の前で》
薬剤師：こちらがすべて風邪薬になります。
　　客：私にはさっぱりわかりません。どれがお勧めですか。
薬剤師：こちらは錠剤で、一回に２錠、一日３回食後に服用してください。そしてこれは粉剤で、一回に１包、一日２回食前に服用してください。
　　客：副作用はありますか。
薬剤師：深刻な副作用はありませんが、これらの薬を飲むと眠くなることがあるので、車の運転はしないでください。
　　客：日本滞在中は運転するつもりはないので。では、錠剤をいただきます。
　　　　《レジで支払いの後、商品を受け取る》
　　客：オーケー、どうも。
薬剤師：すぐによくなるといいですね。

第３章　おいしい郷土料理【飲食編】

3-1　ファーストフード店で

スタッフ：次のお客さま、どうぞ。
　　　客：どうも。
スタッフ：いらっしゃいませ。ご注文をどうぞ。

客：〈メニューを見ながら〉チーズバーガー 1 つ、S サイズのフライドポテト
　　　1 つ、M サイズのコーヒー 1 つをお願いします。
スタッフ：ホットとアイスコーヒーがあります。どちらになさいますか。
　　　客：ホットコーヒーで。
スタッフ：こちらで召し上がりますか、それともお持ち帰りですか。
　　　客：ここでいただきます。
スタッフ：他にご注文は。
　　　客：それで全てです。
スタッフ：はい。768円になります。
　　　客：じゃ、千円で。
スタッフ：232円のお釣りになります。この番号札をお持ちになり、お席でお待ち
　　　　　ください。注文のご用意ができましたら、番号をお呼びします。
　　　客：わかりました。
　　　　　《数分後》
スタッフ：45番の方！チーズバーガー 1 つ、S サイズのフライドポテト 1 つ、M サ
　　　　　イズのホットコーヒー 1 つでございます。よい一日を！
　　　客：ありがとう。あなたもね。

3 - 2　群馬の郷土食

　　　客：いい匂いですね。それ、何ですか。
販売員：焼きまんじゅうです。群馬の郷土の味です。お一つ、いかがですか。
　　　客：団子のように見えますが、中に何か入っているの。
販売員：焼きまんじゅうは基本的には、小麦粉とイースト菌だけでつくられていま
　　　　す。まず、蒸してから、竹串をさして、甘い味噌だれを塗りながら焼きま
　　　　す。
　　　客：この香りは食欲を刺激するね。たまらない。いくらですか。
販売員：一串、300円です。
　　　客：じゃぁ、一つ、いただきます。クレジットカードで支払えますか。
販売員：すみません、カードでのお支払いはお受けしておりません。
　　　客：では、現金で支払います。
販売員：ここで召し上がりますか、それともお持ち帰りですか。
　　　客：ここで。緑茶をいただけますか。
販売員：はい。緑茶は無料で提供しています。
販売員：はい、どうぞ。群馬の食を楽しんでください。
　　　客：ありがとう。

3 - 3　食事処で

給仕人：いらっしゃいませ。空いているお席へどうぞ。
　　　客：どうも。
給仕人：こちらがメニューです。後ほどご注文を取りに伺います。
　　　　《しばらくして》
給仕人：ご注文は決まりましたか。

客　：おすすめの料理はありますか。

給仕人：どの料理もおいしいですが、トンカツ定食が人気です。ポーク・カツレツ、ご飯、味噌汁、漬物がセットとして一緒に出されます。

客　：それにサラダは付いていますか。

給仕人：サラダは付いていませんが、トンカツには千切りキャベツが添えられています。

客　：わかりました。それをいただきます。

給仕人：トンカツ定食が一つ。他にご注文は。

客　：水を一杯いただけますか。

給仕人：ただ今、お持ちします。

3-4　すき焼きの具材は全部メイド・イン・グンマ

スタッフ：卓上コンロの上の鉄鍋は、すき焼き用です。すき焼きを召し上がったことはありますか。

客　：あります。最初、テーブルに生卵を見たときには、信じられなかったです。私の国では生卵を食べることは一般的ではないので。

スタッフ：日本では生卵を食べても安全です。

客　：そして熱いお肉と野菜を溶いた生卵に絡めて食べると、おいしいということもわかりました。

スタッフ：そろそろ、すき焼きをおつくりしてよろしいですか。

客　：お願いします。

スタッフ：この霜降りのお肉は上州和牛でございます。上州は群馬県のもう一つの呼び方です。ですから上州和牛というのは、群馬県で育てられたブランド和牛という意味です。

客　：こんな美しい霜降り牛肉は見たことがない。

スタッフ：焼き具合はどのようにいたしましょう。

客　：ミディアム・レアで。

《客の目の前ですき焼きをつくる》

スタッフ：どうぞ。熱いので気を付けて。

客　：とてもおいしい！和牛が口の中でとろけます。また、味付けがいい。

スタッフ：すき焼きのもう一つのポイントは、味付けです。醤油、砂糖、酒、みりんを混ぜたこの調味料です。

客　：たまらないね。

スタッフ：こちらが、下仁田ネギ、春菊、シイタケ、しらたき、焼き豆腐でございます。これらのすき焼き用の具材もすべて群馬産です。

客　：すき焼きこそが、群馬のお客様へすすめる料理ということね。

第4章　温泉旅館に泊まる【温泉・宿泊編】

4-1　チェックイン

客：どうも。チェックインしたいんですが。

フロント係：はい、予約はございますか。

客：はい。名前はアンドリュー・ジョーンズです。

フロント係：少しお待ちください。

《予約リストを調べる》

フロント係：はい、ジョーンズさん。予約をいただいております。本日より2泊、
1名様ですね。

客：そうです。

フロント係：この書式に記入をお願いします。

客：はい…これで。

フロント係：お客様のお部屋は2階の萩の間になります。これが部屋の鍵です。た
だ今、係りの者がお部屋へご案内いたします。

客：部屋からの眺めはいいですか。

フロント係：とても。部屋は日本庭園に面していますので。

客：いいですね！

フロント係：景色を楽しまれますように。

4-2　予約なしのチェックイン

客：どうも。予約していません。今晩、空いている部屋はありますか。

フロント係：今晩のみで、お一人ですか。

客：えぇ。

フロント係：少しお待ちください。

《空室を調べる》

フロント係：お部屋をご用意できます。料金は夕食・朝食込みで14,000円です。

客：それで結構です。料金は前払いですか、それともチェックアウトの時
ですか。

フロント係：どちらでも結構です。この書式に記入してください。

客：いいですよ…どうぞ。

フロント係：ジョーンズさん、医学的あるいは宗教的理由から、食べられない食
材があれば教えていただけますか。

客：ないですね。

フロント係：苦手な日本食はありますか。刺身や納豆は大丈夫ですか。生の魚と発
酵した豆のことですが。

客：すしが大好きなので、生魚も大丈夫だと思います。でも、発酵した豆
は苦手です。

フロント係：では、明日の朝食は納豆の代わりに何か別の副菜をご用意させていた
だきます。

客：どうも。

付記

205

4-3　客を部屋へ案内する

スタッフ：靴は玄関でお脱ぎください。どこでもスリッパを着用することができますが、畳の上はお控えください。
客：了解です。
スタッフ：お部屋へご案内いたします。こちらでございます。
客：どうも。
スタッフ：ここがお客様のお部屋です。畳のお部屋ですので、ここでスリッパをお脱ぎください。
客：畳の上でスリッパはダメ。了解。
スタッフ：お荷物はこちらに置かせていただきます。浴室とトイレはそちらです。どうぞ、ごゆっくり。今、お茶をお入れします。
客：どうも。〈窓の外を眺めて〉何て美しい庭園だろう！
スタッフ：日本庭園を眺めているだけで、ストレスから解放されますよ。
客：落ち着いた空間が心を和ませてくれますね。
スタッフ：それはよかったです。さあ、お茶をどうぞ。
客：どうも。

4-4　貴重品は金庫に保管する

スタッフ：テレビ台の中に備え付けの金庫がございますので、貴重品はその金庫に保管してください。お客様がいらっしゃらない時でも、私どもはお掃除やお布団敷きで出入りいたします。金庫をお使いになるとよいですよ。
客：どのように使うのですか。
スタッフ：金庫の扉を開けて、貴重品を入れて、鍵を掛けるだけです。
客：簡単ですね。でも、温泉に入るとき、この鍵はどうすればいいの。
スタッフ：このようにブレスレットとして身に着けられます。鍵を紛失することもありませんし。
客：グッドアイデアですね！
スタッフ：どうも。もしくは、フロントに貴重品を預けることもできます。
客：日本は安全な国ですし、誰もが正直ですよ。先日、レストランのトイレにカメラを置き忘れましが、無事に戻ってきたことにびっくりしました。他の国ではあり得ないことです。
スタッフ：もちろん、私どもの旅館は安全ですが、万が一を考えて、お客様には貴重品を放置しないように申し上げております。
客：確かに、その通りです。

4-5　地図で場所を説明する

スタッフ：5時半以降、ご希望の時間にお部屋の方へお夕食をお持ちいたします。何時にいたしましょうか。
客：では、6時半に。さて、夕飯の前に温泉で一浴びしたいですね。
スタッフ：この部屋のお風呂をご使用できますが、大浴場もございます。
客：せっかく温泉地にいるのだから、大浴場を試す方がいい。どこですか。

スタッフ：ここに建物図があります。〈地図を指で示しながら〉大浴室は1階のここです。
　　　客：わかりました。ありがとう。
スタッフ：浴衣はそこの棚にございます。初めての方のために、大浴場の使用についてエチケットが添付されています。お読みください。
　　　客：ええ。そうします。
スタッフ：もし質問がございましたら、いつでも私の方へ。喜んでお答えいたします。

4-6　泉質と効能について説明する

　　　客：すみません。この看板に何と書いてあるのですか。
スタッフ：「源泉掛け流し」と書いてあります。
　　　客：どういう意味ですか。
スタッフ：「源泉掛け流し」というのは、源泉から直接に流れ出る温泉水を意味します。
　　　客：つまり、加水していない湧き出したままの天然温泉ということね。
スタッフ：そうです。
　　　客：ここの温泉は何に効きますか。
スタッフ：当温泉の泉質は、塩化物泉です。簡単に言うと、ナトリウムを含んでいます。神経痛、リウマチ、皮膚炎に効くと言われています。
　　　客：すごい！

4-7　問題を処理する——部屋が寒すぎる

フロント係：はい、フロントでございます。
　　　　客：もしもし、萩の間に滞在しているジョーンズです。部屋が少し寒いのですが。どうすればいいでしょうか。
フロント係：お部屋にエアコン用のリモコンはありますか。
　　　　客：今、手元にありますが、使い方がわかりません。
フロント係：ただ今、係りの者が伺いますので、少しお待ちください。
　　　　客：了解です。
　　　　　　《その後》
スタッフ：失礼します。入ってもよろしいですか。
　　　客：どうぞ、お入りください。少し寒いのですが、温度を調節していただけますか。
スタッフ：承知しました。エアコンのリモコンはどこですか。
　　　客：テーブルの上にあります。
スタッフ：リモコンをエアコン本体に向けて、ボタンを押します。上のボタンを押すと、温度が上がります。温度を下げたいときは、下のボタンを押します。
　　　客：この2つのボタンは必要ですね。覚えておきます。
スタッフ：室温を26℃に設定しました。それが大半の人々が快適だと感じる温度です。後はお好みで調節してください。

付記

客：わかりました。ありがとうございました。

4-8　給仕をする──〔1〕

スタッフ：そろそろお夕飯の時間ですが、お持ちしてよろしいですか。
　　　客：はい。温泉に入って、喉が乾いたし、お腹も空きました。
スタッフ：お食事の際に、お飲み物を召し上がりますか。
　　　客：ビールをいただきます。
スタッフ：生ビール、それとも瓶詰ビールですか。
　　　客：生ビールがいいですね。
スタッフ：生ビールを一つ。ただ今、お持ちします。
　　　　　《数分後》
スタッフ：こちらが生ビールとお料理です。
　　　客：盛り付けが美しい！
スタッフ：こちらが野菜の炊き合せ、そして鮪と甘海老とサーモンのお造りでございます。お醤油はそこにございます。どうぞ、お召し上がりくだい。
　　　客：おいしそうですね！

4-9　給仕をする──〔2〕

スタッフ：お食事はお済みですか。テーブルを片付けてもよろしいですか。
　　　客：えぇ、お願いします。どの料理もおいしかったです。
スタッフ：それはよかったです。
　　　　　《テーブルのお皿を下げる》
スタッフ：後ほどお布団を敷きにまいります。
　　　客：何時頃ですか。これから温泉街をぶらぶらしたいんですが。
スタッフ：どうぞ、いつでも外出なさってください。その間にお布団を敷かせていただきます。
　　　客：あぁ、了解です。

4-10　朝食の時間を確認する

スタッフ：明日の朝食は何時にいたしますか。
　　　客：朝食（の時間帯）はいつですか。
スタッフ：6時から9時までです。
　　　客：では、8時半に。明日の朝は少しゆっくり寝ていたいです。
スタッフ：承知しました。では、朝食の約10分前に、お布団を上げにまいります。
　　　客：わかりました。8時15分にモーニングコールをいただけますか。
スタッフ：はい。フロント係へ伝えておきます。

208

4 -11　朝食バイキング

スタッフ：朝食はバイキング形式になっておりまして、種類も豊富です。お客様に
　　　　　とても好評です。
　　　客：すべて和食ですか。
スタッフ：いいえ。ご飯よりもパン食を好まれるお客様もいらっしゃいますので、
　　　　　パンケーキ、ソーセージ、スクランブル・エッグといった洋風の朝食も
　　　　　ご用意してございます。
　　　客：いいですね。日本に来てから和食が続いています。朝食にベーコン・
　　　　　エッグを食べたいですね。
スタッフ：朝食バイキングは 1 階のレストランで、午前 7 時から 9 時半までです。
　　　客：混みますか。
スタッフ：いいえ、大丈夫です。平日は団体のお客様が少ないので。
　　　客：わかりました。絶対行きます。

4 -12　フロントで部屋の鍵を預かる

　　　　客：外出したいので、部屋の鍵を預かってください。
フロント係：かしこまりました。
　　　　客：この辺は、夜は安全ですか。
フロント係：えぇ。夜でも女性が独りで外出できるほど安全です。でも、温泉街に
　　　　　　は酔っ払いもいますので、注意するに越したことはありません。
　　　　客：おっしゃる通りです。私もほろ酔い気分です。
フロント係：8 時以降は、皆さんほろ酔い気分です。
　　　　客：まだ宵の口です。就寝前に温泉地の雰囲気を楽しみたいです。
フロント係：はい。楽しんできてください。深夜12時までにはお帰りください。閉
　　　　　　館の時間ですので。
　　　　客：了解。

4 -13　宿泊客に情報を提供する

　　　客：こんにちは。昼食をとりたいのですが、この辺りのおいしいレストラン
　　　　　をご存知ですか。
スタッフ：えぇ、何軒か知ってますが。何を召し上がりたい気分ですか。
　　　客：この地域でしか食べられないものがいいです。おすすめは何ですか。
スタッフ：そうですねぇー、おっ切りこみをおすすめします。野菜と一緒に煮込ん
　　　　　だ幅広のうどんです。インターネットで映像を検索してみますね。
　　　客：視覚的な情報は常に役に立ちます。
スタッフ：これがおっ切りこみの写真です。群馬県は小麦生産地域なので、おいし
　　　　　いパスタが作られています。おっ切りこみは、群馬の人々のお袋の味で
　　　　　す。
　　　客：オーケー。お昼はおっ切りこみにします。写真を見てお腹が空きまし
　　　　　た。店の場所を教えてください。
スタッフ：この地域のガイドマップをご覧ください。〈地図上を指で示しながら〉

付記

今、私たちはここです。で、お店はここです。歩いて10分ほどです。
客：歩くのも悪くないね。アドバイスをありがとうございます。
スタッフ：いつでもどうぞ。

4 -14　チェックアウト

客：チェックアウトお願いします。部屋は萩の間です。部屋の鍵をお返しします。
フロント係：かしこまりました。少しお待ちください。
《料金を計算する》
フロント係：お客様の料金は32,000円になります。こちらが明細書でございます。
客：〈明細書に目を通しながら〉ここに4,000円が加算されています。何の料金でしょうか。
フロント係：夕食時にビールをお飲みになりました。その料金でございます。
客：夕食ごとに生ビール2杯ずつ。了解しました。クレジットカードでお支払いします。
フロント係：では、ここに署名をお願いします。
客：はい。
フロント係：ありがとうございました。こちらがカードと領収書になります。よいご旅行を。
客：いろいろとありがとう。とても楽しい滞在でした。
フロント係：当旅館に滞在いただきありがとうございました。またお会いできるといいですね。

第5章　世界遺産の見学【富岡製糸場編】

5 -1　窓口で来場者に対応する

訪問者：〈独り言をいう〉入場料は看板に記されている。大人の入場は千円だな。
窓口の係員：次の方、どうぞ。
訪問者：大人1枚、お願いします。音声ガイドを利用したいのですが、機器のレンタル料はいくらですか。
窓口の係員：200円です。
訪問者：で、どこで支払うのですか。
窓口の係員：ここで結構です。総額で1,200円になります。
訪問者：では、これで。
窓口の係員：入場券と音声ガイド、そしてその取扱説明書です。
訪問者：どうも。この携帯電話のような機器は使いやすいですか。電子機器の操作は得意じゃないので。
窓口の係員：簡単ですよ。それぞれの説明パネルに記されている数字を押してください。音声説明が流れます。

訪問者：えーと。

窓口の係員：例えば、東置繭所を訪れると、説明パネルに1の数字が記されています。あなたの音声ガイド機器でも1のボタンを押してください。2秒後に説明が始まります。解説の終わりに赤いボタンがつく場合があります。そのボタンを押すと、解説項目に関連したさらなる詳細情報を聞くことができます。

訪問者：わかりました。親切なご説明に感謝します。

窓口の係員：どういたしまして。製糸場の訪問を楽しんでください。

5-2　初対面で自己紹介する

まゆ子：こんにちは。本日、ボランティア・ガイドを担当いたします桑田まゆ子です。初めまして。

訪問者：初めまして。カリフォルニア州サクラメント出身のアンドリュー・ジョーンズです。仕事で日本を訪れていますが、知り合った日本人が群馬出身で、富岡製糸場の見学と温泉体験をすすめてくれたものですから、帰国前に小旅行をしているところです。で、あなたはお仕事は何をされてますか。

まゆ子：近くの大学の3年生です。卒業後は地元の観光業界で仕事をしたいと考えています。今日の英語ガイドも、英語コミュニケーション力をつけるよい機会なので引き受けました。ためらわず質問してください。未熟ながら、最善を尽くしますので。

訪問者：どうも、そうするつもりです。

まゆ子：まず最初に、現在富岡製糸場においては、東置繭所と繰糸所内へ入ることが許されています。他の建物の内部には入れません。

訪問者：なぜですか。建物の老朽化のためですか。

まゆ子：えぇ、140年前に建てられた建物ですから、老朽化が進んでいる建物もあります。また、長い年月の間に使われ方が変わってしまい、改造されたものもありますので。

訪問者：了解です。一回りするのにどれくらいかかりますか。

まゆ子：約40分です。1時間を超えることはないですよ。では、見学を始めましょう。

5-3　瓦職人、煉瓦を焼く

訪問者：煉瓦造りの洋風建物は、当時の日本人にとって近代的だったでしょうね。

まゆ子：日本の近代化の象徴でした。

訪問者：これらの煉瓦造りの洋風建築を設計したのは誰ですか。

まゆ子：富岡製糸場の首長であるポール・ブリュナが設計計画し、オーギュスト・バスティアンが設計図を完成させました。彼はブリュナが雇ったフランス人製図技師でした。

訪問者：じゃぁ、フランス人の職人たちがこれらの建物をつくったんですか。

まゆ子：いいえ。実際の建設に携わったのは日本の職人たちでした。でも、当時の日本に煉瓦製造の技術を持っている者はいなかったため、ブリュナやフランス人建築技師の示教を受け、瓦職人たちが煉瓦を焼きました。富岡製糸

場に近い甘楽町福島に窯がつくられ、煉瓦が焼かれましたが、最初はうまく焼けませんでした。

訪問者：すごい職人気質を見せたんですね。
まゆ子：明治の日本人は気骨があったんですね。
訪問者：それは明治魂、それとも大和魂？
まゆ子：あなたの言葉に深く感動しています。

5-4 東置繭所で

まゆ子：この大きな建造物が東置繭所です。建物は木材と煉瓦で建てられていて、「木骨煉瓦造（＝木の骨組みに、壁に煉瓦を積み入れて造る）」と呼ばれています。日本の木造建築の技術が使われている欧風の建物です。つまり、ヨーロッパと日本の伝統が融合されています。
訪問者：ガイドマップによると、西側にも同じ大きさの倉庫があります。なぜ、大きな倉庫を2つも建てたのだろう。
まゆ子：当時この地域では、養蚕は一年に一回だけ行われました。つまり、蚕が繭をつくるのは一年に一回です。買い集めた大量の繭を貯蔵するための大きな倉庫が必要だったのです。
訪問者：倉庫に置いておくうちに蚕が孵化して蛾になってしまわないのですか。
まゆ子：集められた繭は乾燥させてから倉庫に貯蔵されました。
訪問者：なるほど…
まゆ子：次は繰糸所を見学しましょう。

5-5 繰糸所で

まゆ子：ここが繰糸所です。繭から糸を巻き取って生糸をつくるところです。
訪問者：なんて長い建物でしょう！
まゆ子：約140mの長さです。富岡製糸場の中で一番長い建物です。
訪問者：建物にはたくさんの窓がありますね。
まゆ子：自然光が不可欠でした。当時、電灯はありませんでしたから。建物のもう一つの特徴は、トラス構造が屋根を支えるため、中央に柱がないということです。中は広い作業スペースになっています。
訪問者：では、中を見物しましょう。
まゆ子：そうしましょう。

5-6 繰糸所内で──〔1〕

訪問者：うわぁ、これが繰糸機ですね。これらの機械が一斉に動いたら、壮観でしょうね。
まゆ子：そうでしょうね。さて、このパネルの写真をご覧ください。ここで使われた最初の繰糸器です。台の上に鍋のようなものが置かれています。これが繭を煮る釜です。この釜数が工場の規模を示し、ここには300釜がありました。当時、世界の工場が最大150釜の規模であったということを考慮す

ると、この製糸場は世界的にも最大の規模だったということができます。

訪問者：ということは、その当時300人もの女性たちがここで働いていたということですか。

まゆ子：もっと多いです。記録によると、1873年には500人を超えていました。繰糸担当者は300人ですが、工場には他にもいろいろな仕事がありましたから。工女たちは日本中から集められました。彼女たちは繰糸の技術を習得して、その技術をそれぞれの地元へ持ち帰り、工場新設の折に技術を教え伝えたのです。

訪問者：つまり、富岡製糸場の工女たちが繰糸器を使って作業する技術を日本中に広めたんですね。

まゆ子：長野県岡谷市は、そういった経緯から富岡市の姉妹都市です。岡谷市では、現在も生糸の生産が続けられています。

5-7　繰糸所内で――〔2〕

まゆ子：この写真をご覧ください。これは座繰り器と呼ばれ、日本の伝統的な糸繰り装置です。この製糸場ができる前は、女性たちは各家庭でこの方法で繭から糸をとっていたんです。

訪問者：根気を要したろうね。

まゆ子：おっしゃる通りです。それだから、繰糸器は絹産業にとって画期的なことだったのです。高品質な生糸の大量生産が可能になったわけですから。

訪問者：想像できますね。絹はかつてはぜいたく品だったけれど、今は庶民でも身にまとうことができますからね。私の祖母は絹のブラウスを特別な日に着ていました。

まゆ子：お土産店にもいろいろな絹製品がそろっています。よい土産品になりますよ。

訪問者：後で見てみますね。

まゆ子：次に進みましょう。

5-8　ブリュナ館で――〔1〕

まゆ子：さて、私たちはブリュナ館の前にいます。建物の中には入れませんので、ここで説明させていただきます。

訪問者：残念です。暮らしぶりを見てみたかったので。

まゆ子：近く開館することを願いつつ、本日はここでポール・ブリュナについて説明させていただきます。彼は横浜にあるフランス人経営の貿易会社で生糸の検査をしていたフランス人でした。1870年に明治政府から委託され、富岡製糸場の設立とその経営指導を担ったのです。

訪問者：彼は生糸について多くの知識を持っていたわけですね。

まゆ子：彼は繰糸器をフランスから輸入し、数人のフランス人の技術者と指導員を雇いました。フランス人たちは左側に見えるあの宿舎に滞在しました。後に、男性用宿舎は検査人館として使われましたが、女工館はそのまま残されています。

訪問者：日本での生活は大変だったろうね。

まゆ子：えぇ、恐らく。でも、フランス人たちは給料に関して優遇されていたと報告されています。指導者のブリュナは、当時の大臣級の給料を得ていました。彼はこの大きな屋敷に彼の家族と住んでいました。

訪問者：ベランダに囲まれた洋館ですね。長崎のグラバー邸と似ていますね。

まゆ子：その通りです。コロニアル様式の建物です。強い日差しを避けて風通しをよくするために、ベランダ付きで高床構造になっています。

訪問者：異国の人々にとっては、日本の夏は暑かったんでしょうね。

まゆ子：本当に。日本の夏はとても蒸し暑いし、日本人にとっても過ごし難い季節です。

5-9　ブリュナ館で──〔2〕

まゆ子：ブリュナは富岡製糸場の指導者として1873年から1875年までこの家に住んでいました。彼の帰国後、建物は工女の夜間学校として使われました。

訪問者：大きな館じゃないですか。

まゆ子：えぇ。館の地下には煉瓦造りの貯蔵室があって、食料品やワインが貯蔵されていたと考えられています。

訪問者：フランス人にとってワインは生活必需品です。ブリュナがここで優雅な生活をしていたことが垣間見られます。

まゆ子：フランス人たちについては興味深い話が伝えられています。製糸場設立当初は工女が集まりませんでした。その理由は、フランス人たちが人の生き血を飲んでいるという噂が広まったからです。日本人たちは彼らに生き血を吸い取られてしまうと恐れたのです。当時の日本人が赤いワインを生き血と誤解したことから、工女募集が難航したのです。

訪問者：面白い話だけど、異文化理解は容易ではないってことですよ。私も初めて海苔を見たとき、その黒い紙を食べ物とは思いませんでしたから。今では、スシなしでは生きていけませんが。

まゆ子：それ、笑えますね。それはそうとして、その好ましくない噂を打ち消すために、富岡製糸場の初代所長、尾高惇忠（じゅんちゅう）は自分の娘を工女にしたのです。14歳の尾高勇（ゆう）は富岡製糸場で最初の工女になりました。

訪問者：娘さんの意志は尊重されたの。彼女は工女になりたかったの。

まゆ子：勇は父親の意をくみとり、熱心に技術を習得して、一等工女になったと伝えられています。

訪問者：強くて優秀な女性ですね。

まゆ子：えぇ、明治の女性は強かったと聞いています。

5-10　寄宿舎で

まゆ子：前方に見える2つ並んだ建物が工女たちの寄宿舎です。

訪問者：工女たちはどういう生活をしていたのですか。

まゆ子：質素な、規則正しい生活を送っていました。電灯がない時代なので、日の出から日没まで就労しました。つまり、朝7時から休憩と昼食を挟んで夕方4時半まで働きました。週6日働き、日曜日は休みでした。

訪問者：週休1日制はつらい響きがありますね。給料はよかったのですか。
まゆ子：手取り額は少ないですが、食事付きの寄宿舎で、医療も無料でした。食費を給料の一部として計算すると、大まかですが、当時の大工さんの給料の半分ぐらいでした。
訪問者：彼女たちは、勤勉に働いたんでしょうね、だから百年の短期間で日本は工業大国になったんですよ。絹産業に従事した女性たちがその礎を築いたことがうかがえますね。
まゆ子：日本人は働きすぎだとよく言われますが、こういう歴史を垣間見ると理解できますね。
訪問者：でも、仕事が人生のすべてではありませんよ。ワーク・ライフ・バランスの考え方を実現しなくてはね。
まゆ子：その通りです。

5 -11　工女たちの作業着

訪問者：先ほどのパネルの写真から、工女さんたちは日本髪に着物姿だったことがうかがえるけど、裾の広いスカートは、何と呼ぶのですか。
まゆ子：それは袴（はかま）です。普通、袴は礼装ですが、一種のキュロットスカートなので動きやすいです。だから工女たちの作業着になったと思われます。
訪問者：剣道する人も袴をはきますよね。袴はカッコいいですよ！
まゆ子：えぇ、同感です。袴姿は凛として見えますものね。
訪問者：とっても！自分用に欲しいですね。

5 -12　見解を示す

訪問者：今日は、日本の明治時代について多くを学んだと思います。
まゆ子：よかった！明治の人々は西洋諸国から新しい技術をどんどん取り入れて、自分たちのものにしていったんですね。
訪問者：日本がわずか百年で近代化に成功した秘訣は、明治魂だと思います。
まゆ子：アハハ。歴史的に見ると大変な時代でしたけれど、活気に溢れた時代でした。
訪問者：また、女性たちが日本の近代化に一翼を担ったこともわかりました。
まゆ子：よくできました！

5 -13　養蚕と群馬の女性

まゆ子：そして、もう一つ。養蚕は群馬の女性にとって重要だったということに気付いていただきたいのです。
訪問者：えぇ。
まゆ子：養蚕は群馬の女性の収入を保証しました。言い換えると、女性たちは自宅で繭から生糸を紡いだり、機（はた）で布を織ったりすることで安定した収入を得ることができたのです。群馬の女性たちは働き者ですし。

付記

訪問者：つまり、群馬の女性は養蚕によって強い経済力を維持してきたということ
　　　　ですね。
まゆ子：「上州のかかあ天下と空っ風」は、「群馬のいばる奥さんと乾いた風」と翻
　　　　訳されますが、そう言われるように、群馬は強い女性と強い風で知られて
　　　　きました。
訪問者：それは面白い。日本は亭主関白の国なのに。
まゆ子：でも、群馬は例外です。養蚕のお陰で、女性は強く、たくましいです。彼
　　　　女たちは経済的に家族を支えていたんです。
訪問者：群馬の女性は自立しているようですね。あなたはそういう女性の一人であ
　　　　ることを誇りに思うべきですよ。
まゆ子：でも、強い女性は日本ではむしろ敬遠されます。
訪問者：時代が変われば、世の中も変わりますよ。

5 -14　お手洗いの場所を説明する

訪問者：すみません。お手洗いへ行きたいのですが、場所を教えていただけますか。
まゆ子：診療所の近くにあります。ブリュナ館まで戻ると、右側に見つかります。
訪問者：でも、さっき長い列ができていたところじゃないですか。
まゆ子：そこが混んでいる場合には、繰糸所の隣にあるお手洗いをご使用ください。
訪問者：ありがとう。そうします。

第6章　おすすめパワースポット【周辺観光編】

6 - 1　貫前神社はユニーク！

まゆ子：神社仏閣に興味はありますか。
訪問者：もちろん。それらを見ることが旅をする理由の一つです。この近くに神社
　　　　やお寺があるのですか。
まゆ子：ええ。富岡市やその周辺には多くの神社やお寺が散在します。地域の人々
　　　　は昔からそれらに参拝してきました。日本人の心のよりどころです。
訪問者：私はそれらの宗教に属していませんが、神社と仏教寺院を見るのが好きで
　　　　す。心を落ち着かせてくれるので。
まゆ子：では、富岡市にある貫前神社を訪れることに興味を持たれるかもしれませ
　　　　んね。歴史のある古い神社で、ここから近いです。
訪問者：どう行けばいいのかな。
まゆ子：上州富岡駅から三つ目の駅、上州一ノ宮駅で降りて、徒歩で15分ぐらい
　　　　です。
訪問者：簡単そうですね。でも、あの線は電車の本数が少ないから、時間を要する
　　　　かも。
まゆ子：一番簡単な方法はタクシーに乗ることです。ここから10分ぐらいで行けま
　　　　すよ。
訪問者：電車賃の方が安いですが、タクシーを使えば、時間を節約できますね。

まゆ子：総門までタクシーで行けます。そこから楼門まで階段を下り、楼門をくぐって本殿へ行く、という珍しい参拝の形式です。

訪問者：その神社へ行ってみたいですね。タクシー乗り場は、どこですか。

まゆ子：こちらです。タクシーが出払っている場合は、私が電話で呼ぶこともできますよ。

訪問者：ご助力、ありがとう。

まゆ子：いつでも、どうぞ。

6-2　城下町小幡はカッコイイ！

まゆ子：私のお気に入りの一つは、富岡市の隣、甘楽町にある城下町小幡です。

訪問者：お城があるからですか。

まゆ子：今はもうお城はありませんが、城跡と楽山園と呼ばれる立派な日本庭園が残されています。そこでお茶を楽しむことができます。係員が茶道に則ってお茶を入れてくれます。

訪問者：参観とお茶は無料ですか。

まゆ子：どちらも有料ですが、高くはありません。

訪問者：うーん。殿様は茶の湯を楽しみながら、庭を愛でたんでしょうね。そういう気分を味わうのも悪くないですね。

まゆ子：はい、いいんじゃないですか。誰もがとてもリラックスできるところです。それに、庭園の周辺地区には、当時の建物が地域の人々によって保存されています。

訪問者：侍たちが住んでいた建物が残っているんですか。

まゆ子：えぇ。子孫たちによって維持されてきた武家屋敷や庭園を見て回ることができますよ。

訪問者：すごい。

まゆ子：私はその地区の江戸時代の情緒が大好きです。粋な街並が私を当時にタイムスリップさせてくれるんです。

訪問者：訪れる価値がありそうですね。ここから近いし…

まゆ子：きっと気に入りますよ。

6-3　群馬県立自然史博物館

まゆ子：群馬県立自然史博物館は、地球・自然・生命に興味のある方にとっては、素晴らしいところです。

訪問者：興味のない人って、いますか。人類にとっては永遠のテーマですよ。

まゆ子：とりわけ子どもたちにとっては楽しみながら学べるよい場所です。大人にとってもわくわくする展示ですよ。

訪問者：例えば？

まゆ子：そうですね。実物大のティランノサウルスが頭をもたげて鳴き声を上げるんです。

訪問者：ティランノサウルスって、恐竜の？

まゆ子：もちろん作りものです。でもリアルで迫力あるので、泣き出す子どももいるそうです。

訪問者：実物大のティランノサウルスに睨まれたら、私も怖いですよ。

まゆ子：ハハハ。さらに、カマラサウルスの全身骨格が展示されているんです。博物館スタッフによると、この恐竜の骨格を完全に近い姿で保有する博物館は、世界中でも極めて少ないそうです。

訪問者：それはすごいよ！

まゆ子：お見逃しなく。

6-4　アドバイスをする——〔1〕

訪問者：まゆ子、もう一つ質問してもいいですか。

まゆ子：もちろんです。いくつでも受けますよ。

訪問者：前に話したと思うけど。群馬を訪問しているもう一つの理由は、温泉を体験するためです。どこかよい温泉地をご存知ですか。

まゆ子：群馬は温泉王国ですから、多くの温泉地があります。どのような温泉地がお望みですか。遠くても有名な温泉地、それともここから近い温泉地ですか。

訪問者：えぇーと。

まゆ子：そうですね、伊香保、草津、四万は、よく知られている温泉地です。ただし、これらは群馬県中部と北部に位置しますから、移動時間がかかります。

訪問者：どれくらいかかりますか。

まゆ子：ここから伊香保へは2時間くらい、また草津へは3時間くらいかかります。

訪問者：少し遠いかな。

まゆ子：では、富岡に近い下仁田温泉、もしくは安中市の磯部温泉がおすすめです。あなたが田舎の魅力ある静かな雰囲気を好むなら、これらの温泉地はあなたに合っているかもしれません。

訪問者：良さそうですね。

まゆ子：下仁田温泉に行くには、最寄り駅は下仁田駅で、上信線の最後の駅になります。電車で30分ほどです。駅からはタクシーで行けますよ。

訪問者：悪くないね。

まゆ子：で、磯部温泉は安中市にあります。最寄り駅は磯部駅で、高崎駅からJR信越線で10分ほどです。

訪問者：それも悪くない。どっちに行こうかな。

まゆ子：大きな決断ですね。スマホでチェックしてみてはいかがですか。

訪問者：名案ですね。では…

6-5　アドバイスをする——〔2〕

訪問者：どの写真もいいですね。決められないなぁ。どっちがいいと思いますか。

まゆ子：もし日本最古の温泉記号を見たければ、それは磯部温泉にあります。

訪問者：日本最古の温泉記号って？

まゆ子：ボウルから湯気が立ちのぼるシンボルを見たことありませんか。〈メモ用紙に温泉記号（♨）を描く〉こういう記号ですが…

訪問者：私には、このシンボルは温かい食べ物を出す食事処を表しているように見えますが。

まゆ子：外国人はそのシンボルを食事処として誤解するかもしれませんが、それは江戸時代から350年以上にわたり使われてきた温泉記号なんです。

訪問者：ということは、磯部温泉を訪問すると、最古の温泉記号を見ることができるわけですね。

まゆ子：その通り。そして、シンボルの発祥地として知られている温泉を楽しむこともできますよ。

訪問者：うーん。

まゆ子：気が進まないようですね。じゃぁ、下仁田温泉をおすすめします。なぜなら下仁田駅からタクシーで5分ですし、荒船風穴もあるからです。

訪問者：アラフネ…それ、何ですか。

まゆ子：それは蚕の卵を冷蔵した場所です。自然の冷気が岩の割れ目から出ている場所です。その冷気を利用することで、卵の孵化を遅らせることができたのです。蚕を育てる回数を増やすことは、生糸の生産を促進させました。

訪問者：今、思い出しました。それは富岡製糸場と絹産業遺産群の一つですね。

まゆ子：その通りです。荒船風穴を訪れて、地方の温泉を楽しむのはいかがですか。

訪問者：いいね！どうやって行けばいいの。

まゆ子：下仁田駅から乗合タクシーを利用できます。タクシー料金は手頃なはずです。予約が必要なので、よろしかったらお手伝いしますよ。

訪問者：ご親切に感謝します。

まゆ子：荒船風穴の近くに牧場があります。日本で最も古い洋式牧場の一つ、神津牧場です。そこで新鮮なソフトクリームを食したり、牛の行進を眺めたりして休憩することができますよ。

訪問者：牛の行進？

まゆ子：そうです。放牧されている牛たちが午後に集められて、牛小屋へ向かいます。本当に行進しているかのようです。

訪問者：下仁田へ行く価値がありそうですね。

6-6 高崎のバス観光をすすめる──〔1〕

まゆ子：高崎市には観光名所がたくさんあります。高崎駅は新幹線の停車駅ですから、ついでに立ち寄ってみるのも名案ですよ。バスで行けるところもあります。

訪問者：そう言えば、高崎に来たとき、新幹線の窓から白い巨像が見えましたが、あれは何ですか。

まゆ子：あの白い巨像は高崎市のシンボルです。正式名称は高崎白衣大観音ですが、地元では観音様と呼ばれています。それは、高崎市の平和と繁栄を願って1936年に建立されました。

訪問者：仏像ですか。

まゆ子：えぇ。観音は英語では「慈悲の女神」で、人々やあらゆる生き物を救うとされる仏教の聖人の一人です。

訪問者：高さはどれくらいですか。

まゆ子：その像は、高さ41.8mの鉄筋コンクリート造りで、像の内部にも入れます。

訪問者：奈良の大仏よりも大きい！

まゆ子：奈良の大仏は高さ約15mですから、高崎白衣大観音は比較にならないほど大きいです。

訪問者：	そんなに大きいの？近くで見てみたいですね。どうやって行くんですか。
まゆ子：	観音像は観音山の頂上にあります。高崎駅西口から13番もしくは14番のぐるりんバスに乗ります。観音山行のバスで、25分かかります。
訪問者：	13番または14番のぐるりんバス…
まゆ子：	そうです。ぐるりんバスはカラフルなイラストが描かれていて目立ちます。料金は一律で200円です。
訪問者：	どこまで乗っても、200円を払う。いいですね！
まゆ子：	観音様の地域を見守る優しい姿に心が和みますよ。それから、観音山の頂上から市内全域が見渡せます。
訪問者：	絶景スポットの一つですね。
まゆ子：	観音山は、春は桜、秋は紅葉で美しいです。一年を通して素晴らしい景色です。

6-7　高崎のバス観光をすすめる──〔2〕

まゆ子：	少林山達磨寺は高崎市の観光名所の一つで、バスで行けます。達磨寺は英語で Dharma Temple と言います。そのお寺こそ、ダルマ人形の発祥の地です。
訪問者：	丸いマスコットのことじゃないですか。店頭で初めて見たときから、なんで手足がないのだろうと不思議に思ってました。
まゆ子：	達磨は偉い僧侶でした。彼は何年もの長い間瞑想をした人物として知られていますが、瞑想をしているとき手足は衣に隠れて見えなかったことから、彼の姿は丸い形に見えたのです。
訪問者：	なるほど。
まゆ子：	でも、その丸い人形は倒れても、すぐに起き上ることから、縁起がいいと信じられています。
訪問者：	達磨人形が諦めてはいけないことを教えてくれる、ということですか。
まゆ子：	その通りです。「七転び八起き」という日本の諺がありますが、達磨人形はその不屈の心得を象徴しています。
訪問者：	人生は山あり谷ありですから、心に留めておかなくては。ところで、そのお寺への行き方を教えてください。
まゆ子：	高崎駅西口から1番のぐるりんバスに乗って、少林山入り口で降りてください。おおよそ20分です。達磨寺の総門はバス停から近いところにあります。
訪問者：	そこで座禅を体験できるかな。
まゆ子：	飛び入りはどうでしょうか。住職に直接お願いしてはどうですか。最初は「だめ」と言われたとしても、お願いし続ければ、聞き入れてくれるかもしれません。「不屈の心得」を覚えていますか。
訪問者：	オーケー。達磨寺で自分の不屈の心得を実践する、というのはすごい挑戦ですね。
まゆ子：	おっしゃる通りです。ところで、駅へ戻るときは、2番のぐるりんバスに乗ることを忘れないでください。
訪問者：	覚えておきます。ありがとう。

6-8　高崎のバス観光をすすめる──〔3〕

まゆ子：少し遠いですが、バスで行ける観光名所がもう一つあります。
訪問者：どこですか。
まゆ子：榛名山の山腹にある榛名神社です。社殿と榛名山の巨岩が合体していて、実に並外れています。自然の力を感じる場所です。
訪問者：フーン、そこはパワースポットですか。
まゆ子：ええ。関東地方屈指のパワースポットだと言われています。
訪問者：参拝すると、運気が上がりますか。
まゆ子：もちろん。榛名神社は榛名山に宿る火の神と土の神を祭っています。豊作、成功、結婚、あらゆることに御利益があると聞いています。
訪問者：日本の神話のようですね。
まゆ子：その通り。太古の昔に創建されていますから、神話でしか語ることができません。日本で最も古い神社の一つですから。
訪問者：遠くても、行く価値がありそうですね。ぐるりんバスで行けますか。
まゆ子：いいえ。高崎駅の西口で本郷経由榛名湖行きの群馬バスに乗り、榛名神社前で下車してください。およそ70または80分かかります。バス停から神社まで徒歩で15分です。
訪問者：どれくらい頻繁にバスは運行しているんですか。
まゆ子：1時間に1本です。
訪問者：了解。

6-9　吹割の滝で

まゆ子：滝の音が聞こえてきますね。道幅が狭いから気を付けてください。
訪問者：前方に滝が見えてきました。岩の裂け目に水が流れ込んでいる滝は、初めて見ました。素晴らしい！
まゆ子：「東洋のナイヤガラ」と呼ばれています。
訪問者：規模は小さいですが、確かにナイヤガラの滝のような形をしていますね。
まゆ子：そうでしょう。
訪問者：流れの近くで写真を撮っている観光客がいるけど、危険じゃないですか。
まゆ子：白い警告線を越えない限りは、安全です。看板に「白線立ち入り禁止」と書いてあります。
訪問者：面白い！
まゆ子：過去に事故が起きていると聞いています。白線を越えた人が足を滑らせ、滝壺へ落下したそうです。
訪問者：この滝に落ちた人たちは助かったんですか。
まゆ子：いいえ。滝壺が深いため、遺体さえ見つからなかったそうです。
訪問者：訪問者の安全のために他にも何かすべきですよ。転落の危険を知らせる看板だけでは十分な安全対策とは思えないですが。
まゆ子：景観を損ないたくないという考え方は理解できますね。まず、私たちは警告に注意を払うべきです。

付記

解 答

解答

第1章：上信電鉄でお出かけ【交通編】

1-1　高崎駅で──上信線乗り場への行き方

Exercise（p.3）：　目的地（行き先）によって、最寄り駅・路線は異なるため、Provide information を参照し、Exercise を行った後、Practical application の路線図を用いて他の目的地についても練習してください。

1-2　上信線乗り場で──切符の買い方を説明する

Exercise（p.7）：　Prepare で各施設までの所要時間と交通手段を確認後、Exercise を行ってください。

Prepare［解答］：　個々人の住居位置によって各施設までの所要時間と交通手段は異なるため、様々なパターンを考えてみてください。

1-4　行き方を教える──〔1〕

Exercise（p.10）：　Prepare でイラストの示す内容を確認後、Exercise を行ってください。

Prepare［解答］：　(1) go to a movie　　(2) ski　　(3) travel by plane [air]
(4) eat *sushi*　　(5) buy a new smartphone

1-5　行き方を教える──〔2〕

Exercise（p.13）：　Prepare で高崎駅から各施設への行き方（JR 高崎駅周辺地図を参考）を確認後、Exercise を行ってください。
目的地によっては、パターン以外の表現も必要であるため、English Points を参考にしてください。

Prepare［解答の一例］
(1)　the town hall（市庁舎）：
　　Go straight for several blocks. Then you'll see the tall building.

224

(2) a restaurant（ガストレストランの場合）：
      Go straight for three blocks. It's on the corner of the third block.
(3) the Music Center（音楽センター）：
      Go straight for several blocks. It's opposite the town hall.
(4) ○○ bank（横浜銀行の場合）：
      Go straight for two blocks. Then turn right and go one more block.
      You'll find it on your left.
(5) a convenience store（ローソンの場合）：
      Go straight for one and a half blocks. You'll find it on the left.
      （または個人の知識に基づいて）It's on the first floor of the station building.
(6) ○○ hospital（井上病院の場合）：
      Go straight for two blocks. Then turn right and go one more block.
      You'll find it on your right.
(7) ○○ clinic（吉川医院の場合）：
      Go straight for four blocks. It's just around the corner of the fourth block.
(8) ○○ hotel（ワシントンホテルの場合）：
      Go straight for one block. It's right over there.
(9) ○○ square（もてなし広場の場合）：
      Go straight for five blocks. Then turn right and go one more block.
      It's next to Suzuran department store.
(10) ○○ department store（高島屋デパートの場合）：
      It's a five-minute walk from the station. Turn right at the west exit.
      You'll see the building soon.

1-6　客を乗せる

Exercise（p.16）：　　目的地と荷物に関する情報は、乗車客により異なるため、様々なパターンを考えてみてください。

1-7　ぐるりんバスの乗り方を教える

Exercise（p.19）：　　Provide information を参考に Exercise を行ってください。

第2章：物産店でお土産を買う【買い物編】

2-2　土産店で──〔2〕

Exercise（p.27）：　　Prepare のイラストの内容を確認後、Exercise を行ってください。

解
答

Prepare［解答］

(1) *kokeshi* doll   (2) *Gumma-chan* good   (3) wooden chopsticks   (4) silk ties

(5) glassware   (6) wooden cup   (7) *Daruma* doll   (8) silk scarf

2 - 3 　土産店で──〔3〕

Exercise（p.30）：　　Prepare で数字の言い方を確認後、Provide information を参考に Exercise を行ってください。

Prepare［解答］   (1) 257   (2) 4612   (3) 68917

                  (4) 3578   (5) 25740   (6) 13641

2 - 4 　土産店で──〔4〕

Exercise（p.35）：　　Prepare で事物の説明の仕方を確認後、Exercise を行ってください。

Prepare［解答］   (1) *sansho*   (2) *oyaki*   (3) *katsuo-no-tataki*

                  (4) *umeboshi*   (5) *shakuhachi*   (6) *dondoyaki*

2 - 5 　土産店で──〔5〕

Exercise（pp.39-40）：Prepare で比較級の作り方を確認後、Provide information を参考に Exercise を行ってください。

Prepare［解答］

（1）規則的に変化する形容詞

原級の和訳	原　　級	比　較　級
高い	high	higher
短い、（背の）低い	short	shorter
年老いた／古い	old	older
小さい	small	smaller
興奮させる	exciting	more exciting
重い	heavy	heavier
興味深い、おもしろい	interesting	more interesting
速い	fast	faster
若い	young	younger
重要な	important	more important
早い	early	earlier
難しい	difficult	more difficult

（2）不規則に変化する形容詞

原級の和訳	原　　級	比　較　級
（数の）多い	many	more
（量の）多い	much	more
小さい、少ない	little	less
良い、上手な	good	better
順調な、健康な	well	better
悪い、下手な	bad	worse

2 - 8　土産店で──〔8〕

Exercise（p.49）：　ロールプレイする際、各自の情報をもとに Exercise を行ってください。

第 3 章：おいしい郷土料理【飲食編】

3 - 1　ファーストフード店で

Exercise（p.58）：　Provide information を参考に注文の場面を想定して Exercise を行ってください。

3 - 2　群馬の郷土食

Exercise（pp.61-62）：Prepare で動詞活用変化（過去分詞）を確認後、Exercise で受動態のつくり方を考えてください。

Exercise［解答］
(1)　is kept　　　(2)　were eaten by　　　(3)　was written by
(4)　was painted by　　(5)　were hired

解
答

227

Prepare ［解答］

規則動詞の活用

	意　味	原　形	過　去　形	過　去　分　詞
1	掃除する	clean	cleaned	cleaned
2	閉める、閉ざす	close	closed	closed
3	雇用する、賃借りする	hire	hired	hired
4	（絵具で）描く、（ペンキで）塗る	paint	painted	painted
5	停止する、やめる	stop	stopped	stopped
6	勉強する	study	studied	studied

不規則動詞の活用

	意　味	原　形	過　去　形	過　去　分　詞
1	捕まえる	catch	caught	caught
2	切る	cut	cut	cut
3	飲む	drink	drank	drunk
4	食べる	eat	ate	eaten
5	見つける	find	found	found
6	与える	give	gave	given
7	保つ、飼う	keep	kept	kept
8	知る、知っている	know	knew	known
9	読む	read	read	read
10	見る、見える	see	saw	seen
11	取る、受け入れる	take	took	taken
12	書く	write	wrote	written

3 - 3　食事処で

Exercise（p.65）：　Provide information を参考に注文の場面を想定して Exercise を行ってください。

3 - 4　すき焼きの具材は全部メイド・イン・グンマ

Exercise（p.70）：　Prepare で使用具材を確認後、Exercise を行ってください。

Prepare ［解答の一例］

Ingredients for a dish

(1) *Okkirikomi*: wide udon noodles, chicken, taro, Japanese radish, green onion, *shiitake* mushroom, carrot......
(2) Chicken Curry: chicken, onion, carrot, tomato, curry powder......
(3) Chow Mein: pork, cabbage, bean sprouts, chow mein noodles, Worcester-like sauce
(4) *Temaki-zushi*: vinegared rice, sheet of dried seaweed, egg, avocado, tuna, salmon, shrimp......
(5) Spaghetti with meat sauce: spaghetti noodles, ground beef, tomato, onion, garlic......
(6) *Shabu-shabu*: beef, sesame paste, green onion, carrot, *shiitake* mushroom......

第４章：温泉旅館に泊まる【温泉・宿泊編】

4 - 1　チェックイン

Exercise（p.76）：　　Prepare で各スタッフの英語名を確認後、Exercise を行ってください。

Prepare ［解答］

(1) （　　受付　　） receptionist————(C)　(2) （総支配人） general manager—(F)
(3) （ 荷物を運ぶ係 ） porter————————(E)　(4) （ 給仕人 ） wait staff————(I)
(5) （　客室係　） housekeeping staff—(H)　(6) （　女将　） proprietress————(A)
(7) （ バーテンダー ） bartender————(B)　(8) （コンシェルジェ） concierge————(D)
(9) （　料理人　） cook————————(G)

4 - 2　予約なしのチェックイン

Exercise（p.80）：　　Prepare で各自のアレルギー・嗜好を確認後、Exercise を行ってください。

Prepare ［解答の一例］
　　　　・I'm allergic to buckwheat.
　　　　・Japanese foods I don't like include natto and seaweed.

4 - 3　客を部屋へ案内する

Exercise（p.85）［解答］
　　　　(1) （ ！ ）　(2) （ ？ ）　(3) （ ？ ）　(4) （ ！ ）　(5) （ ！ ）
　　　　(6) （ ？ ）　(7) （ ！ ）

4 - 5 　地図で場所を説明する

Exercise（p.89）：　Prepare でイラストの示す標識名を確認後、Exercise を行ってください。

Prepare［解答］
1.（　G　）　2.（　A　）　3.（　F　）　4.（　J　）　5.（　B　）
6.（　I　）　7.（　D　）　8.（　H　）　9.（　E　）　10.（　C　）

4 - 6 　泉質と効能について説明する

Exercise（p.94）：　Prepare で日本語表現の意味内容を確認後、Exercise を行ってください。

Prepare［解答］
(1)　*mottainai*　　（もったいない）　　(2)　*komore-bi*　　（木漏れ日）
(3)　*kuidaore*　　（食い倒れ）　　(4)　*ikumen*　　（イクメン）
(5)　*ichigo-ichie*　（一期一会）　　(6)　*ishin-denshin*（以心伝心）
(7)　*kacho-fugetu*（花鳥風月）　　(8)　*hikikomori*　（引きこもり）

4 - 7 　問題を処理する──部屋が寒すぎる

Exercise（p.98）：　Prepare で和製英語の英語表現を確認後、Exercise を行ってください。

Prepare［解答］
(1)　アイスティー　　(2)　アメリカンドッグ　　(3)　ココア　　　　(4)　シュークリーム
(5)　ショートケーキ　(6)　ソフトクリーム　　(7)　バイキング　　(8)　プリン
(9)　ピーマン　　　　(10)　ホットケーキ　　(11)　フライドポテト

4 -11 　朝食バイキング

Exercise（p.104）：　Prepare で日本の祝日に関する英語表現を確認後、Exercise を行ってください。

Prepare［解答］
(1)（ 正月（元旦））　January 1 ──New Year's Day
(2)（成人の日　　）　The 2nd Monday in January──Coming-of-Age Day
(3)（節分　　　　）　February 3 ──The day before the beginning of spring
(4)（ひな祭り　　）　March 3 ──Doll [Girls'] Festival
(5)（憲法記念日　）　May 3 ──Constitution Day
(6)（子どもの日　）　May 5 ──Children's Day

(7)（七夕　　　　　） July 7 ——Star Festival
(8)（敬老の日　　　） The 3rd Monday in September——Respect-for-the-Aged Day
(9)（体育の日　　　） The 2nd Monday in October——Health-Sports Day
(10)（文化の日　　　） November 3 ——Culture Day
(11)（七五三　　　　） November 15 ——The festival day for children of seven, five and
　　　　　　　　　　　　　　　　　　three years of age
(12)（勤労感謝の日） November 23 ——Labor Day

4 -13　宿泊客に情報を提供する

Exercise（p.109）： Prepare で高崎市および各自のホームタウンにおける情報を確認
　　　　　　　　　　後、Exercise を行ってください。

Prepare［解答の一例］：個々人の情報に基づくため、様々なパターンがあります。

Kind of food   Name of shop or restaurant
(1) *soba* noodle·····················（ *Eki-soba, Fujimi-soba,*　　　　　　　　　）
(2) *udon* noodle　················（ *Men-ichi, Yaokiya*　　　　　　　　　　　）
(3) *yakiniku* ·······················（ *Chōsen-hanten, Yakiniku-kingu*　　　　）
(4) *ramen* noodle ················（ *Nakajū-tei, Seikaken,*　　　　　　　　　）
(5) *okonomiyaki* ················（ *Enya, Kansai*　　　　　　　　　　　　　）
(6) Italian food ····················（ *Shango, Harappa*　　　　　　　　　　　）
(7) French food····················（ *Eteruna Takasaki, Kannon-yama Fūsha*　）
(8) Mexican food ·················（ *Tiotia*　　　　　　　　　　　　　　　　）
(9) Chinese food ················（ *Ryūshō,* Shanghai *Karyū*　　　　　　　）
(10) Korean food ················（ Korean Kitchen *Shijan, Chingu*　　　　　）

解
答

第5章：世界遺産の見学【富岡製糸場編】

5-5　繰糸所で

Exercise（pp.134-135）：Prepare で最上級の作り方を確認後、Provide information を参考に Exercise を行ってください。（同時に既習の比較級も確認する。）

Prepare［解答］

（1）規則的に変化する形容詞

原級の和訳	原　　級	比　較　級	最　上　級
高い	high	higher	the highest
短い、（背の）低い	short	shorter	the shortest
年老いた／古い	old	older	the oldest
小さい	small	smaller	the smallest
興奮させる	exciting	more exciting	the most exciting
重い	heavy	heavier	the heaviest
興味深い、おもしろい	interesting	more interesting	the most interesting
速い	fast	faster	the fastest
若い	young	younger	the youngest
重要な	important	more important	the most important
早い	early	earlier	the earliest
難しい	difficult	more difficult	the most difficult

（2）不規則に変化する形容詞

原級の和訳	原　　級	比　較　級	最　上　級
（数の）多い	many	more	the most
（量の）多い	much	more	the most
小さい、少ない	little	less	the least
良い、上手な	good	better	the best
順調な、健康な	well	better	the best
悪い、下手な	bad	worse	the worst

参考文献一覧

植田一三・他，2010，『英語で説明する日本の文化必須表現グループ100』語研.

上野陽子，2008，『気持ちが伝わる英会話のルールとマナー』日本実業出版社.

上野陽子，2010，『ネイティブに伝わる英会話のルールとマナー』日本実業出版社.

上野陽子，2014，『1週間で英語がどんどん話せるようになる26のルール』アスコム.

左藤　靖，2013，『もう困らない「英語で接客」ができる本』大和書房.

大学英語教育学会基本語改訂特別委員会編著，2016，『大学英語教育学会基本語リスト
　　新JACET8000』桐原書店.

田地野　彰，2004，「日本における大学英語教育の目的と目標について：ESP研究からの
　　示唆」MM News No.7, pp.11-21.

田地野　彰・水光雅則，2005，「大学英語教育への提言」『これからの大学英語教育』岩
　　波書店，pp.1-46.

田地野　彰・寺内　一，2010，「21世紀のESPと大学教育」『21世紀のESP：新しいESP
　　理論の構築と実践』大修館書店，pp.215-224.

寺内　一，2010，「ESPの歴史と定義」『21世紀のESP：新しいESP理論の構築と実践』
　　大修館書店，pp.3-16.

寺内　一・他，2010，「日本におけるESP教育の実践例」『21世紀のESP：新しいESP理
　　論の構築と実践』大修館書店，pp.147-214.

野村真美，2000，『CD BOOK 身のまわりの生活英語表現』ベレ出版.

野村真美，2004，『CD BOOK 日常英会話 Best 表現1100』明日香出版社.

野村真美，2004，『CD BOOK 気持ちを表す日常英語表現』ベレ出版.

野村真美，2010，『CD BOOK とっても短い英会話フレーズ1500』ベレ出版.

野村真美，2012，『CD BOOK 日常英会話の基本の基本フレーズが身に着く本』明日香出
　　版社.

松本　茂，2002，『ネイティブの子どもなら誰でも知っている英単語』七寶出版.

松本美江，2009，『改訂版　英語で日本紹介ハンドブック』アルク.

宮野智靖・ミゲル・E・コーティ，2011，『すぐに使える英会話ミニフレーズ2500』Jリ
　　サーチ出版.

米田貴之，2014，『バンクーバー発！4コマ漫画で体感するから身につくほんとに使える
　　リアルな英語フレーズ』明日香出版社.

渡邉美代子，1993，『14の基本万能動詞で英会話攻略』南雲堂フェニックス.

第1章

上信電鉄，「鉄道運賃」上信電鉄ホームページ，（2019年2月15日取得，http://www.
　　joshin-dentetsu.co.jp/tetudou/untinhyou/untinhyou-top.htm）.

上信電鉄，「路線図」上信電鉄ホームページ，（2019年2月15日取得，http://www.joshin-
　　dentetsu.co.jp/tetudou/rosenzu.htm）.

高崎市，「ぐるりん時刻表・路線図」高崎市ホームページ，（2019年2月15日取得，
　　http://www.city.takasaki.gunma.jp/docs/2014022800027/）.

高崎市，「市内循環バス「ぐるりん」運賃・乗り継ぎ割引・回数券・定期券等の案内」高
　崎市ホームページ，（2019年2月15日取得，http://www.city.takasaki.gunma.jp/
　docs/2014010901088/）．
高崎市，「高崎駅西口・東口バス乗り場について」高崎市ホームページ，（2019年2月15
　日取得，http://www.city.takasaki.gunma.jp/docs/2014010901040/）．

第2章

上毛新聞社編，2014，『ぐんまの手仕事』上毛新聞社．
朝日新聞社・他，「法被」『コトバンク』，（2017年8月24日取得，https://kotobank.jp/
　word/%E6%B3%95%E8%A2%AB-115236#E3.83.87.E3.82.B8.E3.82.BF.E3.83.AB.E5.
　A4.A7.E8.BE.9E.E6.B3.89）．
群馬県，「ぐんまちゃんトピックス」群馬県ホームページ，（2017年8月26日取得，
　http://www.pref.gunma.jp/01/b0110211.html）．
群馬県，「ぐんまの特産品」群馬県ホームページ，（2017年8月24日取得，http://www.
　pref.gunma.jp/01/b2110047.html）．
群馬県総務部広報課，「シルク産業」ぐんまちゃんナビ，（2017年8月26日取得，http://
　www.gunmachan-navi.pref.gunma.jp/industry/silkindustry.php）．
群馬県達磨製造協同組合，「高崎だるまとは」群馬県達磨製造協同組合ホームページ，
　（2017年8月26日取得，http://takasakidaruma.net/daruma01.html）．
JTCO日本伝統文化振興機構，「群馬編　伝統工芸品館」JTCO日本伝統文化振興機構ホー
　ムページ，（2018年3月16日取得，http://www.jtco.or.jp/japanese-crafts/?act=detail
　&id=344&p=5&c=18）．
和製英語・カタカナ英語辞典，「フリーサイズ」和製英語・カタカナ英語辞典ホームペー
　ジ，（2018年3月16日取得，http://www.waseieigo.com/28hugyou.html#freesize）．

第3章

（一社）日本養鶏協会，「たまごの知識」一般社団法人　日本養鶏協会ホームページ，
　（2017年8月29日取得，https://www.jpa.or.jp/chishiki/kigen/index.html）．
群馬県，「ぐんまの特産品」群馬県ホームページ，（2017年3月17日取得，http://www.
　pref.gunma.jp/01/b2110047.html）．
群馬県，「GNN GUNMA News Network〜すき焼き編〜」群馬県ホームページ，（2018年2
　月15日取得，https://www.youtube.com/watch?v=xOSSaLHhUZA&feature=youtu.be）．
「群馬の名物・グルメまとめ！食べておきたいB級グルメ・料理は？お土産にも！」Trav-
　el Note，（2018年2月15日取得，https://travel-noted.jp/posts/1481）．
「群馬の食材だけですき焼きを作ろう！県あげて取り組む「ぐんま・すき焼きアクション」
　とは？！」マガジンハウス：Local Network Magazine「colocal コロカル」，（2018年
　2月15日取得，http://colocal.jp/news/55325.html）．

第4章

群馬県高等学校教育研究会歴史部会編，2005，『群馬県の歴史散歩』山川出版社．
上毛新聞社事業局出版部，2014，『新　ぐんまの源泉一軒宿』上毛新聞社．
上毛新聞社事業局出版部，2016，『西上州の薬湯』上毛新聞社．

スタンロー，ジェームズ，（吉田正紀・加藤将史訳），2010，『和製英語と日本人』新線社.

アイコン，「シルエット AC」ホームページ，（2018年3月11日取得，https://www.silhou-ette-ac.com/）.

朝日新聞・他，「バイキング料理」『コトバンク』，（2018年2月11日取得，https://koto-bank.jp/word/%E3%83%90%E3%82%A4%E3%82%AD%E3%83%B3%E3%82%B0%E6%96%99%E7%90%86-112773#E5.A4.A7.E8.BE.9E.E6.9E.97.20.E7.AC.AC.E4.B8.89.E7.89.88）.

「足湯の効果とは？」足湯でカンタンに健康 Navi!，（2018年3月19日取得，http://asiu-rakouka.sa-kon.net/index.html）.

ASPEC，「間投詞・Interjection」ASPEC（Asian Skills Promotion and Education Consul-tancy）ホームページ，（2018年3月7日取得，http://aspec1.com/index.php?%E9%96%93%E6%8A%95%E8%A9%9E%E3%83%BBInterjection1

「英語の相づちをマスターして、会話上手になろう！」英語学習で世界をもっと身近に DMM 英会話 Blog，（2018年3月7日取得，http://blog.iknow.jp/posts/2001）.

（株）ゆこゆこ，「群馬県の温泉地一覧」ゆこゆこホームページ，（2018年2月12日取得，https://www.yukoyuko.net/onsen/search/L03/P10）.

草津温泉観光協会，「共同浴場」湯 Love 草津，草津温泉観光協会ホームページ，（2018年2月12日取得，https://www.kusatsu-onsen.ne.jp/onsen/list/index.php?g=2）.

草津温泉観光協会，「湯もみの歴史」草津温泉熱乃湯，湯 Love 草津，草津温泉観光協会ホームページ，（2018年2月12日取得，https://www.kusatsu-onsen.ne.jp/netsu-noyu/history/）.

草津温泉旅館協同組合，「草津三湯めぐり」草津温泉旅館協同組合ホームページ，（2018年2月12日取得，http://onsen-kusatsu.com/）.

「草津温泉の共同浴場（外湯めぐり）」antoi.net/te/ ホームページ，（2018年2月13日取得，http://antoi.net/te/spa/kusatsu/sotoyu/index.html）.

「草津温泉の歴史（その1）＆（その2）」，温泉の科学，関東周辺立ち寄り温泉みしゅらんホームページ，（2018年2月13日取得，http://www.asahi-net.or.jp/~ue3t-cb/bbs/special/sience_of_hotspring/sience_of_hotspring_7-2-1-1.htm / http://www.asahi-net.or.jp/~ue3t-cb/bbs/special/sience_of_hotspring/sience_of_hotspring_7-2-1-2.htm）.

草津町，草津町ホームページ，（2018年2月12日取得，http://www.town.kusatsu.gunma.jp/）.

群馬県，「群馬県内泉質別温泉一覧」群馬県ホームページ，（2018年2月12日取得，file:///C:/Users/Owner/AppData/Local/Microsoft/Windows/INetCache/IE/8G3CZ3S3/000277058.pdf）.

群馬県，「群馬県の温泉状況について」群馬県ホームページ，（2018年2月12日取得，http://www.pref.gunma.jp/04/d5000026.html）.

群馬県温泉協会，「上州温泉入浴10訓」（一社）群馬県温泉協会ホームページ，（2018年3月17日取得，http://www15.plala.or.jp/gunma-spa/nyuuyoku10.html）.

国土交通省観光庁，2014，「観光立国実現に向けた多言語対応の改善・強化のためのガイドライン」国土交通省観光庁ホームページ，（2019年2月22日取得，file:///C:/Users/Owner/AppData/Local/Microsoft/Windows/INetCache/IE/82GN5XC6/001029742%20

(2).pdf)

国土交通省総合政策局観光事業課, 2008,「多様な食文化・食習慣を有する外国人客への対応マニュアル」国土交通省観光庁ホームページ, (2017年8月28日取得, http://www.mlit.go.jp/kankocho/shisaku/sangyou/taiou_manual.html).

「『真田丸』真田昌幸が築いた！伊香保温泉石段街」ニッポン旅マガジン, (2018年2月13日取得, https://tabi-mag.jp/ishidanikaho/).

渋川伊香保温泉観光協会,「石段」渋川伊香保温泉観光協会ホームページ, (2018年2月13日取得, http://www.ikaho-kankou.com/ishidan.cfm).

勝月堂,「湯乃花まんじゅうの歴史」全国の温泉まんじゅうの発祥のお店"勝月堂"ホームページ, (2018年3月19日取得, http://www.shougetsudo.net/history.html).

「水沢観音と日本三大うどん「水沢うどん」」いにしえの日本を思う寺社巡り, (2018年2月13日取得, http://japantemple.com/2018/02/09/post-2590/).

"Ryokans in Japan: A Virtual Tour," Boutique Japan website, (2018年2月12日取得, https://boutiquejapan.com/ryokan/).

宿.com,「温泉の泉質/効能一覧」宿.com ホームページ, (2018年2月12日取得, http://www.yadyad.com/en/onsen/effect).

「和製英語・カタカナ英語辞典」和製英語・カタカナ英語辞典ホームページ, (2018年2月12日取得, http://www.waseieigo.com/).

第5章

小野　博（監修）, 2006,『English Quest Basic—CD-ROM で学ぶ英語の基礎：初級編』桐原書店.

群馬県広報課, 2018,『ぐんまがいちばん！』群馬県広報課ぐんまイメージアップ推進室.

東京書籍編集部, 2014,『世界文化遺産　富岡製糸場』東京書籍.

富岡製糸場伝道師協会編集, 2005,『世界へはばたけ！富岡製糸場　まゆみとココのふしぎな旅』上毛新聞社.

富岡製糸場伝道師協会編集, 2011,『富岡製糸場事典』上毛新聞社.

和田英,（森まゆみ解説）, 2011,『富岡日記』みすず書房.

群馬県警察,「運転免許保有者数（2018年12月末現在）」群馬県警察ホームページ, (2019年2月22日取得, https://www.police.pref.gunma.jp/koutuubu/04menkyo/menkyohoyuusya.html).

「群馬県のランキング」都道府県別統計とランキングで見る県民性ホームページ, (2018年3月12日取得, http://todo-ran.com/t/tdfk/gunma).

「コレならどこにも負けない！！【群馬県の日本一】」never まとめ, (2018年3月12日取得, https://matome.naver.jp/odai/2133734020301825201).

「日本遺産　かかあ天下：ぐんまの絹物語」ホームページ, (2018年3月1日取得, http://worldheritage.pref.gunma.jp/JH/).

深谷市, 深谷市ホームページ, (2018年2月15日取得, http://www.city.fukaya.saitama.jp/).

富岡市,「富岡製糸場 CG 映像ガイドツアー」富岡製糸場ホームページ, (2018年2月14日取得, http://www.tomioka-silk.jp/tomioka-silk-mill/visit/group.html).

富岡市, 富岡製糸場ホームページ, (2018年2月14日取得, http://www.tomioka-silk.jp/

tomioka-silk-mill/).

第6章

小野忠孝，1959，「龍宮の椀」『日本の民話20　上州の民話　第1集』未來社，pp.15-18.

北爪智啓・他，1997，『群馬県立自然史博物館　展示ガイドブック』群馬県立自然史博物館.

久保田順一・他，2015，『真田道を歩く　改訂版』上毛新聞社.

群馬県高等学校教育研究会歴史部会編，2005，『群馬県の歴史散歩』山川出版社.

群馬県立自然史博物館編集，2000，『群馬県立自然史博物館　総合案内』群馬県立自然史博物館.

下仁田町ふるさとセンター　歴史民俗資料館編，2014，『世界遺産　富岡製糸場と絹産業遺産群「荒船風穴蚕種貯蔵跡」』(普及版)，下仁田町教育委員会.

タウト、ブルーノ，(篠田英雄訳)，1939，『日本美の再発見』岩波書店.

タウト、ブルーノ，(篠田英雄訳)，1950，『ニッポン：ヨーロッパ人の眼で観た』春秋社.

タウト、ブルーノ，(森とし郎訳)，1992，『日本文化私観』講談社.

タウト、ブルーノ，(篠田英雄訳)，2008，『日本雑記』中央公論新社.

榛名神社(監修)，2018，『榛名神社詣で』榛名神社.

安中市，安中市ホームページ，(2018年2月26日取得，http://www.city.annaka.lg.jp/).

(一社)安中市観光機構，あんなか観光ガイド，(2018年2月26日取得，http://www.annaka-city.com/).

一之宮貫前神社，一之宮貫前神社ホームページ，(2018年3月1日取得，http://nukisaki.kazelog.jp/).

川場村，「真田氏と川場村」フォレストタウン・かわばホームページ，(2018年3月1日取得，http://www.vill.kawaba.gunma.jp/gyosei/n_publicinfo/backnumber/no491/feature/index.html).

甘楽町，「織田氏七代の墓」甘楽町ホームページ，(2018年2月25日取得，http://www.town.kanra.gunma.jp/kyouiku/bunkazai/bunkazai/kanra/62.html).

甘楽町，甘楽町ホームページ，(2018年2月25日取得，http://www.town.kanra.gunma.jp/index.html).

甘楽町，「国指定名勝　楽山園」甘楽町ホームページ，(2018年2月25日取得，http://www.town.kanra.gunma.jp/kyouiku/bunkazai/map/20120330191558.html).

甘楽町，「歴史民俗資料館（ぐんま絹遺産）」甘楽町ホームページ，(2018年2月25日取得，http://www.town.kanra.gunma.jp/kyouiku/bunkazai/map/01.html).

「群馬県高崎市　榛名神社」佳景探訪，(2018年2月28日取得，http://www.natsuzora.com/dew/gunma/harunajinja.html).

群馬県立自然史博物館，群馬県立自然史博物館ホームページ，(2018年2月25日取得，http://www.gmnh.pref.gunma.jp/).

群馬サファリパーク，群馬サファリパークホームページ，(2018年2月26日取得，http://www.safari.co.jp/).

(公財)神津牧場，神津牧場ホームページ，(2018年3月1日取得，http://www.kouzubokujyo.or.jp/index.html).

真田街道推進機構事務局，「川場村」真田街道ホームページ，（2018年3月1日取得，
　　http://www.city.ueda.nagano.jp/contents/sanadakaidou/kawaba-vill.html）．

真田街道推進機構事務局，「沼田市」真田街道ホームページ，（2018年3月1日取得，
　　http://www.city.ueda.nagano.jp/contents/sanadakaidou/numata-city.html）．

慈眼院，高野山真言宗 慈眼院ホームページ，（2018年2月27日取得，https://takasaki-
　　kannon.or.jp/）．

少林山達磨寺，黄檗宗少林山達磨寺ホームページ，（2018年2月27日取得，http://www.
　　daruma.or.jp/about/fair.php）．

高崎市，高崎市ホームページ，（2018年2月27日取得，http://www.city.takasaki.gunma.
　　jp/）．

「高崎の「だるま市」が大変なことになっていた！」NEVER まとめ，（2018年2月27日取
　　得，https://matome.naver.jp/odai/2148413818790997501）．

富岡市，「[国指定重要文化財]貫前神社」富岡市観光ホームページ，（2018年3月14日取
　　得，http://www.tomioka-silk.jp/spot/sightseeing/detail/Nukisaki-shrine.html）．

沼田市，「吹割の滝」沼田市ホームページ，（2018年3月1日取得，http://www.city.nu-
　　mata.gunma.jp/kanko/fukiware/index.html）．

沼田市観光協会，「吹割の滝」沼田市観光協会ホームページ，（2018年3月1日取得，
　　http://www.numata-kankou.jp/sight/fukiwarenotaki/index.html）．

沼田商工会議所，「上州真田の里沼田」沼田商工会議所ホームページ，（2018年3月1日
　　取得，http://www.numata-cci.or.jp/kanko/sanada.htm）．

榛名神社，「榛名神社　歴史」榛名神社ホームページ，（2018年1月1日取得，http://
　　www.haruna.or.jp/?page_id=14）．

毎日新聞社，「真田用水でできる奇跡の米「真田のコシヒカリ」とは」毎日メディアカ
　　フェホームページ，（2018年3月1日取得，http://mainichimediacafe.jp/event-
　　arc/1155/）．

ヨコオデイリーフーズ，こんにゃくパークホームページ，（2018年2月26日取得，
　　http://konnyaku-park.com/）．

著者紹介

渡邉 美代子（わたなべ みよこ）

サンフランシスコ州立大学卒業。同大学大学院修士課程修了。専門は、認知意味論・認知言語学、異文化コミュニケーション。獨協大学講師、東京経済大学講師などを経て、現在、高崎商科大学商学部教授。

著書に『英語基本動詞活用辞典―認知的アプローチ』（南雲堂フェニックス）『しぐさでわかる異文化・異性―ことばのいらないコミュニケーション心理学』（共著、北樹出版）がある。

論文に、「地域ニーズに基づいた英語教材の開発に向けて：富岡製糸場とその周辺における英語コミュニケーション活動」（『高崎商科大学コミュニティ・パートナーシップ・センター紀要』第2号）、「コトバの意味問題：クオリアを中心に前言語的な観点から」（日本コミュニケーション学会『ヒューマン・コミュニケーション研究』第33号）、「自然言語カテゴリーに見る言語相対性と普遍性：身体性に基づく認知・概念理解・言語構築」（神田外語大学異文化コミュニケーション研究所『異文化コミュニケーション研究』第8号）他がある。

おらが群馬のおもてなし英語
Hospitality English in Nostalgic Gunma

2019年3月28日　初版第1刷 発行

著 者　渡邉美代子

企 画　高崎商科大学地域連携センター

発 行　上毛新聞社事業局出版部

〒371-8666　前橋市古市町 1-50-21
TEL 027-254-9966　Fax 027-254-9966
E-mail：book@raijin.com

※定価は裏表紙に表示してあります。
※本文、写真、地図、イラストなどの無断転載を禁じます。

©Takasaki University of Commerce　2019　Printed in Japan

本誌は高崎商科大学平成27-28年度地域志向教育研究費による研究助成（研究者：渡邉美代子　課題名：地域ニーズに基づいた英語教材の開発：富岡製糸場とその周辺における英語コミュニケーション活動）を受け、制作したものです。